AF540488

Land Reforms in States and Union Territories in India

About the Author

Dr. P.K. Agrawal is the writer of repute of about forty books on various subjects especially of public interest including three on land reforms.

Dr. P.K. Agrawal belongs to the Indian Administrative Service, 1976 batch. At present, Dr. P.K. Agrawal is the Additional Chief Secretary and Commissioner General Land Reforms to the Government of West Bengal. He comes from Barwa Sagar, District Jhansi, Uttar Pradesh.

Dr. Agrawal has a long experience of eleven years of working in the field of land reforms in West Bengal from the field level to the top policy level.

Dr. Agrawal, before his retirement, has captured his practical experience to analyse and present important aspects of land reforms in all States and Union Territories of India.

Land Reforms in States and Union Territories in India

Dr. P. K. Agrawal

CONCEPT PUBLISHING COMPANY PVT. LTD.
NEW DELHI-110059

Assistance by: Ankur Agrawal and Sagar Agrawal

ISBN-13: 978-81-8069-687-9

First Published 2010

Published and Printed by

Concept Publishing Company Pvt. Ltd.
Regd. Office:
A/15-16, Commercial Block, Mohan Garden
New Delhi-110059 (India)
Phones : 25351460, 25351794, *Fax* : 091-11-25357109
Email : publishing@conceptpub.com,
Website: www.conceptpub.com

Editorial Office:
H-13, Bali Nagar, New Delhi-110 015, India.

Cataloging in Publication Data-- *Courtesy:* D.K. Agencies (P) Ltd. <docinfo@dkagencies.com>

Agrawal, P. K. (Pramod Kumar), 1950-
Land reforms in states and union territories in India / P.K. Agarwal.
p. cm.
Includes bibliographical references (p.).
Includes index.
ISBN 13: 9788180696879 ISBN 10: 8180696871

1. Land reform--India. 2. Land tenure--India. 3. Land use, Rural--Government policy--India. I. Title.

DDC 333.3154 22

Preface

Land reforms have been an important agenda of our development strategy since Independence. For our visionary leaders, it was a must to unlease productive forces in our vast rural areas and to ensure law and order in the country.

The basic concept of the Indian Polity enshrined in Article 39(b) and (c) of the Constitution of India has not been changed with liberalization. The gains of liberalization should trickle down to the vast rural populace by providing them more opportunities to grow. In fact both are and should be complimentary to each other. Unless purchasing power is given in the hands of the teeming millions, liberalization cannot sustain. Agriculture provides 'food security'. In populous country like India, 'food security' is the first requisite. Economy cannot be left exclusively to market or stock upheavals. It is a well proven and accepted fact and principle that production increases with implementation of land reforms. West Bengal is a good example in this regard. It is unfortunate that India has not succeeded in transferring land to the person who tills the land even after 62 years of the independence. It can, therefore, be safely concluded that land reform is an evergreen measure with multilateral dimension. The Naxalite violence has become a major problem in the country because of neglect of land reforms so far. It is high time that we correct our error as a nation and devote seriously and sincerely to the implementation of land reforms.

I had the opportunity during my career as a civil servant to work for about eleven years in the field of land-reforms in West Bengal from the ground level to the top level of policy making. West Bengal is the undisputed leader in the field of land reforms in the country. I, therefore, thought it germane to record my experience in the form of book before retirement which has also been done by some of my illustrious predecessors in service. But I noticed that there is no book which contains details about land reforms in all the States and Union Territories. There are voluminous works on various states separately on land reforms which the practical administrators have no time to go through.

To fill up the gap, I have attempted to write about the present status of land reforms in a capsular form without oversight of main points required for attention or implementation in that particular State or Union Territory. It was an uphill task as adequate material is not readily available regarding land reforms in some smaller states, North Eastern States and Union Territories.

I have avoided repetition. The problem of neglect of Scheduled Castes and Scheduled Tribes is there more or less in each State but I have touched it in details concerning forest issues in case of Madhya Pradesh as an example. Similarly, issue of contract forming has been dealt with in Punjab and Haryana and partly in Karnataka.

In Orissa, the newly created problem of land acquisition has been analysed. In Andhra Pradesh, the topic of land distribution has been analysed in all its practical aspects *vis-à-vis* demands of Naxalites. Topics have been entitled in an interesting way so that these may catch eyes of the administrators or political executives specially in Naxalites infested states. Articles on States of Madhya Pradesh and Chhattisgarh and States of Bihar and Jharkhand have to be read conjointly. General topics to elaborate land reforms have been dealt in the beginning. Topic 'Implementation of Land Reforms' gives idea how land reforms can be implemented. I could have indulged into detailed analysis in case of each State or Union Territory. But I have noticed that in the process, the action points are lost sight of. And only historical and theoretical aspects get dominance.

I have generously used the previously published material on the subject. I express my gratitude to all the publishers and writers whose works have been borrowed in this work. Volumes published by the L.B.S. Academy of Administration on land reforms in various States and Government of India's reports (Department of Land Resources, Ministry of Rural Development) has been quoted frequently. Department of Land Resources has been working for all these years like an 'yogi' on the subject without the public glare. Time is ripe when they and their subject land reforms are going to get attention from the policy makers at the Centre. I am sure that the states will follow the suit as land reform is basically the state-subject.

I am indebted to Late Benoy Krishna Chowdhury, Minister of Land and Land Reforms, West Bengal and my senior colleagues in Indian Administrative Service who guided me in the field of land reforms.

I thank my P As and other officials for typing the manuscript.

I am sure that this book will be very useful to the practical administrators, revenue officials and policy makers. I am sure that the subject of land reform will be a part of curriculum in management and in rural development institutions. Then, this work of mine will be accepted as a text book.

Dr. P.K. Agrawal

Conversion Table for Measurement of Land

Area

1 Hectare	=	2.471 acres = 10,000 sq. metre
1 Acre	=	3 Bigha 8 chhatak = 4840 sq. yards = 43,560 sq. feet = 100 decimal
1 sq. km.	=	247.1 acres = 100 hectare
1 Metre	=	1.0936 yard = 3.28 ft.
1 K.M.	=	0.62 mile
1 Mile	=	1.61 K.M.
1 Gunter's chain	=	66 ft.

Contents

Preface v

1. Land Reform Defined 1
2. Factors Constituting Land Reforms 11
3. Legal and Economic Factors in Land Reforms 19
4. Implementation of Land Reforms: A Case Study 24
5. Performance by Various States and Union Territories Under Land Reforms 43
6. Need for Recording of Sharecroppers and Distribution of Government Surplus Land in Uttar Pradesh and Uttarakhand 56
7. Bottlenecks in Implementation of Land Reforms in Maharashtra 67
8. Institutional Road Blocks to Land Reforms in Bihar 75
9. Naxalite Movement and Land Reforms in Jharkhand 84
10. Strategy to Tackle Naxalism in West Bengal Through Land Reforms 88
11. Need to Implement Radical Land Reforms in Andhra Pradesh 98
12. Great Strides of Land Reforms in Tamil Nadu 113
13. Changes in Forests Management as Part of Land Reform Measures in Madhya Pradesh 121

14. Problems of Implementation of Land Reforms in Chhattisgarh 128

15. Land Reforms to Counter Feudalism in Rajasthan 134

16. Institutional Financing and Political Will as Essential Components of Land Reforms in Karnataka 143

17. A Lot To Do toward Land Reforms in Gujarat 152

18. Need for Protection of Land Rights of Tribals in Orissa 160

19. Implementation of Land Reforms in Kerala 168

20. Land Reforms in Punjab and Haryana 174

21. Achievements of Land Reforms in Jammu & Kashmir 182

22. Land Reform Scenario in Himachal Pradesh 187

23. Land Reforms in Goa 192

24. Land Reforms in North Eastern States 195

25. Land Reforms in Union Territories 222

26. A Scheme to Purchase and Distribute Land by the State 231

27. Streamlining Revenue Administration for Implementation of Land Reforms 237

Bibliography 247

Index 250

1

Land Reform Defined

Land Reform can be defined as the redistribution of rights and interests in land in favour of the landless and the poor cultivators.

According to Shri S.R. Sankaran, "the term land reform encompasses the entire institutional framework of property relations or relations of production pertaining to land."[1]

Thus, land reform provides a means for redistribution landed property through structural reforms which can bring about revolutionary improvements in the standard of life on the rural poor who have been deprived of their due rights in land due to domineering influence of the landed class in all spheres of rural life including political, administrative, social and religious spheres.

Even if land reforms did not lead to effective redistribution in favour of the landless yet it helped in bringing about a less skewed distribution amongst the land-owners. The reforms had a favourable impact on the conditions of agricultural labour because of loosening of hold of monopoly in the rural economy in general.

In India 7.5 per cent of households owned 59 per cent of the nation's land. In Mexico 1 per cent of the population owned 97 per cent of land whereas 96 per cent population only 1 per cent of the land. This skewed distribution of land resulted into social imbalances which surface in the form of social distortions like violence, suicide by farmers or rise in crimes in rural India.

This results into absentee landownership. The zamindari systems of India and Pakistan provide notable examples. As a rule, zamindars and the middlemen neither did any agricultural work nor lived on their farms. In Egypt, almost all the big landowners resided or were settled in towns.

Ayub Khan as dictator of Pakistan mismanaged the land reform in East Pakistan (now Bangladesh) to woo the middle class or big landlords as supporters and to act as instruments of his exploitative regime. According to him, "A Land Revenue Commission set up for East Pakistan in 1958 led to an amendment of the East Bengal State Acquisition and Tenancy Act (of) 1950, by which I was able to raise the ceiling of self-cultivated land from 33 acres to about 120 acres or so.[2]

The result is known to everybody. Pakistan was ultimately dismembered.[3]

The extent of land redistributed was 43 per cent of agricultural land in China, 37 per cent in Taiwan, 32 per cent in South Korea and 33 per cent in Japan whereas in India, it resulted in redistribution of only 1.25 per cent of the operational area.

In developing countries, the agricultural sector has the maximum weightage. In India it had been 46 per cent in 1960s (now less than 35%) and in Colombia, Pakistan and Philippines it had been 31 per cent, 50 per cent and 35 per cent respectively whereas in developed countries like Japan and America it had been 13 per cent and 4 per cent respectively.

Therefore, a 1970 UN resolution correctly says that this structural reform is an integrated programme with the aim to remove the barriers for economic and social development which follows from defects in agrarian structure.

National integration or communal harmony is the main problem of our country today. Land reform gives it the best and permanent solution.

United Nation's Fourth Report says that "the redistribution of land can lead to the spread of national consciousness which is a necessary pre-condition for a popular National Government. The greater awareness among farmers can lead to psychological integration. On the other hand, lack of land reforms, high mechanization, capital and intensive agriculture can cause agitation."[4] Land reform measures aim at alleviating the rural poverty in the following manner:

(a) By distributing land among the landless by taking over excess land from large landholders.
(b) By providing security of tenure and ownership rights to tenants and sharecroppers and by regulating rent payable by them to the landowner.

(c) By protecting tribal interests in land against alienation and encroachments of non-tribals.

(d) By consolidation of landholdings and thereby bringing about rearrangements of land for better productivity.

(e) By development of public lands for providing better access to the rural poor for fuel wood and fodder.

(f) By regulating usurious money lending and providing alternative sources of credit.

(g) By providing access to women to land and other productive assets.

(h) By protecting homestead rights of the rural poor on lands owned by them and providing them with house sites for construction of residential houses.

In India the landed property is the most important property because India lives in villages. Article 39 (b) and (c) of the Constitution of India in the Chapter of Directive Principles of State Policy directs that the State shall ensure:

(a) that the ownership and control of the material resources of the community are so distributed as best to subserve the common good; and

(b) that the operation of the economic system does not result in the concentration of wealth and means of production to the common detriment.

It talks of proper distribution of landed property among the Indian citizens. There was obstruction in implementation of this directive earlier because Articles 31 and 31(A) was in the Part III of the Constitution of India relating to Fundamental Rights. Now the 'right to property' has been taken away from this Chapter and has been made only a constitutional right. In view of this, the Government can ensure egalitarian society through redistribution of landed properties.

"Economic growth without social justice is inhuman, but social justice without economic growth is impossible. And economic growth is equally impossible unless we combine the humanism of true socialism with the dynamism of private initiative which is loosely called capitalism."[5]

In India since the First Five Year Plan, Land Reforms have remained a major issue of National Agenda for achieving agrarian reforms, for reconstruction of rural economy, ensuring social justice to "actual tillers" as well as landless rural poor and thus for creating sustainable base for overall growth of industrial and tertiary sector of our economy. The Central Government is playing an advisory and coordinating role in the field of land reforms as the subject is under exclusive legislative and administrative jurisdiction of the States as per Entry No. 18 of the List II (State List) of the VII Schedule of the Indian Constitution.

The major objectives of Land Reforms consist of re-ordering agrarian relations to achieve an egalitarian social structure, elimination of exploitation in land relations, realizing the age-old goal of "land to actual tiller", enlarging the land base of rural poor, increasing agricultural production and diversification of agricultural economy etc. The major components of the strategy of land reforms are the abolition of Zamindari and intermediary tenures, tenancy reforms, ceiling on ownership of agricultural holdings, distribution of government wastelands including Bhoodan land, modernization and updating of land records system, special measures for prevention of alienation and restoration of alienated tribal land, improving empowerment of women to ensure greater access to land and abolishing gender bias in land legislations.

The Land Reforms Acts contained in IXth Schedule to the Constitution enjoy protection of the Constitution. The objects of Land Reform Acts included in the IXth Schedule to the Constitution are:

(i) Abolition of intermediate interests, zamindaris, jagirs, inams;
(ii) Putting a ceiling on the quantity of agricultural land to be held by a person, prevention of consolidation of holdings in excess of the prescribed ceiling, distribution of surplus land;
(iii) Encouragement of co-operative societies to hold land other than individuals;
(iv) Tenancy reforms for fixity of tenures regulation of rents, conversion of tenants into ownership; and
(v) Preventing the fragmentation of holdings by prescribing a standard area below which no fragmentation will be allowed by transfer, partition or settlement.

In any land reform measure, the primacy goes to the redistribution of lands. It means and includes that the State should take over the lands from the landholders in order to distribute to the needy persons, *i.e.* the persons who actually cultivate the lands. Generally, the landless people constitute the poorest section of the rural areas. This is what layman understands by land reform measure. All other measures support to achieve the right of cultivation for them. Under this category, second largest number of the landless or the land-hungry people are covered by recording them as sharecroppers, *bataidar*, *bhagidar* or *bargadar* in West Bengal to assure them some sort of permanence in their right of cultivation. This is, therefore, given a second priority under land reform. Though this right does not mean transfer of ownership of land, yet the landowners become unnecessarily panicky. This right is just to provide better security to the tenants like the *ad hoc* or temporary government employees or workers in factories are given some soil of protection to continue in their jobs.

Historically, traditionally and conceptually, therefore, the following are suggested as guidelines for better implementation of land reform measures:

1. The excess land should be taken over from the big landholders. The surplus land should be distributed expeditiously and accompanied by timely supply of inputs and investment support. J.R. Yojana/P.M. Rojgar Yojana, NREGP may be resorted to in order to assist the land reform beneficiaries. In areas not covered by such schemes, direct financing by government will be necessary.
2. The ceiling laws should be amended according to the national guidelines based on the conclusions reached at the Chief Ministers Conferences on Ceilings of Agricultural Holdings and should be included in the IXth Schedule to the Constitution.
3. Loopholes in existing laws should be plugged so as to secure complete tenurial and ownership rights on under-tenants and sharecroppers.
4. Priority should be given to comprehensive programmes for preparation and maintenance of land records even where there is no statute for preparation of such records.

5. Special attention need to be paid to tribal areas. Loopholes in laws applicable to tribals need to be plugged and administrative machinery need to be strengthened. Cadastral survey of tribal areas should be completed where it has not already been done.
6. All tenants including sharecroppers should be identified, their right should be recorded and permanent heritable rights should be conferred on them before consolidation operations are started. In the programme for consolidation of holdings, land of small holders and surplus wastelands available for distribution should be consolidated in compact blocks to facilitate the future public or government investments for irrigation etc. to the underprivileged.
7. Publicity requires to be intensified to familiarize the beneficiaries and even the government servants charged with the implementation of land reform laws with the provisions of the law.
8. The administrative set-up requires to be strengthened at different levels and should be imbued with a sense of direction and purpose.
9. Adequate Plan Allocation: Adequate financial provision is required for financing of land reforms.
10. Associations or committees of beneficiaries réquire to be established at village and block levels to fight for the rights of underprivileged and to advise on implementation of all measures of land reforms and provision of supporting facilities to beneficiaries. Landless and sharecroppers and small land holders should be adequately represented on these committees.

The above can form basis to work out factors of land reforms in a generalized way:

1. Distribution of government wasteland and implementation of Bhoodan Act, where such legislations exist.
2. To detect benami lands; to analyse about lands under court's injunction and to gradually reduce the limit of land ceiling to accommodate the less poor.
3. Granting permanent rights of homestead to landless/homeless

persons and implementation of homestead tenancy legislation where such law exists.

4. Removal of encroachment on government lands and redistribution of such lands to landless persons.
5. Restoration of land alienated by the tribals in contravention of the law, in tribal areas.
6. The definition of personal cultivation should lay stress on the following ingredients:

   (a) The person claiming to be in cultivation of the land must bear the entire cost of cultivation;
   (b) He must cultivate his own land by his own labour or by the labour of any member of his family;
   (c) He or member of his family should reside for the greater part of the year in the locality where the land is located; and
   (d) Cultivation should be the main source of his income.

7. No transfer of agricultural lands should be permitted to any non-agriculturist.
8. The tenants (whether occupancy or non-occupancy) dispossessed by force or by fraud or by any other illegal means from their land must be restored to their possession as expeditiously as possible.
9. The field data has shown that there are large number of share-croppers/tenants at will, who have been working with the same landowner for a number of years and are entitled to be conferred the status of occupancy tenant/owner within their respective states. All such tenants should be conferred with the status of occupancy tenant/owner with retrospective effect. Even those who have been evicted or shifted from earlier plots should be restored to the status of occupancy tenant/ownership right. The recognized Kisan Sabha/Peasant Organization/Voluntary Organization/Activist Organization should be associated in such effort and their evidence on the tenancy status of an incumbent should be made admissible.
10. If the landowner does not give receipt to the non-occupying tenant, the share-cropper should be allowed to deposit share

of the produce of landowner with the nearest authority. The landowner should be made liable to criminal prosecution for refusal to grant receipts. Onus of proof should be shifted to the landowner to establish that the latter is not cultivating the land.

11. The tenants in the cultivable lands of religious institutions, trusts, mutts, etc., should also be conferred with ownership right in respect of those lands. Those institutions may be provided with annuity.
12. Resumption of land by landowners from tenants for self-cultivation should not be allowed except in case of physically-handicapped or serving army personnel.
13. Ejection of tenants for non-payment of rent should be prohibited.
14. The small and marginal farmers who are compelled to lease out to big landowners should be linked with institutional agencies, anti-poverty programmes and rural development schemes (like Jawahar Rojgar Yojana/P.M. Rojgar Yojana, ITDP[6], etc.) to make their farms viable. If they lack implements, irrigation facility and inputs, such facilities should be extended to them.
15. In case of a dispute between the landowner and the persons claiming to be tenants/sharecroppers, the burden of proof should be on the landowner to prove the negative.
16. Sharecroppers should be legally included as tenants within the tenancy-reform laws.
17. Special drives should be launched to identify informal tenants/sharecroppers in all the States who should be immediately conferred occupancy tenant/ownership status. In this drive, the local Peasant Organizations/Agricultural Labour Organizations/Voluntary Organizations/Kisan Sabhas and other activist groups should be actively associated.
18. Inadequacies in the administrative organisation should be removed. It should be land reform oriented.
19. The recognized local Peasant Organization/Agricultural Labour Organization/Voluntary Organization/Activist Organization should be permitted to file claims for the conferment of occupancy right/ownership right to

sharecropper/non-occupancy tenant before the appropriate authority.

20. Cooperative fanning should be encouraged in villages on the pattern of Egypt. Panchayats may be nodal agencies to organize these. Arrangement for marketing, implements and servicing should be available at Panchayat.
21. General awareness and concretization camps should be organized in every state having pockets of high tenancy.
22. Implementation of legislation relating to money lending and abolition of money lending.
23. Updating and maintenance of land records in a computerized form and implementation of legislation if any, enacted therewith.
24. Political will should be created. For this landless, small and marginal farmers' representatives should be given place in local panchayat bodies and ministries so that they are associated at each decision-making level.
25. Emphasis should be given to social reforms so that the farmers enjoy the benefits of reforms as healthy contributors to society.
26. Panchayats should be organized and should be really independent in their affairs. They should be associated in implementing land reforms measures. They may be given power to dispose of petty land matters and development of farmlands also.
27. The poor peasants may be provided legal aid up to the level of the Supreme Court. The various stages of land litigation should be reduced. Land tribunals may be set up to reduce the pondicherry at the High Courts as substitutes for speedy disposal of cases. The Lok Adalats should be empowered to dispose of land reforms litigations along with prompt disposal of cases by rural courts, *i.e.* Nyaya Panchayat/Rural Nyayalaya.

NOTE & REFERENCES

1. Yugandhar, B.N. (ed); *Land Reforms in India—Andhra Pradesh—People's Pressure and Administrative Innovation*, p. 17.

2. Ayub Khan, *Friends Not Master*, p. 91.
3. Recently constituted three new States in India, i.e. Chhattisgarh from Madhya Pradesh, Jharkhand from Bihar and Uttarakhand from Uttar Pradesh have regions which were also neglected by their parent States from the point of view of land reforms.
4. Dr. Agrawal, P.K.: *Land Reforms in India*, p. 56.
5. Dr. Arnold Toynbee in 'We, the People' by N.A. Palkhivala, p. 73.
6. ITDP stands for Integrated Tribal Development Programme.

2

Factors Constituting Land Reforms

The following factors can be considered to arrive at a mathematical formula for quantifying land reform. The following linear equation has been suggested.

The term factor analysis "embraces a variety of techniques". Our discussion focuses on the one procedure 'principal component analysis' and the factors derived from the analysis are expressed as linear equations. These linear equations are of the form:

$$T(LR) = R_1L_1 + R_2L_2 + R_3L_3 + R_4L_4 + R_5L_5 + R_6L_6 + R_7L_7 + R_8L_8 + R_9L_9 + R_{10}L_{10} + \ldots\ldots + R_nL_n$$

T(LR) is the Total/Resultant Land Reform.

R is the weightage or ranking of the factor.

L indicates factor related to land reform on the basis of conclusions arrived at earlier. It may represent one factor or combination of factors. The factors are thus as follows:

L_1: Existence or implementation of Employment Generating Schemes like Jawahar Rojgar Yojana, N.R.E.P.[1] I.T.D.P. or I.R.D.P.[2] or P.M. Rojgar Yojana or National Rural Employment Guarantee Programme (NREGP).

L_2: Whether Tenancy or share croppers are recorded or unrecorded and are given their rights. They should not be ejected.

L_3: Practice of cooperative farming or assistance by Panchayats by developing local leadership and helping the cultivators locally in all matters.

L_4: Distribution of Government surplus land after vesting in State and giving possession to the pattadars or assignees of the vested lands after distribution of surplus lands and thereafter.

L_5: Position of land records, detection of benami lands and whether land has been equitably distributed and passbooks of land-details have been issued.

L_6: Extent of social and religious reforms.

L_7: Availability of legal aid to the landless agricultural labourers, pattadars, sharecroppers or poor peasants.

L_8: Financial assistance or credit for supply of timely inputs and other investment support.

L_9: Success of consolidation operation.

L_{10}: Allotment of house sites and restoration of alienated tribal land or lands transferred due to distress.

The above equation can be thus, represented as:

$$T_{j(LR)} = R_i L_i \text{ and } R_i \text{ is the multiplication factor, where}$$
$$i = 1, 2, 3, 4, \ldots\ldots 10 \ldots\ldots n$$

The co-efficient R_i may be determined for each factor depending on the relative importance of that factors. R_1, R_2, R_3, R_4, R_5, R_6, R_7, R_8, R_9, R_{10} or any other co-efficient or factor taken later on.

The weightage *inter se* can be determined by developing closed-ended response based on the concept or decision of the research. Here, one cannot avoid subjectivity. To reduce the subjectivity, even detailed discussion can be made to determine the allocation of the weightage. For this purpose, a rating scale may be fixed. Rating scales, by and large, try to secure the intensity of the respondents' feelings on a pre-defined sets of response alternatives. Here, guidance has been taken from Likert Scale which is also called a 'summated ratings' scale. Let us construct the following six statements or decisions relating to issues under investigation, very adequate, adequate, so so, inadequate, very inadequate, nil. Let us assign the numerical values or rank ranging from 0 to 10 different categories as follows:

very adequate	assigned	10 marks
adequate	assigned	8 marks
so so	assigned	4 marks
inadequate	assigned	2 marks
very inadequate	assigned	1 mark
nil	assigned	0 mark

Using this method of scoring, total scoring is calculated depending on the strength of the factor.

Let us, therefore, assign percentage importance to each factor taking clues from discussion in chapter 1 of this book.

T(LR) is taken as 100 per cent. Therefore, each factor will be determined on the basis of 'a'/100 where 'a' represents percentage weightage *inter se* of each factor. L_t: 4 per cent is given maximum value for Employment Generating Schemes during lean season of work or otherwise. This can be maximum as R_1L_1 = 10* .04 = .4 Similarly,

L_2: 20 per cent weightage is given to recording of sharecroppers and protection to their rights of cultivation. Therefore, L_2 factor will be 20 per cent in ideal condition but on-rating scale, it will vary from zero to 10* .2 = 2

L_3: Local Assistance, it is given 10 per cent weightage. If the Panchayats are established and are functioning well, there is semblance of co-operative farming or pisciculture and there are organizations of pattadars, agricultural labourers or sharecroppers, the adequate weightage will be given. In case of ideal situation of covering the entire village through co-operative farming, full weightage or very adequate category will be given. However, before the stage of co-operative farming, rural organizations are necessary to safeguard rights of cultivators.

L_4: 40 per cent weightage is earmarked for distribution of government vested lands. This is the main target specially in the Indian context. In fact, aim of Imposition of Ceiling Acts is to take away excess lands from the big landholders and to affect redistribution. It is not sufficient that the lands have gone to government but also should be distributed. Therefore, if the lands are still with the local landlords, it will be of very inadequate category. If the lands are vested to government but possession is not taken over, and benami lands are not unearthed, it will be within inadequate category. If the Acts have been implemented, this will be 50-50 category of case. If the lands are distributed but the possession is not given, it will be classified as adequate category. Only in case of lands properly allotted along with possession given over, it will be classified as 'very adequate' category allocating 10 marks.

L_5: Weightage 8 per cent is given to the position of land records and existing position of landownership or landholding. If lands are more or less equitably distributed and there is no cultivation beyond ceiling limit in the village, it will get allocation of rank within 50-50 category. If land records along with village maps properly do exist, then it will have a ranking in adequate category and if passbooks detailing individual holdings are distributed, it will be a perfect system in 'very adequate' ranking with full 10 marks.

L_6: Total weightage 3 per cent is given to social and religious reforms. Poor people spend a lot of money on festivals and ceremonies and do not go for work on a number of days to celebrate many unknown local festivals or rituals due to superstition or orthodoxy. They also indulge in indebtedness and drinking. If there is lot of indebtedness, it will be 50-50 or normal category or average category. Social reform like keeping villagers away from gambling or drinking, will earn "adequate classification". If the agriculturists are free from religious dogmas, they will be placed in the highest ranking.

L_7: Weightage 3 per cent is allocated for legal aid to the poor. If legal aid is available only through mutual conciliation without any statutory system, it will fall in very inadequate ranking. If conciliation or disposal of disputes are done through the aegis of Panchayat bodies or Nyaya Panchayats or through official agencies, it will fall within inadequate category. If legal aid facilities are available up to revenue courts, it will be in 50-50 or normal category. If legal aid is available up to District Judge court's level, it will be adequate. And if legal aid system free of cost actually is available up to High Court, Supreme Court level, it will be given the highest ranking.

L_8: 5 per cent weightage is given for financial assistance for crops through government or cooperative or Panchayat agencies including subsidies. This also reflects the credit facilities available for cultivation to delink the share cropper or pattadar from the moneylender. In this category, mostly crop-credit finances are included, i.e., credit available to purchase plough, cattle, manures and seeds etc. However, if soil conservation work has been done or Irrigational facilities are available, the village will be placed in very inadequate or inadequate rankings respectively. If credits from banks are available, it will be of adequate category. If government subsidies are available fully, then the situation will be of very adequate nature.

L_9: Only 1 per cent weightage is given to consolidation operations. Without co-operative farming consolidation has come under criticism due to corrupt practices. Therefore, if the consolidation operations are started, it will be of 50-50 category. If the *chaks* or plots are finally demarcated, it will be of adequate category. If the plots are dispute free, it will be placed in 'very adequate' ranking.

L_{10}: 6 per cent significance or strength is given equally to allotment of house sites to the rural poor as 3 per cent and 3 per cent for restoration of alienated land due to distress. As tribal population is very scanty, the restoration of tribal land has also been put in the latter category. If the house sites are allotted, it will be adequate ranking. If the house sites are so made that the poor classes are free from fear of the upper classes, and they are properly put in effective possession, the ranking will be very adequate. In ideal case R_{10} is ten.

In case of ideal situation, all R_{is} will have 10 ranking points. Accordingly, the estimate may be made whether a village, subdivision, district or state comes within the type of category i.e., very inadequate, adequate, 50-50, inadequate or very inadequate state of affairs of land reforms.

The coefficients in the factor equations are called "factor loadings". They appear in each factor column, corresponding to each variable. The equation may be depicted in a random case as $R_{(LR)} = 10L_1 + 8L_2 + 0L_3 + 0L_4 + 4L_5 + 0L_6 + 0L_7 + 2L_8 + 1L_9 + 1L_{10}$ where L_1... to L_{10} are fixed already.

The factor loadings depict their relative importance of each variable with respect to a particular factor. In the above equation, we have got positive loading factor indicating that they are variables of importance in determining the extent of land reform in a given sample. Similarly, some factors with negative attribute may be included which pull back land reforms. But as this study is a part of legal study, there is not much scope to go into acute niceties or finer details. It is to concretize the ideas so that real focus may not be lost sight of while viewing the land reforms as an integrated whole.

The above equation, is reduced in number form as follows:

$T_{(LR)} =$ $10 \times 0.04 + 8 \times 2 + 0 \times .1 + 0 \times .4 + 2 \times .08 + 4 \times .03 + 0 \times .03 + 0 \times 03 + 2 \times .03 + 0 \times .01 + 2 \times 0 = .4 + 1.6 + .16 + .12 + 0 + 0 + .06 + 0 + 0 = 2.34$ which is in inadequate category.

It means that the important factors to contribute for land reforms are distribution of surplus land, recording of sharecroppers and organizing the rural folk for implementation of land reforms. The three factors will amount to 70 per cent of resultant land reform, i.e. $T_{(LR)}$.

In the ideal solution, the factors derived will explain 100 per cent of the variance in each of the original variables or factors.

There are two important subjective issues which should be properly resolved before employing factor analysis model.

1. How best the factors should be employed in attempting to reduce the data? How best the criteria should be used in establishing that number?
2. The labelling of the factors is intuitive and subjective.
   The following resultant land reform (LR) is obtained for the State of Uttar Pradesh.

$$T_{(LR)}^{3} = .003\,(I) + 2\,(II) + .1\,(III) + 1.6\,(IV) + .32\,(V) + .03\,(VI) + 00\,(VII) + .1\,(VIII) + .4\,(IX) + .48\,(X) = 3.23, \text{ i.e. about } 32.3 \text{ per cent.}$$

Applying preceding empirical formula, we find that land reform beyond over 50 per cent category should be good. Beyond 80 per cent, it should be adequate. On the basis of above formula we find extent of land reform in two States of India i.e. U.P. and West Bengal, is as follows: 32 per cent and 67 per cent respectively.

Similarly, the formula can be successfully applied to assess total land reforms from macro to the micro level, i.e. from national level to state, district, sub-divisional/taluka/tehsil, block or village level and accordingly, corrective steps can be taken to improve the extent of land reform at that level.

In West Bengal we may give following weightage:

L_1 = As landless and poor farmers get only about 15 days work out of 150 days required. The work is allotted more or less equitable except little party colouring which should not be there. Poor is poor irrespective of caste, creed, community, colour or political affiliation.

Therefore, weightage will be just below average, i.e. inadequate = 2.

L_2 = This factor of recording of sharecroppers is very successful. Though as per an estimate there are more sharecroppers and there can be conferment of ownership rights to them like in Maharashtra. Yet this factor gets full marks due to very poor performance of other States in this regard. Therefore R_2 = 10.

L_3 = This factor also gets good marking as Panchayats and Krishak Organizations are very strong so much so there is hardly any scope of injustice to the poor farmers unless contrary takes place. Moreover, as co-operative farming is yet far off and efforts by governmental agencies are nil, this may get adequate marking, i.e. 8.

L_4 = There is equitable distribution of land more or less but all lands could not be distributed yet as about 1.70 lakh acres of land is locked in litigation. Therefore, this factor can only get at the most adequate category, i.e. 8.

L_5 = Position of land records is as backward as any other state. There is no provision of regular updating. However, by induction of lowest level functionaries, i.e., revenue inspectors at the Gram Panchayat levels, the situation is likely to improve. Therefore, it is averaged R = 5.

L_6 = Social and religious factors are little dormant in society but are very much effective in personal lives. Therefore, farmers are occupied with the rites and rituals. L_6 is, therefore, very inadequate with 1 rating.

L_7 = Neither Panchayats nor religious reformers Court and is also inadequate. Therefore, R_7 = 5.

L_8 = Facility of crop credit is satisfactory through Panchayats but due to poor recovery, bankers retard progress. It will be of average category, i.e. R_8 = 5. Allotment of house site is O.K. but construction is inadequate.

L_9 = Neither consolidation taken up nor is likely to be taken up. Therefore R_9, = 0.

L_{10} = Restoration of alienation land due to distress is done but restoration of land to tribals shows lethargy as cases before Special Officer, Scheduled Castes and Scheduled Tribes are not processed expeditiously. The factor gets a weightage as adequate = 8.

Calculating above factors, we find:

$$T(LR) = .4 \times 2\,(I) + 2 \times 10\,(II) + .1 \times 8\,(III) + 4 \times 8\,(IV) + .8 \times 5\,(V) + .3 \times 1\,(VI) + .3 \times 5\,(VII) + .5 \times 5\,(VIII) + 0 \times 1\,(IX) + .6 \times 8\,(X) = .8 + 20 + .8 + 32 + 4 + .3 + 1.5 + 2.5 + 0 + 4.8 = 66.7\% = 67\%.$$

Which is over 50 per cent category but is below adequate category (80 per cent).

NOTES

1. N.R.E.P stands for National Rural Employment Programme.
2. I.R.D.P. means Integrated Rural Development Programme.
3. I. stands for Employment Generating Scheme
   II. stands for Position of Sharecroppers
   III. stands for Cooperative Farming
   IV. stands for Distribution of Surplus Land
   V. stands for Status of Land Records
   VI. stands for Social and Religious Reforms
   VII. stands for Availability of Legal Aid
   VIII. stands for financial assistance for crops.
   IX. for consolidation and
   X. for allotment of house sites

REFERENCE

Dr. Agrawal, P.K.: Issues in Land Reforms, RGICS working paper, no. 18,000, Rajiv Gandhi Institute For Contemporary Studies, Rajiv Gandhi Foundation, Jawahar Bhawan, Dr. R.P. Road, New Delhi-110001, pp. 16-23.

3

Legal and Economic Factors in Land Reforms

Land reforms are basically redistributive measures of landed properties:

Rural population is 72.2 per cent as per 2001 census

The share[1] of agriculture in GDP of India is as follows:

1950-1960	49.4%
1990-2000	27.7%
2001-2002	22.5%

Purchasing power in rural India should improve.

1. Constitutional Background

The Constitution (First) Amendment Act, 1951 added two new Articles 31A and 31B and added the Ninth Schedule to the Constitution:

It provided right of property of greater segment of population

One of the Directives to the State under Article 39(b) reads that 'the ownership and control of the material resources of the community are so distributed as best to subserve the common good'.

In Golaknath Case the Supreme Court held that the amendment cannot be made by Parliament so as to take away or abridge the fundamental rights enshrined therein including right to property.

The concept of property right in Part IV is conditioned by social interests and social justice.

State List entry 18 reads as: "Land that is to say right in or over land tenures, including the relation of landlord and tenant and the collection of rents, transfers and alienation of agriculture land, land improvement and agriculture loans, colonization.

Re-enacting Article 31(1) in the form of Article 300-A by the Constitution (Forty Fourth Amendment) Act, 1978 provided remedy by a civil suit or statutory remedy, if any, say by way of damages.

Land reform measures involve joint efforts by the States and the Union.

2. Cases Pending in Courts

Table 3.1: Cases and Area in Litigation in High Courts (Implementation of Land Ceiling Laws)

S. No.	*States*	*High Court*	
		Cases	*Areas*
1.	Andhra Pradesh	1254	44424
2.	Assam	61	23596
3.	Bihar	648	50098
4.	Karnataka	1165	94402
5.	Kerala	1501	27657
6.	Madhya Pradesh	271	21232
7.	Rajasthan	201	21800
8.	Uttar Pradesh	2060	40496
	Total	**7161**	**323705**

High Courts can dispose of huge pendency of about seven thousand cases involving about 3.2 lakh acres of surplus government land by constituting specialized benches.

3. Ceiling Limits on Various States[2]

Table 3.2: Actual ceiling limits in various States (Area in ha)

State	*Irrigated with one crop*
Andhra Pradesh	6.07 to 10.93
Bihar	10.12
Gujarat	6.07 to 19.73
Haryana	10.90

(*Contd.*)

(*Contd.*)

State	Irrigated with one crop
Karnataka	10.12
M.P.	10.93
Punjab	11.00
Rajasthan	10.93
Tamil Nadu	12.14
U.P.	10.95
West Bengal	5.00

* 1 ha = 2.42 acres = 11712.859 yards

4. Personal Cultivation

The Apex Court consistently upheld the practice of personal cultivation.

Resumption of Land by the Landlord

The Supreme Court cautioned the High Court that it should not go into the merits of the case and decide questions of facts not before it in its writ jurisdiction.

Land Held by Deity to Continue as Debuttar

In the garb of large religious and social organizations, many individuals are satisfying their piety ego at the cost of the landless and the downtrodden of the society.

5. Tenancy Reforms

Tenancy reforms more or less depend on quality of drafting of legislation.

Publicity of tenancy movements by tenants like bargadars certainly affect the minds of courts favourably as judges do not work in vacuum.

The Government of Maharashtra is turning the clock back by acquiring lands of many of the landless in the Konkan division.

Ceiling on Land Holdings

The Supreme Court demolished the way-out to evade ceiling by planting the trees on surplus land. (Justice D.P. Mohapatra)

Bar to Civil Jurisdiction

The Supreme Court agrees that the jurisdiction of civil courts stands ousted in matters where revenue courts are empowered to grant relief.

Records of Rights

The rors produced through computers can only claim presumption until they are challenged.

Allotment of Surplus Land

The Apex Court is inclining to support the protagonists that the larger plots are more beneficial for productivity.

6. Land Reorms and Productivity

It is a bogy spread by the vested interest that fragmentation of lands result into less mechanism and less investment in agricultural sector. The measures of land reforms contribute to the higher productivity in land due to following reasons:

(i) Human Resource Development (HRD)
(ii) All economics matrix/calculations take into consideration the cost of human labour while arriving at the cost of production. In old age, when a person is unable to do any hard labour, he at least can grow some vegetables, forest or cash-crops without feeling useless in life.

In fact experiments by two major NGOs in Gujarat and Maharashtra have proved beyond doubt that even small patches of land have been instrumental to increase production by way of harvesting water and joint agricultural operations supported by government schemes, cooperative credits, mutual cooperation and joint efforts. Implementation of land reforms has definitely resulted into higher productivity in few States like in West Bengal.

Advantages

The higher productivity due to land reform has two pronged advantages:

The assignees of the vested lands or the share croppers can make farming cooperative societies without disturbing the individual ownership on the Egypt pattern.
The diversion of middle class youths to their lands will reduce unemployment and law and order problems in rural India.

Indifference to Land Reforms

The first and the foremost reason is that the present administrative or political elite are apt in the art of fire fighting. Secondly, the political elite don't want to work hard. The public also believe in 'personality cult'.

It is in this context that even sometimes the socialists have regarded land reforms measures as opium for masses as they delay the onset of blood revolution.

FAO now, so late, has supported the concept of small farms.

According to FAO, redistribution of only 5 per cent of farm land in India, coupled with improved access to water, could reduce rural poverty level by 30 per cent under what they would otherwise be, so that in Indian conditions of land, water reforms would be a key approach.

Thus, the process of land reform is required to be hastened in India.

Conclusion

The solid base of land reforms will provide a strong platform to the economy to take off. Both are complementary to each other.

REFERENCES

1. Government of India's Report published by Department of Land Resources, Ministry of Rural Development & Department of Justice, Ministry of Law and Justice: Quarterly Progress Report (Cumulative) on Implementation of Land Ceiling Laws for quarter ending in December, 2000 (Area in acres).
2. Dr. Agrawal, P.K.: *Actual ceiling limits in various States, Land Reforms in India*, M.D. Publications, New Delhi-2, p. 198, Year 1993, Total pages 273.

4

Implementation of Land Reforms: A Case Study

The innovation is about the methodology of implementation of land reform measures. The need for implementation of land reforms has been accepted by one and all. The doubt and curiosity is how these measures can be successfully implemented. Land reform as a solution to extremists' agitations in various states has by and large been agreed upon.

I was associated with the implementation of land reforms in West Bengal from day one of the Left Front Rule in West Bengal since 1977 as an IAS officer.

I have projected in my book 'Land Reforms in India' how the land reform measures can be successfully replicated in the largest state of India, i.e. U.P. without any change in laws relating to land in U.P.

In this paper, I have lucidly stated how the twin measures of land reforms, i.e. recording of sharecroppers and distribution of surplus government lands were implemented in West Bengal so that these could be easily replicated. To simplify, the procedure, more emphasis is on practical experience rather than on academic or semantic discussions

I am sure that some of the public conscious energetic and dutiful bureaucrats and politician will take some clues and implement the land reforms in their own way in the changed circumstances.

1. Introduction

Land reform basically is the redistribution of rights and interests in land in favour of the landless and the poor cultivators. In this paper only two major land reforms innovations are being dealt with which were actually undertaken in West Bengal.

Every political party promises to implement land reforms measures before elections but few of them take it seriously after they win election. But it was an exception after the landslide victory of the left front parties in West Bengal in 1977 led by the Communist Party of India (Marxists) [CPI (M)]. The Left Front allies had come in power with a specific mandate to implement land reforms. I was one of the Presiding Officers in this election. After the Left Front came into power, they reorganized the state apparatus for this purpose and gave it first priority in their governance. They were lucky that their predecessor government had passed requisite pro-land reform legislations. The only need was to implement in the field. The predecessor government had made about 7 ha. as maximum permissible land to be held by any raiyat/person. In addition, they had provided under Section 16 of the WBLR Act, 1955 that anybody cultivating land of another person on condition to deliver a share will get 75 per cent share of produce if the person, who cultivates the land, known as bargadar[1] provides plough, seeds, cattle, fertilizers, irrigation and other inputs.

2. Operation Barga

(i) Need

Without waiting for administrative arrangements for implementation of the above provisions, relating to the tenancy cultivation/barga cultivation, the Krishak Sabha, peasants' wing of CPI(M) started harvesting crops of landowners in an organized manner and removal of the produce to their place (*khamar*) for separation of grains. Earlier these harvested crops used to be taken to the central place controlled by the landlord or the landowner where he used to control the process of separation of produce and then he used to distribute to the bargadars at his sweet discretion. The landowners in such cases, never allowed more than 50 per cent of produce after harvesting to the sharecroppers or bargadars. The sharecroppers started claiming 75 per cent of produce where there were dispute with the landowners or the relations between the landowners and the sharecroppers were strained. In few cases, so far exploited sharecroppers or local peasants' organizations also wanted to score with the landowner, who used to enjoy unhibited power in the village so far. The administration stood by the side of the sharecroppers as per the changed political scenario. As a result, the landowners approached the local administration like Block Development Officer (BDO) and Junior Land Reforms Officer (JLRO) now known as Block Land & Land Reforms Officer (BLLRO). The BDO was authorized to mediate between the two but in the presence of the local peasants organization on behalf of the sharecropper. As the peasants organizations were tough and uncompromising in most of the cases as they had earlier experience of rough behaviour of landowners with them. Now law and administration both were on their side. Earlier landowners could do this only by keeping administration specially police administration on their side. Thus, the administration slowly veered around the sharecroppers and poor cultivators in the villages and all demanded to get the sharecroppers/bargadars recorded. In the melee, many unscrupulous bargadars under the umbrella of the peasants' organizations also took undue advantage and started cultivating land and harvesting crops which they had no right. It was essential to show the cultivation through sharecropper and the landowners did not cultivate land personally. He cultivated through him and there was an agreement to allow him to cultivate his land. This agreement in the village is to be inferred through conduct because village economy runs mainly paperless and cashless. Therefore, if the alleged bargadars had been cultivating land of the landowner peacefully for past two/three years, he was presumed to be bargadars unless otherwise it was contradicted. Or the landowner could show that he cultivated through daily labourers and that he maintained lists of those daily labourers and the proof of payment of their due daily wages. The landowners in rural West Bengal never gave receipt of produce from the bargadars nor maintained register for cultivatior and through daily labourers. The peasants' organizations took advantages of these legal lacuna and slowly they controlled the cultivation scene in rural Bengal. I was young IAS officer used to settle such harvesting disputes as BDO which wee questioned by the Commissioner as regards their legal basis. Seeing one-sided swing in the rural area, creation of law and order and legal problems, the local administration approached the policy makers unanimously to get bargadars recorded. This is what the political elite at the state level wanted. Without creation of demand for amendment of rule on law, the rule or law is not implemented in spirit and with speed. The top bureaucrats headed by

Shri D. Bandyopadhyay, IAS with the requisite will drafted programme for barga recording throughout the State. Operation Barga accordingly as a programme was launched in West Bengal on 5th July, 1978. As per report before 1977, the total number of bargadars recorded were:

154,816 (CS) + 30,681 (RS) = 1,85,497

As per estimate of peasants organizations, there were 7,47,716 bargadars whereas as per census there were about 6,86,188 bargadars in the State. Therefore, it required special attention. Apart from this, the then Minister-in-Charge of Land and Land Reforms Department Shri Binoy Krishna Chaudhury declared in the West Bengal Legislative Assembly on 13th March, 1978 that recovery of benami lands will be another priority of the State Government. These lands after identification will be vested in the State which will be in due course distributed among the landless persons as per the well laid down norms which are more or less same all over the country. With these twin objectives in place, the new Left Front Government in West Bengal started its journey towards social engineering and formation of egalitarian society in rural West Bengal. I was associated in Operation Barga as Sub-divisional Officer, Barasat where VIPs used to come to see the new methodology from its beginning.

The legal provisions were strengthened by amending Rule 21 and Schedule A of the West Bengal Land Reforms Rules, 1955. The Schedule A was amended by amending the second proviso by providing that "the Settlement Officer could direct that names of bargadars shall be incorporated in the record-of-rights by the Revenue Officer subordinate to him after holding such enquiry and after giving the persons claiming as bargadars and the owners of the land concerned such opportunity of being heard as the Revenue Officer may deem fit." On the question whether individual notice or general notice should be given for the purpose of giving opportunity of being heard, the relevant rule was amended in 1981 [Proviso 2 was added to clause 1 of Schedule A appended to W.B. L.R. Rules, 1965]. It was now laid down that opportunity of being heard would be deemed to have been given if within one week before the enquiry, the Revenue Officer publishes a notice of his intention of enquiry by fixing a notice at conspicuous place in the office of the Gram Panchayat concerned. Two "Explanations" were further added, thereby legalizing the issue of bargadars' certificates. The second amendment closely followed, and the Revenue Officer was authorized to incorporate in the record-of-rights changes on account of barga cultivation by making necessary enquiries. These amendments accorded the required legal sanction to the methodology of Operation Barga. The immediate impact of Operation Barga was encouraging, as was reflected in the budget speech of the Minister mentioned earlier. It was indeed a matter of satisfaction to note that the rate of recording accelerated by 357 per cent compared to the rate of Rs. recording, within a span of 6 months from July to December, 1978. The table below gives the figures in detail:

Table 4.1: Recording of Bargadars upto 31.01.1979

Name of District	*Number of Bargadars*
(1)	(2)
Bankura	40,709
Birbhum	32,749
Burdwan	36,805
Coochbehar	35,405
Darjeeling	7,870
Hooghly	42,433
Howrah	23,187
Jalpaiguri	31,777
Malda	46,421
Midnapore	88,678
Murshidabad	31,614
Nadia	24,439
Purulia	—
24-Parganas	75,443
West Dinajpur	55,164

As Operation Barga gained momentum a counter-propaganda by the land owners, and sometimes their counter-move, was discernible in the publicity media and in the law courts. This was not unexpected, as there must be some reaction to attempts at structural changes. One of the criticisms was that adequate notice was not being given to the land owners through the existing system of giving notice was legalized by an amendment of the West Bengal Land Reforms Rules, 1965. According to this amendment, parties interested would be deemed to have been given an opportunity of being heard if the Revenue Officer published a notice of his intention to make an enquiry for recording names of bargadars by affixing the notice to a conspicuous place or by beat of drums. This amendment was followed by another by which granting of a barga certificate under Section 50 of the West Bengal Land Reforms Act, 1955 was legalized. Originally, Operation Barga was to be completed by 30th June, 1979. The Board of Revenue extended the date to 31st December, 1979. An assessment of the result showed downward trend in the rate of recording of bargadars. While extending the date of Operation Barga to 30th June, 1980, the Board of Revenue issued a departmental circular in which it was stated that while there was no need to change the methodology of Operation Barga, there was a great deal of need for the officials to follow the procedure laid down with more sincerity. As a result of the further drive, by 30th April, 1980, 8,54,740 bargadars were recorded, as compared to 5,72,694 bargadars recorded by 31st January, 1979. The monthly average recording in this period was 18,803.

The programme of Operation Barga was further extended first by two months—to 31st August, 1980, and then again by 3 months, to 30th November, 1980. Total number of bargadars recorded by August, 1980 was about 9.5 lakhs. Thus, in two years' time names of about 4.5 lakhs bargadars was recorded under the crash programme of the Operation Barga continued and upto September, 1987, 13,75,284 bargadars were recorded. Later on the addition per year was gradually declining. As on date, i.e. upto October, 2007[3], 15,10,173 number of bargadars have been recorded covering a area of 1,11,12,71 acres.

Further assuming that in the present set up and legal framework, 25 per cent of the bargadars will remain outside the records. Thus, we may reasonably conclude that the total number of bargadars in West Bengal will be around 20 lakhs[4]. On the other hand, the excess vested land in the State would be around 15 lakh acres.

(ii) Salient Features of the 'Operation Barga'

The entire State of West Bengal (except areas of Purulia district and Islampur Sub-Division which were ceded from Bihar), was for the purpose of scheme, divided into two areas: (i) Area 'A' consisting of about 24,000 mouzas already covered by Khanapuri Bujharat, and (ii) Area 'B' comprising the remaining 18,000 mouzas not covered by K.B. For the purpose of hastening the process of recording the names of bargadars, it was decided that in Area 'B', a crash programme called 'Operation Barga' was to be undertaken so as to cover the entire area within one year, i.e. 30th June, 1979. Priority pockets with large concentration of bargadars would have to be selected in consultation with peasants' organizations and composite squads of officers consisting of Junior Land Reforms Officers and Kanungos would have to cover the specified priority pockets within a very short time. In respect of Area 'A', 'Operation Barga' would be taken up in a selective basis on information received on joint or individual petitions or from other sources.

The methodology was: A squad will, after giving due notice, hold an evening meeting on the first (D-l) day at a venue which is a place of habitual congregation of bargadars and agricultural labourers. A group of mouzas may be taken at a time and a general public notice will be given. Care will be taken that these four points are clearly discussed in the meeting: (i) legal and economic benefits that will accrue to recorded bargadars, (ii) security of the right of cultivation, (iii) pooling of funds flowing of like FFW, ITDP, NREP, IRDP, etc.[5] The similar programmes are still there with changed nomenclatures, and (iv) need for a supportive organization of their own for the enduring benefits of land reforms. During and after the meeting names of bargadars will be tentatively enlisted. On the next (D-2) day, field enquiry and verification will be made and the verified list will be hung up at a public place so that objections if any could be raised. On the third (D-3) day after hearing objections, if any, names of bargadars will be recorded and bargadar's certificates will be distributed. In this way, names of bargadars would be speedily recorded within the four walls of West Bengal Land Reforms Act, 1955 and the Rules framed thereunder. This is the programme of 'Operation Barga'.

3. Vesting and Distribution of Government Surplus Land

Upto 1977, 11,22,000 acre of lands were vested to the State. Out of that, only 6,12,000 acre of lands were distributed among the landless poor. There were three problems in this area of land reform:

Firstly, the beneficiaries who were given government surplus land (known as assignees of the vested lands or *pattadars*), were not put in possession of land. Some of the land continued with the erstwhile owners or their agents.

Secondly, the assignees of the vested lands or *pattadars*, were arbitrarily selected, because the local Member of the Legislative

Assembly (MLA) indirectly controlled the selection process of beneficiaries. He had no time and his representative indulged in all sorts of malpractices with the connivance of the local land revenue wing of the Collector of the District.

Thirdly, lot of land was still lying outside the net of vesting as these lands belonged to influential persons of ruling political party mainly Congress or to other local influential persons including so called charitable organizations or to big money lenders or strong Zamindars.

First problem was solved easily, because the CPI (M) had their own wing of amins or land experts who were conversant with those lands. They with the help of block level land reforms officials then known as Junior Land Reforms Officer (JLRO) put these persons in real possession with the help of their peasants' organizations. The land owners could not procure assistance of block level administration or police station as they were scared of strong backlash by the ruling party.

As regards second problem, self-contained circulars were issued for preparation of lists of beneficiaries. By that time, panchayat bodies also came into existence. It was laid down that all lists of beneficiaries or pattadars will be processed through the *sthayee* or sub-committee on land reform of the Panchayat Samity (block level panchayat body). This provided double check and also provided scope to activate the land reform machinery for this work. The priority in distribution was given to the persons in possession of land. Under Section 49 of the WBLR Act, the preference in settlement of government land shall be given to the persons belonging to Scheduled Tribe and then to the Scheduled Caste. No person holding 1 acre (0.4047 ha) land will be entitled for government land. He will have to personally cultivate the land and land was not made transferable. However, sometimes while considering priorities, political favouritism was shown by the panchayat sub-committee pressurizing lower level land reform officers.

To tackle third problem, efforts started to unearth benami lands kept by the erstwhile landlords in the names of their agents, dogs, animals or other distant relatives or friends. The test was as to who was enjoying the usufructs from the lands. The WB Land Reforms Act further restricted the exemption only for the public religious and charitable trusts. It imposed family ceiling but the ceiling remained more or less around 25 acres.

Exemption for tank fisheries, orchard and private forests were also taken away. All lands were made at par. Thus, possibility under garb or disguised classifications was done away with. This gave all the impetus to track down benami lands, bring them under ceiling net and then distribute among the landless poor cultivators.

Methodology Adopted

The distribution of government vested land also was taken up in the drive mode. It was decided to organize patta distribution camps or patta distribution programmes which was attended by a State or District VIP. In this camp, beneficiaries will be brought to a block level venue where some pattas will be distributed from the stage. Then, rest of the pattas will be distributed through counters like in the election. The pattadars will be given advice that they should preserve the patta/lease documents with safety and security like their own mother as land is mother. They should not mortgage this land whatsoever adverse situation they come across. Transfer of patta land in any form including mortgaging is prohibited by law. Thirdly, they should cultivate land themselves or through members of their family. In some of the camps, even bankers were invited who had got filled in application forms by the new assignees of the vested land for loan and gave them bank credit at a minimal rate of interest of about 4 per cent. This was essential because once a bargadar or pattadar is recorded in government records, his traditional link with the village landowner is cut-off and usual flow of credit to him is barred. This gave lot of momentum to the land distribution programme. The land reforms functionaries also worked hard day and night and prepared patta documents which otherwise were neglected due to other routine works in the block/taluka level revenue offices. This work was also accomplished in a drive mode. It is unfortunate to mention that the administration at all levels in the country has lost their focus on their mission. They get indulged into day-to-day affairs so much mainly in court cases and employees' matters that main work programme becomes the last priority. Therefore, the main work of the land reform office was to be done through the camp or programme so that under the fear of VIP visit the surplus land could be distributed. The villagers enjoyed the programme as they were transported either by the panchayat functionaries or by the land revenue functionaries to the venue and were given sweet or tiffin after the function along with land document under plastic covers. At some places, they were also given the copy of record of rights/r-o-rs known as *parcha* in West Bengal or *khatauni* in other parts of India and had not to pay any extra money to receive land. The programmes were extensively covered by the Press and TV channels. That created competition among district heads to come in limelight. The VIPs like the Land Reforms Commissioner could also satisfy himself on the spot that the lands were being distributed to the deserving persons and they were actually handed over the pattas otherwise lower level functionaries keep on prolonging the same on one pretext or the other.

During the camp, the local land reforms functionaries were clearly instructed to hand over possession of land for which documents were distributed. Thus, they could not take any plea subsequently. In West Bengal, the villagers under the panchayats and peasants' organizations are quite conscious and vigilant and they ensured that possession of lands were handed over to them. This way, the possessions of lands were restored to the old and new pattaholders in rural areas.

I successfully implemented this programme during my five years tenure as Additional District Magistrate (Land Reforms) in Districts of Purulia (1980-84) and Murshidabad (1985-86) and carried it further as District Magistrate and Collector of Coochbehar District (1986-87), I also distributed land identity cards personally signed by me to all tribal pattadars and most of the scheduled caste pattadars in these three districts making an innovation at the district level which was subsequently approved by the State Headquarters. Then, as the Director of Land Records and Surveys (1992-93), I organized various patta distribution camps attended by the then Minister-in-Charge, Land and Land Reforms Late B.K. Chaudhury who was next to the Chief Minister in status in the Government of West Bengal. I have been repeating the same thing since I took over the Principal Secretary, and Land Reforms Commissioner of the Department of Land and Land Reforms and I find to my utter surprise contrary to general expectation, that all lands have not been distributed. In fact, I find government surplus land in continuous flow like the flow of a stream. The lands are otherwise kept under cover by the local land revenue or land reform machinery because distribution of land always creates ripples in otherwise peaceful set-up of the officer or the village. In West Bengal alone, 1.8 lakh acres land is beyond the reach of the landless peasantry because the courts have yet to decide whether these lands will go to the State or to the landowners. The dumb majority of the landless persons does not find its spokesmen easily and they leave their situation on the fate. If the land is given to them, this is the dearest and the best. They certainly bless the officials as well as politicians who arrange land documents to them for life. Their loyalty is not wavering like the loyalty of the Indian middle class which changes after every five years. Therefore, everybody should participate in the 'yagna' for the good of the society.

4. Benefits from the two Measures

(i) From the Operation Barga

In the first place, the very name "Operation Barga" has become a familiar term all over the country. It has become synonymous with recording of tenancy rights of cultivators. The bargadar cultivators on the one hand feel secured of their tenure of cultivation which will not depend on whims and fancies of the land owners. On the other side, the landowners immediately felt a sense of deprivation that they will lose their land once names of bargadars were recorded. Slowly and gradually both reconciled and have accepted a situation where both will co-exist side by side. Both are happy as production has since considerably increased because land is cultivated by the actual tiller who has permanent right of cultivation which is heritable. Therefore, on the whole the land owner continues to get at least share which they were getting before 'operation barga'. But it is surprising that under pressure from the political elite, no bargadar has been terminated for not giving proper share or getting the land cultivated by another person through informal letting out. This should not happen. But in the field of land reforms, developments are guided to certain extent by political will apart from the administrative will and statutory requirements.

The land price of land with bargadar has gone down considerably because the bargadar cannot be generally evicted. The widows and old men will suffer most because they cannot till their own land and their land cannot be sold at an economic price as no purchaser would like encumbrance of a bargadar. Thus, they fear to lose their land and livelihood. But in rural areas, the families are still joint and these incidents are stray. The land owners have organized themselves under the banner of Bhumijivi Sangh and are trying to stall these measures but have failed to go to the Supreme Court. The Operation Barga is not an end itself. It is a means to an end to carve out a secure existence for the bargadars in the hostile social environment in the interest of public good. This public good is achieved in two ways. Growth and prosperity depend on peaceful situation, and most of the cases of breach of the peace in the country-side have their genesis in land disputes. Unrecorded bargadars are always prone to eviction and insecurity and form the subject-matter of a law-and-order problem. Secondly, optimal food production of the country has a direct casual relationship with security of land tenure, no matter whether the parcel of the land is an economic holding or not. Recent researches have proved that on the whole, the rate of food-crop production is size-neutral to the holding and that on the contrary, motivation and security being equal, unit production rate by the owner of a smaller holding is generally greater and more efficient than by the affluent owner of a large holding having even the advantages of mechanized farming. In a labour-intensive economy like ours, with little capital-formation, ensuring social security and motivation to the actual tiller can undisputedly hasten growth. What else will these people do if there is no other employment in the village ? Operation Barga, by hastening the process of barga-recording, is likely to hasten the pace of security and motivation of the bargadars. According to a Chinese proverb, more number of times a cultivator visits his farm, more is production.

The 'Operation Barga' has also provided security of tenure to the Left Front Government to some extent in West Bengal who have been ruling the State for last thirty years. This has proved to be a good impetus to other political parties to implement land reforms measures in their own states otherwise none was coming forward even to listen about land reform measures what to say of their implementation. The main target of all political parties is how to win election. Now-a-days, a lobby of neo-liberalization of economy has been advocating against sharecropping system as the real estate companies or entrepreneurs cannot purchase or acquire land for making housing and malls without compromising with bargadars, at a higher price of land by way of arranging additional premium to the bargadars on land. This is not been accepted by the Left Front Government who are generally against real estate boom as it does not generate adequate employment. There is no objection if real estate companies give jobs to bargadars after eviction even menial jobs like guards etc. Even they are averse to employ them during construction stage. How can a popular government neglect major segment of the society for the benefit or profit to few ?

The World Bank has suggested to advance grant or credit to make bargadars as *raiyats* or owners in case the land owners want to sell their lands. But it is a mere suggestion. Who can afford huge finance to purchase land in rural areas where the land prices are touching astronomical figures ? There is also a suggestion to create a State Land Corporation and Regional Land Corporations for bargadars where the Corporation will advance credit for purchase of lands intended to be sold by the sharecroppers[6] 'which will be recovered in easy installments. If bargadar does not agree to purchase, the Land Corporation will purchase on grounds of need or distress of the landowners, and settle with pattadars. In the changed scenario, reverse tenancy has started. Even small cultivator, have started leasing out their land due to lack of credit facilities and inputs. This is a wrong tendency. Fear of recording sharecroppers can check this practice. If it is not done immediately the rural India will become very unstable and violence will erupt now and then. Insecured and uncertain individuals are potential source of violence and resultant instability in the society.

It will be agreed by all that mere recording of bargadars' names will not guarantee them security and motivation. A whole basket of measures will be necessary to free them from the clutches of their exploiters who sometimes appear to them to be benevolent. Liquidation of rural indebtedness provision of alternative sources of input-and-maintenance-finance, protection from legal persecutions, effective implementation of the lawful rights of the bargadars, provision of social security by way of old age pension etc., implementing minimum needs programmes, State programmes for effective organization of bargadars, all these and many similar others will be the meaningful package deal for the bargadars.

(ii) From Distribution of Government Vested Land

Before drive for distribution of government surplus land was undertaken, the total lands distributed was 6,12,000 acres to 9,63,000 beneficiaries[7]. The same figure in October 2007 stood 11,18,341 acre to about 29,54,749 (Oct-2007)[8]. It means that about 1 crore population was benefited by this innovation by creating 20 lakh additional pattadars.

Area of vested agricultural land increased from 11,22,000 acres to 13,12,227 (October 2007). Thus, the main impact was due to drive to distribute the land not by way of vesting through unearthing benami lands. There is a limit of land as it cannot be stretched like rubber. This included 1096600 scheduled caste pattadars and 532857 scheduled tribe pattadars. This exposes governments like U.P. and Bihar who are projecting themselves as champions for schedule castes but are not making basic impact on the living of scheduled castes in rural areas. Similarly, it is an eye opening to separatist agitation or extremists' agitations for the cause of scheduled tribe pockets of North Eastern States, Darjeeling, MP, Chhattisgarh, Andhra Pradesh, Bihar, Jharkhand, Orissa. This is where the strength of Left Front Government lies. The Naxalite agitations etc. get diluted because of this basic work done by the administration in West Bengal after 1977 as a drive and with the full support of the strong political will of the ruling parties.

The wide gap between land legislation and its implementation was plugged to a large extent. It was ensured that the pattadars were given possession of their lands which were well protected by the local peasants' organizations. Institutional financing from banks, cooperative societies etc. was also arranged so that these pattadars could develop their land and contribute to the increase in production of foodgrains of the State. It really happened in practice. The State which earlier used to be food-deficit State became a food surplus State and started exporting foodgrains like rice, potatoes to other states. This has been accepted by all governments. The Chief Minister of Orissa Mr. Biju Patnaik[9] unequivocally accepted that the increase of productivity in West Bengal was due to extensive land reforms measures and he ordered for their replication in Orissa. But before he could gear up his party and administration for the purpose, he died. Now, further innovations are added to this drive. The name of wife appears as first beneficiary on patta document so that that male pattadars may not mortgage or transfer patta land due to debt, drinking habit, gambling etc. Secondly, self-help groups are being formed so that they may get credit from banks and may purchase high cost equipments like tractors, harvesters etc. centrally and also arrange also for marketing products centrally. Thus, cooperative farming is being promoted keeping the individual membership intact. This will ensure entry of West Bengal in new era of agriculture production and marketing without exploitation by intermediaries at the second stage of land reforms. The ultimate purpose of land reforms measures is to increase the productivity of foodgrains in the country. The panchayat bodies, have enthusiastically come forward to assist the pattadars and bargadars through various labour generating schemes and through rural housing and rural sanitation schemes like the Indira Avas Yojana. As panchayats are dominated by the real leaders of the village folk, they care for their fellow poor people. Even few bargadars and pattadars head local gram panchayats. Many are members as such. Thus, it is not the lip service but is actual administrative structure which helps the poorest of the poor in West Bengal.

As the quantum of land left is not much for distribution, land is being distributed in small parcels so that a person can make his home and do some vegetable cultivation on adjoining area along with rearing his cattle. Thus, at least, he will not die due to starvation. Under the Acquisition of Homestead for Agricultural Labourers etc. Act, 1975 3.18 lakh beneficiaries have been given pattas for homestead purpose. An innovative scheme[10] is under implementation in West Bengal where the land is purchased and distributed to the BPL landless persons upto 16 decimal to construct their homestead and for garden cultivation. This is most essential in areas where land is no longer left for distribution but there is a huge demand for land from the poorest of the poor section of the society.

Thus, if we take total beneficiaries 'under the land reforms measures in West Bengal, these 48 lakhs are covering about 2.4 crore population out of 9.25 crore population of the State at present. This is the population which is satisfied and forms the bedrock of peace and tranquillity in the village from where the State can take off for any development including industrial development to cater specially for the urban poor.

(5) Replication

There is no problem in replication of these innovations by adoption these types of procedural strategies within the existing framework of law and rules prevailing in every state. It has been shown that in U.P.[11] similar 'Operation Barga' for recording of sharecroppers or bataidars or bhagdar can be undertaken within the framework of land, i.e. the U.P. Land Revenue Act as amended by the U.P. Land Laws (Amendment Act, 1977). The land reforms laws of Orissa and Bihar have similar provisions. Similarly, an operation barga type drive was undertaken in Kerala and it was successful. States of Andhra Pradesh,

Bihar and Jharkhand are sincerely looking for such options in near future. In Northern India, there is a large presence of informal tenancies not less than 11 per cent and similar operation, can be undertaken easily. In Maharashtra,[12] and Tamil Nadu the system is for conferment of ownership to the tenants. Moreover, it might be difficult in North Eastern States, where lands belong to the community and land laws are different.

As far as vesting of excess land from the landowners is concerned, the Benami Transactions (Prohibition) Act, 1987, a Government of India statute can be applied in all the states. So far only 60.27 lakh acres of lands[13] have vested in States which should be at least double of that. The State laws are otherwise competent enough to unearth and recover benami excess lands from the clutches of landowners. The distribution of government vested land requires drive on the pattern of West Bengal which can be easily followed because it is only procedural change which has made the difference. For undertaking distribution of government vested land, a technically sound machinery will be required which can measure and demarcate the land promptly. Secondly, number of revenue staff and officials will be required to be increased along with imparting them training. In West Bengal, the Department of Land and Land Reforms is a major Department of the Government having about 30,000 employees. IAS officers having top reputation are posted in the Department. Then the Department is held in high esteem by all the Departments and political executive. This can be easily done by other states. In other states, at present, the Department of Revenue is a neglected one and its voice is not given proper heed. Its power is further diluted by setting up of the Board of Revenue with more senior officers than the Principal Secretary. If Board of Revenue is entrusted with land reform measures then they should also be accountable before the State Assembly. Power and accountability should go side by side. In West Bengal, Board of Revenue no longer exists. Attempts are to be made to impart training to the revenue staff and officials in computerization of land records. Attempts are to be made so that records of rights[14] are fed in computers including maps which can be continuously updated with each transfer of land or change in plot size or boundary which is being done in West Bengal as a second phase of land reforms. Moreover, West Bengal has yet to integrate its land records with the Registration Department like Andhra Pradesh and Karnataka so that the records of lands can be continuously updated.

(6) Factors Contributing to the Success

Main factors contributing to the success of land reform measures in West Bengal are:

(i) The peasants/cultivators are well organized under the umbrella of strong and powerful different peasants' organizations like Krishak Sabha, Samjukta Kishan Sabha, Agragami Krishak Sabha under political parties—CPI (M) and CPI, RSPI, FBI and others in their respective pockets of influence.

(ii) The new and young administrators are trained and motivated to involve in the land reform works by the political executives in a friendly environment and thus, a group of IAS officers are well grooved and motivated in this field who can be regarded as experts in the field. Their expertise is further passed on through training and interactions with the lower level functionaries.

(iii) The Government of West Bengal attaches top most importance to the Department of Land and Land Reforms and Directorate, Land Records and Surveys and tries to assist and support them in all ways. They try to give them maximum allocation of fund and personnel within the budget constraint. Such is the will of the Government in West Bengal to implement land reforms. The officers and officials in the Department are not transferred or victimized at the instance of landowners or powerful persons whose lands are to be subjected to cultivation by the sharecroppers or are to be vested being excess beyond the prescribed ceiling limit as per relevant law.

(7) The Future

After farmers' agitations in Singur and in Nandigram in West Bengal, recent long march of Tribals of Vidarbha from Central India to the Capital Delhi, incidents of suicides by farmers in Vidarbha (Maharashtra) and Andhra Pradesh and Naxalite agitations in Andhra Pradesh, MP, Chhattisgarh, Bihar, Jharkhand, Orissa, all governments have woken up to pay due attention to the rightful causes of farmers, sharecroppers, cultivators and the landless. None can dispute if poor tribals parade to the capital of the country to demand land for them which is their basic necessity. None should deny the right of cultivation to the villagers if their lands are acquired for industrial or commercial purposes to accommodate requirement of new liberalized era to take India into the 21st century. An appropriate, due rehabilitation package has come forward for them preserving their right of cultivation. A villager is not generally fit and expert to do any other thing except cultivation. How can one deny this basic right of life and livelihood to him? If this great army of disgruntled landless persons and poor cultivators, is not given their due rights, it will run over the prosperity created by the neo-liberalized era of economic activities in the country.

Karl Marx has, therefore, termed land reform measures as anti-revolution as these delay blood revolution. In the era of most powerful states, even blood revolution is not the reality. Therefore, future lies only in implementation of land reforms with all sincerity and earnestness. It will help to create a peaceful and stable society in India which will be ready to take up any challenge in coming times towards development and progress.

NOTES AND REFERENCES

1. Section 16(1) (b) of the West Bengal Land Reforms Act, 1955.
2. Land Reforms in West Bengal—A Statistical Report compiled by Government of West Bengal, 1979.
3. *Source*: Monthly Progress Report for the month of October, 2007 published by Director of Land Records & Surveys, WB 35, Gopalnagar Rd., Alipur-700029.
4. Ghosh, T.K., *Operanon Barga & Land Reforms*, p. 99
5. Food for Work Programme, Integrated Tribal Development Programme, National Rural Employment Programme, Integrated Rural Development Programme.
6. As per Section 21C WBLR Act, 1955.
7. Left Front Government in West Bengal, p. 14.
8. Monthly Progress Return of Land Revenue Works, Director of Land Records & Surveys, WB. pp. 1, 9 and 12.
9. *Land Reforms in India*, p. 206.
10. The scheme is known as "Scheme for donation of land for homestead and cultivation" (*Chas-Basobaser Bhumi dan Prakalpa*) and is in vogue since 2005-06 in West Bengal with provision of fund of Rs. 30 crore initially)
11. *Land Reforms in India* (PKA) pp. 146-147.
12. In Maharashtra, 1.492 million tenants were declared owners of land on

2.512 million hectares. But they had to pay price of land which was between 20 to 200 times, the annual land tax. About 30 million tenants got ownership rights. Of which 66 per cent got without any payment. As per an estimate there are 15 million concealed tenants.

13. *Annual Report, 2006-07*, Ministry of Rural Development, Government of India.
14. Other Land reform measures are employment generating schemes, development of peasants' organizations, social and religious reforms, legal aid to the poor peasants, credit for cultivation, consolidation and allotment of house sites ref: *Issues in Land Reforms*.

5

Performance by Various States and Union Territories Under Land Reforms

Successful reform of land tenure in densely populated states, as in Kerala and West Bengal, leads to a slow change of rural social relations and power restructure, but does not overcome other socio-economic problems, like un- and under-employment. "The legalistic approach, observance of all juridical procedures, compensation payments etc. slow down the pace of change and diminish the re-distributive effect, thus it also limits the new investment in the farming sector."[1]

The West Bengal[2] is the leader in the field of land reform for following reasons:

(a) Intermediary tenures have been done away within agricultural and non-agricultural land.
(b) About 15 lakh share-croppers known as bargadars have been recorded and their rights of cultivation are heritable.
(c) The ceiling in West Bengal is 5 hectares for irrigated area and 7 hectares for non-irrigated areas inclusive of both agricultural and non-agricultural land.
(d) Land in possession of small and marginal farmers is 60 per cent in place of 29 per cent which is the national average.
(e) Land Tribunals have been proposed.
(f) Over 2.5 lakh persons have been given homestead instead of land.
(g) Tenantwise records or rights are being planned and computerization is being introduced.

(h) The percentage of land owning cultivators has increased to 41.9 in 1981 from 31.2 per cent in 1971.

In Karnataka, occupancy rights are conferred on dwelling houses, constructed by agricultural labourers on lands belonging to others. Land tribunals have 4 non-official members, out of which one shall be from S.C./S.T. community. Lands held by institutions are brought under the ambit of the Act.

Gujarat has done fairly well in the field of land reforms because of its sound administrative base through active Panchayat System. The following steps have been successfully taken:

(a) Occupancy rights have been conferred on the inferior holders or permanent tenant numbering about 12.41 lakhs including tenants.
(b) Absentee ownership has been effectively eliminated by the provision requiring personal cultivation.
(c) The records are regularly rewritten after 10 years.
(d) As recommended by the Government of India, the Ceiling Act was amended to provide a maximum ceiling of 10 to 18 acres of perennially irrigated land and 30 to 54 acres of dry crop land.
(e) Allottees of surplus land get financial assistance of Rs. 2,500 per hectare which is treated as subsidy under the Centrally Sponsored Scheme.
(f) Land held by the Scheduled Tribe will not be transferred without the previous permission of the Collector.

The achievements under land reform measures are encouraging in Tamil Nadu. There are about 4,94,000 registered tenants cultivating lands belonging to individuals and Public Trusts to an extent of about 6,85,500 acres. The Government is also seeking the cooperation of social workers in the rural areas for proper implementation of the land reform laws. Finally, steps to reorient the attitudes of the revenue and police officials in the matter of protection of the rights of the rural poor *vis-a-vis* the land rich have been effectively taken.

In Maharashtra, by 1970, ownership of leased land was partly or fully transferred to the tenants in about 18.75 lakh tenancy cases, out of a total of about 26 lakh recorded tenancy cases in the State. The ceilings were lowered in 1975, as a consequence of which an area of 1,60,962 ha was declared as surplus. Out of the total area of 2,85,455 ha declared as surplus under these enactments, 2,51,522 ha have already been distributed.

State of Madhya Pradesh is leader in the maintenance of land records. There is a mechanism for continuous updating of records of rights and maps. The individuals have also been provided with their up-to-date land details in the form of passbooks.

In Assam, the ceiling in rural areas has been fixed at 6.68 ha per family while in urban areas the ceiling is 2000 sq. metres per family. Recently, in March 1990, the Government has made penal provisions for violations regarding purchase of tribal lands.

In Andhra Pradesh, voluntary declaration of concealed land by the land owners will save them from the punitive actions provided in the Act. In Andhra, the tenancies were based on oral contract and those too, were recorded and thus established the tenants rights and legitimacy.

In smaller States, the State-wise specialties were noted as follows:

In Jammu & Kashmir, under Agrarian Reforms Act, 1976, the rights in a holding of land of any person not cultivating it personally, were extinguished and vested in the State.

In Orissa, raiyati rights have been conferred on more than 1.6 lakh temporary lessees. In Tripura, civil court's jurisdiction has been barred.

In Goa, where the tenants are cultivating on communidade (community) land, they have been so recorded in the land records. In Sikkim, there are effective provisions to ensure that there is no arbitrary termination of cultivation. In Pondicherry, the right of resumption for personal cultivation was withdrawn totally except for the armed forces personnel. In Manipur, the Revenue tribunal is dealing with cases under the Manipur L.R. & Land Reforms Act in place of conventional judicial courts. In Meghalaya, there is community ownership of land and land cannot be acquired even for public purposes without scrutiny by people's representatives and community. In Mizoram, the Government is deeply concerned with the non-productive development of land by the allottees and also allotment and transfer of land to non-agriculturists.

Computerisation of Land Records (CLR)[3]

The Centrally Sponsored Scheme on Computerisation of Land Records (CLR) was started in 1988-89 with 100 per cent financial assistance as a pilot project in eight Districts, viz. Rangareddy (A.P.), Sonitpur (Assam), Singhbhum (Bihar), Gandhinagar (Gujarat), Morena (M.P.), Wardha (Maharashtra), Mayurbhanj (Orissa) and Dungarpur (Rajasthan) to remove the problems inherent in the manual systems of maintenance and updating of Land Records and to meet the requirements of various groups of users. It was decided that efforts should be made to computerise CORE DATA contained in land records, to assist development planning and to make records accessible to people/planners and administrators.

The main objectives of the scheme are:

- Ensuring that landowners get computerized copies of ownership, crop and tenancy and updated copies of records of rights (RoRs) on demand.
- Realizing low-cost and easily-reproducible basic land record data through reliable and durable preservation of old records.
- Ensuring accuracy, transparency and speedy dispute resolution.
- Facilitating fast and efficient retrieval of information for decision making.
- According legal sanctity to computer-generated certificates of land records after authentication by the authorized revenue official.
- Setting up a comprehensive land information system for better land-based planning and utilization of land resources.
- Focusing on citizen-centric services related to land and revenue information.

Under the CLR scheme, financial assistance is provided to States and UTs for completing data entry work, setting up computer centres at the tehsil or taluk or block or circle level, sub-divisional level, district level and a monitoring cell at the State level. Funds are also provided for imparting training on computer awareness and applications software to revenue officials for regular updating of records of rights and smooth operation of computer centres. Digitization of maps has also been allowed under the CLR scheme.

Initially, it was decided that basic infrastructure would be created at the district level for undertaking data entry. After completion of data entry (including verification and validation at the district level), data has to be ported to tehsil or taluk computer centres for regular operation. Therefore, in 1997-98, it was decided to extend the scheme to the tehsil or taluk level to facilitate better accessibility to computerized copies of RoRs for landowners.

Phased coverage under the scheme:

- During the VIIth Plan, 24 districts were sanctioned;
- During the VIIIth Plan, an additional 299 districts were sanctioned;
- During the IXth Plan, an additional 259 districts and 2787 tehsils or taluks were sanctioned;
- Tehsils or taluks sanctioned during the first four years of Xth Plan period (2002-03 to 2005-06) are in Table 5.1.

The Budget provision during the financial year, viz. 2006-07 under the scheme of CLR was Rs.100.00 crore (Rs.90.00 crore for States/UTs and Rs.10.00 crore for NE States). Funds to the tune of Rs. 51.14 crore were released to the States for data entry work and scanning and digitization of land records including cadastral maps.

Table 5.1

Year	*Sanctioned Locations*	*Funds released (Rs. in crores)*
2002-03	183 taluks	31.18
2003-04	172 taluks, 201 sub-divisional and 191 district land records data centres	35.77
2004-05	178 taluks, 361 sub-divisional and 51 district land records data centres	45.62
2005-06	207 taluks, 457 sub-divisional and 122 district land records data centres	99.24
Total	**740 tehsils/taluks, 1019 sub-divisional, 365 district land records data centres**	**211.81**

Since inception, the scheme has been sanctioned to 582 districts, 3527 taluks/tehsils and blocks and 1019 sub-divisions. In 3324 tehsils, taluks and blocks computer centres have been set up and in 2877 tehsils, taluks and blocks computerized copies of RoRs are being issued to landowners on demand. The States of Karnataka, Goa, Tamil Nadu and Gujarat have stopped manual distribution of RoRs by totally relying on the computerized system for more than a year now. Many other States are also making good progress in shifting to the computerized system. Some States have also placed land records data on the Internet websites for easy access and dissemination of this information. Digitization of maps has also been allowed under the scheme.

So far Rs. 496.52 crore has been released to States and Union Territories, of which Rs. 292.52 crore (59%) have been utilized by States/UTs.

1. Statewise Achievements Under the CLR Scheme

The States of Karnataka, Goa, Tamil Nadu and Gujarat have stopped manual distribution of RoRs by totally relying on the computerized system for more than a year now. Many other States are making good progress in shifting to the computerized system. Some States have also placed land records data on the Internet websites for easy access and dissemination of this information.

- *Goa*—This is the first State which has completed land records computerization. The *Dharni* project is an integrated system in which mutation has been automated and updated copies of RoRs are being issued to landowners along with vocational details. Though legal sanctity has been accorded to computerized copies, issue of manual records has not been stopped because the State is providing computers to the village officers in a phased manner.
- *Karnataka*—The *Bhoomi* project integrates mutation and updation of land records to ensure that RoRs provided to farmers are in sync with the times. The workflow has been automated and secured using security mechanisms. Manual issue of the RoRs has been stopped in 177 taluks and legal sanctity is accorded to computerized RoRs. Under the project, 1.5 crore landowners have taken computerized copies of the RTC from taluk computer centres earning Rs. 22.58 crores as user charges for the State.
- *Tamil Nadu*—A computerized land records system called *Tamil Nilam* is operational. Regular mutation and updation is being done through computers. This is an integrated system

with interface to other citizen-centric services such as old age pension, lodging complaints relating to mutation, etc. The manual system of issue of RoRs has been abandoned throughout the State.

- *Gujarat*—A computerized land records system called *e-Dhara* is fully operational with mutation, updation and distribution of copies of RoRs being done through taluk computer centres. The State has notified computerized copies of RoRs as legally valid documents. Digital data of all districts have been kept at the State level and is hosted on the Internet.
- *Madhya Pradesh*—Computerized copies of the khasra (RoRs) are being distributed in 257 of 273 tehsils on demand. Gram panchayats are empowered to certify undisputed mutations at the village level and other types of mutations are being approved by revenue officials. Efforts are being made to register all mutations on tehsil computers and distribute only computerized copies of RoRs. Land records data have been put on the website for easy access and display.
- *Orissa*—Data entry work for RoRs has been completed and the scheme is operational in 161 of 171 tehsils where computerized copies of RoRs are being distributed on demand. Land record data have been hosted on website.
- *West Bengal*—Computerized copies of RoRs are being distributed to land owners in all blocks on demand. Manual issue of RoRs have been banned and legal sanctity provided to computerized copies of RoR.
- *Rajasthan*—Copies of computerized jamabandi RoRs are being issued in all the 241 tehsils. Land record data is available on the Internet.
- *Andhra Pradesh*—Data entry work has been completed and computerized RoR copies are being distributed in 308 *Mandate,* which are sub-taluk level small revenue units.
- *Pondicherry*—Data entry work has been completed in all taluks and verification is in an advanced stage. The scheme has been made operational in 5 out of 8 taluks and computerized RoR copies are being distributed to landowners on demand.

- *Sikkim*—Data entry has been completed for the entire State, and in 4 sub-divisions distribution of updated copies of RoRs has started.
- *Chhattisgarh*—Computer centres have been set up in all tehsils and computerized copies of RoRs are being distributed to landowners on demand. The land records data has been hosted on the website.
- *Kerala*—45 per cent data entry has been completed and the balance work is expected to be completed by December, 2006. Computer centres have been set up in all taluks but computerized copies of RoR are yet to be issued to landowners.
- *Maharashtra*—Computerisation of land records had been completed and all the tehsils were on-line. State government has started distribution of computerized copies of RoRs in all 358 taluks on demand.
- *Uttar Pradesh*—Data entry work along with backlog data verification and validation has been completed. Computerized copies of RoRs are being distributed to landowners from all the 305 tehsils. Manual issue of RoRs has been stopped.
- *Haryana*—Data entry work has been completed and verification and validation work is at an advanced stage of completion. The scheme has been operationalized in 67 out of 115 tehsils with issuance of copies of computerized *jamabandies* to landowners on demand. The State has developed an integrated land records and registration system—*HALRIS,* which enables entry of mutations immediately after registration of land.
- *Himachal Pradesh*—The scheme has been operationalized in 76 out of 108 tehsils with landowners getting computerized copies of RoRs on demand.
- *Uttarakhand*—Computerisation of land records has been completed and the scheme is operational in all 84 tehsils with landowners getting computerized copies of RoRs on demand. Manual issue of RoRs have been stopped. The land records data have been hosted on the website.

- *NCT of Delhi*—99 per cent data entry work has been completed and computerized copies of RoRs are being issued to landowners in west district.
- *Assam, Arunachal Pradesh, Mizoram, Manipur, Bihar, Tripura and UTs of Andaman & Nicobar Islands and Chandigarh*—Data entry is under progress. Software for mutation and updation through computer centres has been developed by the NIC.
- *J&K, Punjab, Jharkhand, Nagaland and the UTs of Dadra & Nagar Haveli and Daman & Diu*—Data entry has not been completed, and the scheme is yet to gain momentum.
- *Meghalaya & Lakshadweep*—The scheme has not yet started because of non-availability of land records. They have been asked to undertake survey work for creating land records so that the scheme could be implemented.

2. Centrally Sponsored Scheme of Strengthening of Revenue Administration and Updating of Land Records (SRA & ULR)

The importance of land records in the rural areas cannot be over-emphasised. The causes of rural conflicts have often been traced to improper maintenance of land records. Updation is vital for systematic maintenance of land records to reflect ground realities in synchronization with ownership changes, ensure genuine land transactions and implement rural development programmes for effective enforcement of land reforms. It will minimize land disputes and create social harmony in villages.

Although the importance of a proper land records system has been emphasized from the First Five Year Plan, land records in most parts of the country are not in good shape largely due to resource constraints. As per existing instructions, records of rights are prepared by carrying out cadastral surveys followed by settlement operations; these are time consuming, call for huge staff and is expensive. Equipment used in these operations is also outdated. Even where there is a system of periodical updating of land records, lack of adequate revenue machinery and proper infrastructure and absence of training are responsible for poorly maintained land records.

With a view to assisting the States and UTs in the task of updating of land records and strengthening revenue administration, a Centrally Sponsored Scheme of Strengthening of Revenue Administration and Updating of Land Records (SRA & ULR) was started in 1987-88 on 50:50 sharing basis between the Centre and the States. Union Territories are provided full Central assistance. Initially, the Scheme was approved for the States of Bihar and Orissa in 1987-88 and extended to other States/UTs during 1989-90. The Scheme is being implemented by the State Governments through their Revenue/Land Reforms Departments.

The main objectives of the scheme are:

(i) Strengthening survey and settlement organizations for early completion and preparation of land records in areas where this work is yet to be completed.

(ii) Setting up survey and settlement organizations especially in the north-east, where no land records exist.

(iii) Imparting pre-service and in-service training to revenue, survey and settlement staff and strengthening training infrastructure for this purpose.

(iv) Providing facilities for modernization of survey and settlement operations, printing survey maps, reports and documents and storage, copying and updating of land and crop records using, among other things, latest science and technology inputs.

(v) Strengthening revenue machinery at the village and immediate supervisory levels on a selective basis to make the work load of functionaries manageable.

Under the scheme, States and UTs have been given assistance for purchase of modern survey equipments [like Global Positioning Systems (GPS), EDM, total stations, theodolites, work stations], carrying out aerial surveys, office equipment (like photocopiers, laminating machines and binding machines) and basic facilities to improve work efficiency at lower levels of revenue administration, construction of record rooms for proper storage of land records, construction of office-cum-residence for patwaries and construction, repair and renovation of training institutes and equipments for training.

Release of funds during first four years of Xth Plan.

Table 5.2

Year	*Funds released (Rs. in crores)*
2002-03	20.73
2003-04	24.21
2004-05	19.43
2005-06	39.49
Total	**103.86**

A provision of Rs.49.00 crore (Rs.5.00 crore for NE States and Rs.44.00 crore for non-NE States) existed under the Scheme during the financial year, viz. 2006-07. Funds to the tune of Rs.8.83 crore have been released to the States for purchase of modern survey equipment, continuation of survey works, training of staff etc.

Since inception (1987-88), financial assistance to the tune of Rs.333.72 crore have been provided to State governments and UTs as the Central share, of which Rs.253.81 crore (76%) have been utilized by States.

North Eastern Region

Land Reforms Division is implementing the Schemes of Computerisation of Land Records (CLR) and Strengthening of Revenue Administration and Updation of Land Records (SRA & ULR) in the region. The position of release of funds under these Schemes to the North Eastern States including Sikkim since inception is quite satisfactory.

National Land Resources Management Programme (NLRMP)

Significant progress has been made by the States and UTs under the existing two Centrally sponsored schemes of Computerisation of Land Records (CLR) and Strengthening of Revenue Administration and Updating of Land Records (SRA & ULR) in the field of computerization and digitization of land records, strengthening of survey and settlement organizations by purchase of equipments of various kinds including modern survey equipment such as Global Positional Systems (GPS), Electronic Total Stations (ETS), maintenance and storage of land records by construction of record rooms, improvement in training infrastructure for revenue and survey staff by construction/renovation of new/existing training institutes etc. However, the emphasis of CLR and SRA & ULR so far, has *inter alia* been more on computerization and digitization of land records, strengthening of State revenue, survey and settlement organisations, maintenance and storage of land records and less on having a system that maintains accurate and up-to-date records of rights and securely generates such records on demand. Also lacking, are the integration of textual and spatial data on RoRs, integration of relevant map with r-o-r, linkage of registration with mutation and updating of RoRs, backend reconciliation of village records, and a comprehensive and standard database of land records across the country that is necessary for understanding land and immovable property markets and for efficient administration and policy making in a modern economy.

Further, some progress has been made in a number of States in computerization of the property registration. However, the prime focus of these initiatives has been on automation of the deed registration procedures, and there is hardly any linkage with the land records management system.

Keeping in mind the overarching goal of comprehensive and all-round development, the key deliverables that need to be provided to our citizens would include computerized RoRs with maps to scale, other land data based certificates, e.g. domicile certificate, caste certificate, income certificate, etc., and also the necessary documents/ information for securing agricultural and non-agricultural credit based on land assets and so on.

With this backdrop, a National Land Resources Management Programme (NLRMP) has been conceptualized as a major e-governance and systems reforms initiative that is concerned not merely with the computerization, updation and maintenance of land records or the validation of titles, but as a programme that will add value and provide a comprehensive data base for planning and decision-making for development planning as well as regulatory activities where there is need for location-specific information. The disconnects and redundancies in the system would be reduced and a better reform model would be re-engineered, so that the spatial and non-spatial land-related data for the entire country could be available as a *national enterprise knowledge base* for both public and private stakeholders.

The NLRMP will, *inter alia*, focus on citizen services like computerized Records of Rights (RoRs) with maps; certificates (domicile, caste, income, etc.); web-based "anytime-anywhere" access to land data; services through facilitation centres in tehsils and other places; speedy and efficient property registration; automatic initiation of mutation notices; land passbooks—smart cards with all land information including charges and encumbrances; facilitated access to land-based credit/Cooperative Banks, etc. It envisages creation of core GIS with cadastral layer for the entire country, 100 per cent digitization of cadastral maps, integration of textual and spatial data, updating of land records using modern technology (aerial photogrammetry, DGPS, ETS), National and State Land Data Banks with specific plot IDs and details, use of uniform land data codes with Indian language script computing, integration with National Spatial Data Base (NSDB) and National Natural Resources Management System (NNRMS), full training and capacity building of the functionaries and National and State Missions for effective implementation.

This comprehensive programme to manage land data and information will support the entire spectrum of land resource management, and all developmental, regulatory and disaster management activities needing location-specific information will be benefited.

REFERENCES

1. Bergmann, Theodor: *Agrarian Reforms in India*, Agricole Publishing Academy, p. 192.
2. Dr. Agrawal, P.K.: *Issues in Land Reforms*, RGICS Working paper series No. 18, 2000 Rajiv Gandhi Foundation, New Delhi, p. 24, year 2000 total pp. 54.
3. *Annual Report 2006-07,* Government of India: Department of Land Resources, Ministry of Rural Development (www.rural.nic.in) p. 140, year 2007, total pp. 277.

6

Need for Recording of Sharecroppers and Distribution of Government Surplus Land in Uttar Pradesh and Uttarakhand

U.P. is the most populous state in the country. As one of the pioneer states in the country in the field of land reforms, Government of U.P. enforced the Uttar Pradesh Zamindari Abolition Act, 1950 which prohibited leasing of land except in special circumstances like the disabled persons, defence services, widows and minors. As a result the tenancy went underground. Sharecropping exists in all states of India. West Bengal recognizes it in all its aspects and about 15 lakh share-croppers have been recorded in West Bengal. Even in Bangladesh and America, share-cropping is recognized. If self-cropping is agreed to be the best alternative, let us accept that in most situations, share-cropping is the second best alternative.

With the changing times, U.P. revenue administration has to realize the need for change of their approach towards tenancy. In fact, in U.P., the hidden share-cropping is rampant. The person who cultivates the land of another person on condition to share crop is known as *bataidar, bhagdar* or *adhiar*. In U.P., there are millions of instances where people are leasing out and in land for cultivation. The transactions are like ordinary business transactions for a season for a year or more. Seeing these types of cultivation in U.P., one tends to support contract farming, though contract farming is anti-farmer and it has to be adopted only in limited way in a well defined conditional environment.

As per field survey[1] done by me during 1990-92 and reflected in-the book "*Land Reforms in India*", there are approximately 16 per cent sharecroppers in Uttar Pradesh. Thus, there will be about 30.37 lakh unrecorded tenants in Uttar Pradesh out of total holdings 187.85 lakh (1981).

However, from 1981 to 1991, there was an increase of agricultural labourers to the tune of 25 lakh. This is very serious. The reason partly is that the unrecorded share-croppers are driven out of their fields and they then have no other alternative except to resort to daily labour. The average acre leased in by pure tenant is 0.61 ha.

In West Bengal, due to land reform, the productivity has increased manifold and the state has become self-sufficient in food production. Small and marginal farmers who constitute the base of land reform measures, pay fuller and whole-hearted attention in their cultivation after getting security of tenure due to recording their right of cultivation as tenants.

The farmers are well entrenched and organized in villages. They cannot be subjected to exploitation, injustice and terror.

(A) How to Record Share-croppers in U.P.?

Within the framework of existing laws, the share-croppers can be recorded in U.P. by following procedure:

Under Section 33-A[2] of the U.P. Land Revenue Act, 1901 by UP Act No.8 of 1977 a provision has been substituted as under:

"The provisions of sub-section [1] shall *mutatis mutandis* apply to a person who has been admitted as a sirdar of any land u/s 195 of the Uttar Pradesh Zamindari Abolition and Land Reforms Act, 1950, before the commencement of the Uttar Pradesh Land Laws [Amendment] Act, 1977 or as a bhumidhar with non-transferable rights under said section after such commencement, or as an asami of any land u/s 197 of the first mentioned Act."

The State should arrange for recording of asami on a large scale as a policy as kanungo and other lower officers will not be able to face the powerful lobby of landholders in villages. This can be achieved on the same pattern as 'Barga Operation' in West Bengal. For the purpose of the programme the State can be divided into two broad areas.

Area A: Where neither K-B [settlement and Survey] operations have been undertaken recently nor consolidation operations have been started.

Area B: Where the consolidation operations and survey and settlement operations had finished long time back.

The areas under category A have to be covered under a crash-programme. "Operation Bataidar" composite squads of the land revenue machinery and settlement department could be organized; Kanungo or as per the changed designation made its in-charge as he is legally authorized to sign the certificate of recording. A squad will work in a specified priority pocket to be selected by Settlement Officer and Chief Revenue Officer in consultation with Gram Panchayats/ Khand samiti/Zilla parishad or peasants organizations working in the area for recording u/s 33-A[2] to be accomplished within a short, specified time. A methodology may be prescribed for the purpose. Each squad will preferably take up a group of mouza at a time. A meeting has to be held in the area either in the afternoon or evening whenever it is convenient for the larger number of subtenants, bataidars and agricultural labourers and asamis by issuing a general public notice. Places of habitual congregation of such persons may be selected as venues of such meetings. Meeting places should be generally near the residence of potential beneficiaries. In evening meetings, discussions regarding rights and duties should be held partly for dissemination of information and partly for helping the poor people, asamis, bataidars and agricultural labourers, more specifically about the right of cultivation which can be ensured by recording, about the pooling of funds following from IRDP [Integrated Rural Development Programme], Jawahar Rojgar Yojana, NREGP [National Rural Employment Guarantee Programme], ITDP [Integrated Tribal Development Project], Prime Minister Sadak Rojgar Yojana, 100 days Rojgar Yojana or Area [like Hill, etc.]. Development programmes and other Central or State Sector schemes for agricultural development and about the need for organizations of their own to secure enduring benefits either from land reform or from any other general development programme. Wholehearted cooperation should be sought from the Panchayati Raj institutions. Review should be regularly held at district, Division and State levels. Under Section 40[2] it has been provided that if the Collector or the Tahsildar is unable to satisfy himself as to which party is in possession, he will ascertain by summary inquiry who is the person best entitled to the property, and shall put such person in possession. This power can also be delegated to the squads during the "Operation Bataidar" or operation u/s 33-A[2]. Similar action can also get support from provisions in Sections 48, 49 etc. In fact, record officers, have been appointed in Kaimur Range in the then Mirzapur district, now Sonbhadra district, for recording of tribals on their lands under instructions from the Supreme Court as a result of a PIL.

(B) Distribution of Government Surplus Land in U.P.

Uttar Pradesh lags behind in distribution of land. Being the one of the largest states in the country only 2,63,225[2] acres of agricultural lands could be distributed out of 3,39,385 acres of land available for distribution. Total number of beneficiaries are 3,03,867, whereas in West Bengal total number of beneficiaries are about 29 lakh.

Land under litigation is about 50,000 acres. And wasteland distributed is 24.89 lakh acres as per 2006-07 report published by the Ministry of Rural Development, Government of India in April 2007.

There is lot of hunger for land in U.P. and number of agriculture labourers is gradually increasing.

Many of the assignees of government vested lands have not yet got actual possession of their land and erstwhile powerful landowners continue to get these lands cultivated by their musclemen. Encroachments should be immediately removed from their lands by the respective District Magistrate. Some of the pattadars or AVLs have not cultivated their land because institutional finance is not available to them. As a result, they have leased out their small parcels of land to other farmers having means and resources for cultivation.

This does not mean that the state should encourage leasing out by these poor men. On the other hand, state should arrange crop financing to them at a concessional rate of interests (4%) so that they can cultivate their land by their own labour which is the greatest satisfaction for a villager. Contract farming can never be another alternative for these poor farmers. It will mean that the state wants to increase the number of landless persons and agricultural labourers.

According to one Chinese proverb, the number of times a farmer puts his foot on land, production will increase. Naturally, he will visit his own field. One cannot go and trespass land belonging to another person. Owning land gives so much satisfaction and security to the poor person that he puts best of his labour and attention to the land. Labour constitutes 30-40 per cent as input in agriculture. As a result, the production increases automatically. Secondly, there is no other alternative employment available to this army of unemployed persons in rural areas. There are about 27 per cent persons below poverty line even today. They require land to take benefit under some scheme or the other of the Government. Banks will not allow any credit to the persons below poverty line unless they have land which is an identification for a villager.

Out of 96.36 per cent persons found in possession land, only 66.59 per cent were recorded in revenue records as per survey in 1992. This gap needs to be filled up immediately.

The ceiling limit for irrigated land with one crop is 10.95 ha and for irrigated crops is 7.30 ha and for dry land it is 18.25 ha. This should be reduced to 7.5, 5 ha and 12 ha respectively and process of vesting should go on. After the implementation of ZA&LR Act and the U.P. imposition of Ceiling on Land Holdings Act, 1960, some new landlords have sprung up. They should be taken care of and equitable distribution of rural landed properties should be a continuous process to establish an egalitarian society in the State where there is so much flagrant class-discrimination and class-differences. The society has to be an integrated society.

Exemptions of religious and charitable trust from imposition of ceiling, exemptions of groves and abadi, benami transactions, transfers by the adverse possessions, arithmetical mistake, incorrect compilation of 61-B (total landholding of a person in Uttar Pradesh), hibba name by Muslims and problems in the definition of family, were some of the reasons behind failure of land ceiling. Complication in deciding ceiling limits for various qualities of land and defining family, leads to prolonged trail of cases, leading of higher possibility of mischief. Many people were shown 'dead' before 1973 on the basis of certificates given by Gram Pradhans. Many divorces were obtained on paper, many children were adopted and many other children were shown to be adults on the basis of 'Farzi Parivar' register. Even a factory that had already been conceived on 24-1-71, was conceded a share in the property. Some other provisions in ceiling law are chiefly responsible for poor availability of surplus land. These are:

(a) Provision to give separate ceiling limit for major sons in the family.
(b) Provision for holding land up to twice the ceiling limit for families with over five members.
(c) Provision for treating every shareholder of the joint family as applicable in personal law as separate unit for ceiling limit.

(d) Misclassification of land

(e) Misapplication of appropriate ceiling for land very newly irrigated by public investment etc.

(f) Allowing every share holder of a company as a separate unit for ceiling limit.

Performance of Uttar Pradesh regarding the imposition of ceiling on landholdings has not been very satisfactory. The imposition of ceiling on land holdings has not been very satisfactory. The 1960 Act could not cut much ice. So it was not drastically modified in 1973. But by that time the coming of 1972 Act only 2.87 lakh acres out of estimated 7.50 lakh owners have been declared surplus.

Between verbal discussions, introduction of ceiling legislation and final passing of the bill in the form of an Act, there was such time gap that people could always conveniently make nami or benami transfers of all lands above the expected ceiling, although benami and nami transfers after 24-1-71 were declared ineffective for the purpose of ceiling and mechanism was provided to defect such cases. The law provided for only filing of returns by the landowners. Since big landowners had the support of local administration, ceiling law existing only on paper was natural. Ceiling cases linger for many years. Due to delay in allotment, allottees become unable to take effective possessions over the allotted lands. Land is sometimes not allotted to deserving persons. In courts, State is represented by naib-tahsildars, who are very often not aware of the up to date position of laws and rules and also are no match of the lawyers engaged by parties in marshalling laws and evidence. Minor officials are at the mercy of influential large landowners. Land allotted is more often *usar* and *banjar*. Weaker sections are not organized and are not vocal. Supervision of senior officials is slack.

Loopholes in ceiling laws are also required to be plugged. There should be no relaxation of ceiling limit for religious or charitable trust or wakf, endowment or institution.

Conclusion

State of U.P. is at critical juncture. The poor people have asserted and the new Government has been installed. State of U.P. had to do away with Uttarakhand because the Z.A & LR Act, 1950 was not applied there.

Similarly, some exemptions were made in Mirzapur South District and Banaras State. Now, Naxalite agitation is raising head up there. State owned Nazul land is also excepted. And it is a bone of contention and source of corruption. Land reform is the best solution to the problem of naxalism which is flourishing in U.P.

It is, therefore, suggested that serious attention should be given to implement twin measures of land reforms i.e. recording of sharecroppers and distribution of government, surplus land. Political will as well as administrative will is required to implement the land reform measures. I am sure that U.P. can enter into new era of agricultural production and egalitarian society if land reform measures are properly implemented with immediate effect.

Status of Land Reforms in Uttarakhand/Uttaranchal

State of Uttaranchal which was carved out from Uttar Pradesh on 9th November, 2000, has a population of 84.9 lakh (approx.) as per 2001 Census. It has 17.87 per cent Scheduled Caste population whereas it has only 3.02 per cent Scheduled Tribe population unlike other hilly regions. It has 53,484 sq. km. areas. The Zamindari Abolition and Land Reforms Act, 1950 and other land related Acts are still applicable to Uttarakhand. The ZA&LR Act, 1950 aimed at:

"All the rights, titles and interests of the Zamindars (intermediaries) in every estate shall cease and be vested in the State of Uttar Pradesh free from all encumbrances."

However, Tehri-Garhwal and Jaunsar Bawar Parganas of Dehradun 'have been excluded as the Legislatures did not consider it proper to legislate for those areas.'

The following areas were exempted in Tehri-Garhwal and Jaunsar-Bawar Parganas of Dehradun district:

1. The districts of Almora and Garhwal
2. In the district of Nainital
   - (a) the Nainital sub-division
   - (b) the following villages of the Terai and Bhabar Government estates

Parganas Buzpur

Bajawala	Barathni	Gulzarpur
Banakhera	Bhainsia	Hezira

Banakhara Seni	Gulria Gabra	Ratanpuri
Banskhera	Haripura	Simalpuri
Banskheri	Herson	Sheopuri
Bhajwanagla	Khamani	Thapagnagla
Bhikampuri	Maindeya	Kalabandwari
Bijai Rampura	Halttoo	Faridpur
Chanakpur	Rajpura No. I	

Parganas Gadarpur

Alkhdai	Buxaura	Kulha
Andkhera	Khanpur	Madanpur
Beria	Pachcham	Mahali Jungle
Bari Rain	Khanpur	Mukandpur
Nandpur, Pipalia, Kopa, Jafarpur, Gaderpuri		

North Kashipur

Kamdebpur	Lalitpur	Thari
Beria	Karailpur	Kandela
Birpur Lau, Birpur Tar, Raipur, Pipalsona		

In Khusalpur circle

Khusapur, Lampur Moti, Lampur Lachi, Shahbazpur

(c) The Bhabar villages in the Tarai and Bhabar sub-division which are settled with Zamindars.

The reasons for exemption were examined: Tehri-Garhwal is included in the Himalayan district of U.P. The Himalayan district is the tract within the Himalaya bounded by the Tons on the west and the Kal or Sarda on the east. According to the Census taken on 18th March, 1921, the area is 16,060 square miles and the total population is 1,44,95,727. The Khasiyas were termed as Sudras in Garhwal and as Kshatriyas in Kumaon, i.e. Almora District and the hill pattis of Nainital district. They numbered, 3,11,817 in Kumaon and Garhwal and formed nearly half of the entire population of these districts. As the Khasa form about 90 per cent of the entire Brahman and Rajput population in the Himalayan district, they would number over 820,000.

The villages are, with a few exceptions, universally small and are in fact nothing more than detached hamlets, scattered along the sides and bases of the mountains. The area is thinly populated with the exception of the hill stations of Nainital, Ranikhet, Almora, Lansdown and Chakrata, the population is extremely rural. In 1921, the number of villages with population under 520 was as follows in Tehri-Garhwal.[2]

Total Inhabited Towns and Villages	*Total Population*	*Villages under 500 in population*	*Population*
2,736	318,414	2,734	313,224

There are less than 3 villages per 4 square miles and this large rural population is supported by agriculture. More than 90 per cent of the people are agriculturists. They are mostly cultivating proprietors. The Almora district, like the rest of Kumaon is land of small proprietors holdings, each man owning and tilling his own land. There are few large zamindars and those that exist approximate more to the type of superior proprietors with few legitimate rights beyond the collection from the real owners of the soil of an allowance for malikana.

On the other hand, there was an existing cooperative farming in the hills known as Gaon Sanjait. All the proprietors of the village are jointly and severally liable for the land revenue assessed on the whole village. Perfect partition is altogether unknown in the hills and we have a village proprietary system resembling to the commonest cases either pure pattadari or imperfect pattadari. Therefore, the system could have been turned into cooperative farming by defining the shares rather than postponing the matter for a long time which subsequent governments did not bother for a long time.

Later on, State Government applied the provisions of the ZA & LR Act, 1950 to former Banaras State (Notification 35), Mirzapur District (Notification 36), the former Rampur State (Notification 61) & other State owned Nazal lands. The notification was held valid.

For Uttarakhand region, Kumaon/Uttarakhand Zamindari Abolition Act (KUZA) was passed and is in force since 1960.

At present, the discrimination is removed and all lands of zamindars and big landlords stand vested though lot of work is yet to be done by the revenue machinery to legally vest the land and to physically take over possession of the lands of ex-landlords otherwise the subsequent enactments will just remain golden pieces of papers. By removing clauses 117 to 128 of UPZA Act, this Act has done away with Panchayats for managing and distribution of land. As a result, nothing has happened. On 15th December, 2001,[3] the landless peasants of three villages of Sameshwar Valley in Almora district of Uttaranchal-Padaulia, Pokhti and Brahmpokhri—seized 80 acres (1600 Nali) of land at the call of CPI (ML) and distributed it among themselves. On 17 and 18 December, landless peasants belonging to Naughar and Badyudo villages of the same valley organized and seized 20 acres (400 Nali) of land and distributed it themselves. These lands belonged to the category of benap land, which is called Panchayati land elsewhere in the country.

To guard the local hilly people, restrictions were imposed in 2003 to acquire land by the outsiders who have no immovable land in Uttarakhand by purchase or otherwise firstly beyond 500 sq. metres and at present beyond 250 sq. metres which is sufficient to make the dwelling unit in rural areas. However, to promote competition and free market flow as a part of globalization, there is no restriction on acquisition or purchase of land by the outsiders in municipal areas. This is to promote industrialization in the new State. Uttarakhand is one State which has been quite successful to attract investment. It shows a way how industrialisation can be promoted without compromising interests of the tillers of the land. The State Government has tactfully made the unutilized government land or large chunks of land lying unutilized with the government departments or government institutions. Thousands of acres surplus land of the Pantnagar Agriculture University alone was made available to industries along with concessions in sales tax, income tax and excise duty. As a result, all big industrial houses have set up their units in different parts of Uttarakhand. Time is not far when per capita income of Uttarakhand will match that of Himachal Pradesh just next to Delhi or Goa. Before doing that, the hill people have to be given back at least 20 per cent land for cultivation out of the total land and land subsequently added to 'forest' should be taken back for agriculture. However, more steps as suggested in U.P. are required for recording of sharecroppers and distribution of government vested land among the deserving landless or poor cultivators of Uttarakhand. Then, we shall term the development in Uttarakhand as 'inclusive' or sustainable or integrated development encompassing all sections of the society.

REFERENCES

1. Dr. Agrawal, P.K. (1993): *Land Reforms in India*, M.D. Publications Pvt. Ltd., New Delhi, p. 170.
2. Dr. Agrawal, P.K. (1993): *Land Reforms in India*, p. 72, *op. cit*.
3. Sharma, Purushottam (2008): *Land seizure movement in Almora district. A historical background through Internet*.

7

Bottlenecks in Implementation of Land Reforms in Maharashtra

The implementation of agrarian reform laws was periodically reviewed by the State Government and the first such comprehensive review was undertaken as far back as in 1972. The only intermediary tenures that are being continued today are the Devasthan and Wakf Inam grants.

Abolition of the intermediaries resulted in the conferment of occupancy rights on a very large body of under-right holders and some tenants in all parts of the State. This could indeed be said to be the first major step towards the transition of a feudal order to democratic social order.

The Maharashtra Agricultural Lands (Ceiling on Holdings) Act, 1961 came into force on 26th January, 1962. An area measuring 1,24,493 ha was declared surplus under the provisions of the said Act.

The ceiling were lowered in 1975, as a consequence of which an area of 1,60,962 ha was declared as surplus. Out of the total area of 2,85,455 ha 2,51,522 ha have already been distributed.[1]

Lands measuring 18,422 ha had to be excluded from distribution because this was either uncultivable or was needed for a public purpose or was involved in exemption claims. An area of 6,204 hectares is involved in litigation.

The proportion of scheduled castes and scheduled tribes allottees in Maharashtra has been as high as 53 per cent. The ceiling which was initially imposed on agricultural holdings in 1962, was substantially lowered within a short span of just about 13 years.

The very fact that the lands declared surplus under the amended Act of 1975 were considerably more than what had been acquired under the Principal Act is proof enough of the fact that the Act was implemented quite successfully in Maharashtra. Maharashtra's performance as far as implementation of the Ceiling Act is concerned therefore, speaks for itself. Those ceilings will be further lowered with the passage of time by the operation of the laws of succession.

Tribal Land Alienation

The law relating to the prevention of alienation of tribal holdings in favour of non-tribals is sufficiently stringent in Maharashtra. Government has also taken steps to ensure restoration of land which had been transferred by the tribals in favour of non-tribals under due process of law, to the tribals. Lands measuring 43,351 ha have been restored to the tribals under these measures. As a matter of fact, the State Government's major concern as of now is to augment the compensation admissible to the non-tribals.

Though a redistribution of the ceiling surplus land has gone a long way in the expansion of the owner cultivation in the State, the greatest expansion of owner cultivation came by a "politically costless" means unavailable to other more dense States like Kerala and West Bengal. This was the distribution of just over a million acres of cultivable wasteland.

However, it will be wrong to presume that the political leaders in Maharashtra had all intention or the political will to implement the land reform legislation seriously and honestly. It is a well known fact in Maharashtra that the dominant political class comes from the rich peasantry. The rich sugar barons control the political leadership of the State. Even the well known Chief Minister Mr. Vasantrao Patil, who is known for his concern for land reforms, had spoken publicly of the economic, political and the administrative arguments for retaining the old ceiling limits in 1971. At the time, even the lower rank of hegemonic Congress Party in Maharashtra came in open revolt against the new ceiling law, to be promulgated and implemented. As a result, the Ceiling Act of 1975 (implemented in 1978) did not change the ceiling limit for the most valuable land (irrigated land) at 18 acres.[2]

As the Revenue Department has become a general administration department, it has utterly neglected its original revenue work. The records were not updated. In backward and hilly districts, where Naxalites are active, the landowners nor revenue officers cared to record the changes in revenue records. As a result, the landlords as well as small and marginal farmers were harassed by the talathis who are custodian of records of rights.

If records of rights are not up-to-date, further lands cannot be vested to the state nor benami lands can be unearthed. The poor people who were given patta or government land were not recorded in revenue records. They thus became at the mercy of revenue officials (*talathis*) or the erstwhile landlords who continued to occupy their earlier lands though it got vested to state by law.

Tenancy Reforms

The Tenancy legislations are different for the three regions of Maharashtra. The Mumbai Region is covered by the Bombay Tenancy and Agriculture Land Act, 1948 and the (Amendment) Act 1955; the Marathwada region is guided by the Hyderabad Tenancy and Agriculture Land Act, 1950 and the Bombay Tenancy and Agricultural Act, 1958 (Vidarbha Region and Kutch Area) applies to the rest. The provision of each are similar. They provide for fixity of rent, security of tenure and compulsory transfer of land to the tenants which are non-resumable by landlords.

State of Maharashtra gives two extreme situations. Towards Vidarbha region, the sharecroppers or the landless persons feel deprived of their rights whereas tenant in Pune, Kolhapur belt is sometimes richer than the landowner himself. Most of them have been working with their landowners for more than 10 years. The tenants after the 'Tillers Day' were entitled to purchase the tenancy within one year. The Government run co-operative farm under Maharashtra State Farming Development Corporation in Pune demonstrates an ideal system where the individual farmer can retain the ownership and can cultivate collectively. The cause of disparities in various regions in Maharashtra requires a close look. The experiment has been done in Maharashtra itself. The problem is to undertake the implementation of successful experiment to all parts of the State without caring for political backlash. Then, only the extremists movement which is raising head here and there, can be tackled effectively and its further spread can be checked engulfing other regions of Maharashtra which happens to be one of the richest and most forward looking States of India.

Suggestions

(1) After the 'Tillers Day' no attempt has been made so far to enrol the new informal tenants. A special drive should be

undertaken to identify informal tenants and confer ownership rights on them.

(2) The definition of 'Tenancy' should be broadened so as to include cash rent/kind rent and crop-shares.

(3) No surrender of tenancy should be permitted as these surrenders are generally forged or are managed in an emergency situation to a tenant or sharecropper.

(4) In Vidarbha Region, the resumption of land by the landowners for personal cultivation upto three family holdings (i.e. from 21 to 120 acres) should be reduced. The definition of 'Personal Cultivation' should not include cultivation by hired labour under one's personal supervision at all.

(5) Tenants conferred with ownership rights have to be directly integrated with the anti-poverty programmes.

In Maharashtra, by 1970, ownership of leased land was partly or fully transferred to the tenants in about 18.75 lakh tenancy cases out of a total of about 26 lakh recorded tenancy cases in the State.

In Maharashtra it is found that the incidence of tenancy is very low which was found on survey by the IAS probationers to the tune of 2.4 per cent. As per the NSS (National Sample Survey), 26th and 37th Round in 1971-72 it was 6.15 per cent and 1981-82 it was 5.20 per cent. This is very poor as compared with other States. Some efforts should have to be made for recording of tenants. There is a phenomenon of 'reverse tenancy' whereas some small landholders holding land below 2 ha lease out their land to relatively big holders who made good output of sugarcane by merging leased-in land with their own land. However, State of Maharashtra have done quite a good job by giving finance to the land allottees.

In fact, many tenants were neither aware of the provision of the '*Tillers*' Day' nor they were allowed to exercise this right of purchase. The landlords were obviously not only reluctant, but even opposed the acceptance of the tenancies they feared that they would lose these lands permanently and the tenants would become owners of their lands. The phenomenon prevailed all over Maharashtra, but especially in four districts of the Konkan region where it was quite rampant. In Konkan district, the informed tenants got organised to record their tenancy rights. Similarly in Vidarbha region and Marathwada region, they joined Naxalite outfits as they virtually got no support either from the ruling party or from the revenue administration for preserving their right of cultivation which is very basic to the rural poor.

Following weaknesses or bottlenecks were further noticed in implementation of land reform measure like the foregoing ones:

(1) Absence of correct and updated records and lack of knowledge on the part of sharecroppers to know the details of lands, they cultivate.
(2) Lack of financial support for land reform programmes. As a result, they talk refuge of the local moneylenders who exploits them fully.
(3) Weakness and irregularity of the reporting system and of evaluation.
(4) Delay in disposal of cases by revenue courts as well as civil courts and the High Court.

In Maharashtra, Sawant (1991) estimated that about 44.6 per cent of the total tenancy area was under concealed tenancy during 1981-82. Secondly, the type of exemptions allowed included exclusion of a landlord who was a minor, widow, serving in the armed forces or mentally and physically disabled. In addition to these, exemption was also given to a landlord who preferred to retain the land for self-cultivation in case the landlord did not have any other means of livelihood. Thirdly, the clause of voluntary surrender (voter name, service agreement) by the tenant of his claim on the land had also rendered the legislation ineffective in many cases.

As in September 2006, 14.92 lakh tenants have been conferred ownership rights on 42.90 lakh acres[3] of land which is a better figure than West Bengal.

Distribution of Land

Maharashtra has also been during a good work in the field of distribution of government wasteland. Total about 10.22 lakh acres[4] of Government wastelands have been distributed in Maharashtra and the process is still continuing since April 2007 to February 2008, Maharashtra is leading in distribution of government wasteland which is 1,72,059 ha.

However, Maharashtra is lacking behind in distribution of Bhoodan land though it is the native land of Vinoba. Maharashtra has still to distribute 77,000 acres of Bhoodan land[5]. Similarly, Maharashtra does not maintain proper account of land vested to government and distributed. The total percentage of land distributed is 97.15 per cent as per an estimate in December 1995. However, there is lot of gap in taking over possession of lands because lands get involved in court cases before it is taken over. This is an area of vigorous action in the State.

Some major implementation problems of the ceiling are:

(1) The definition of the family unit, which included minor children, caused a serious problem. The limit of members to enjoy family ceiling should be restricted to five. Then, some additional area can be allowed. For less number of members in family, proportionate land for family should be deducted.
(2) The partition of land was undertaken immediately so as to create separate family units.
(3) The emergence of benami transactions was huge. The enquiry should be done in case of non-existing persons and should be disallowed.
(4) The law provides that if a portion of land was leased out to a tenant, then such land should be excluded for the total size of holding of the family. This provision should not be there. Taking clue for this, a number of landholders created temporary false tenancy records in the names of permanent servants and avoided land surrender.
(5) The categorisation of land was generously misappropriated to retain larger holdings of land. No landholder in record has more than 3 acres of irrigated land in his land. Thus, falsification of records is a major problem.

Land Acquisition and Displacement

In Maharashtra, the tribals are 9.27 per cent of the population. But among those displaced persons, the tribals were about 27 per cent. Some of the major projects were M/s. Enron and Sardar Sarovar Projects. In 1979, Maharashtra had the largest number of large dams in the country, 631 dams were either completed or are in the process of being completed. This is projected as dispossession of the local tribal people by the State. These tribals, finding no satisfactory rehabilitation package, take recourse to the Naxalites. Five rehabilitation schemes are there on papers but these are meant for persons who can take advantage of these schemes. Illiterate and simple tribals cannot perhaps, take proper advantage of these schemes. As a result, they are denied their rights. After having lost their agricultural land and home, they have no other place to go except to join the Naxalite outfits. Thus, the resettlement and rehabilitation work under land acquisition schemes by the government should be given similar priority as land acquisition. Land should be handed over only after the resettlement issues are decided and finalised in the field not only on papers. This is a very strong dictum for the present day regulatory administration but the government has to choose whether they want to deliver fruits of development only to few and leave the affected persons in lurch compelling them to join violent/armed outfits. On the other hand, the Press, NGOs and armed groups are now equally vocal and publicity prone to ballooning these adverse effects of any development project. Thus, more caution and proactive action is required on the part of the government as a whole.

Cooperative Farming

There is a proactive experiment going in Pune successfully for many years on the State arm under the Maharashtra State Farming Development Corporation.[6] The land is owned by the individual cultivators but arrangement is made for cultivation through modern implements and inputs collectively. The marketing is also done on cooperative basis. Thus, it is the ideal system of cooperative farming keeping individual ownership intact.

Conclusion

Though the incidents of Naxal violence is increasing in prosperous State of Maharashtra, yet everything is not lost. Maharashtra has lot of resources of fund and personnel. The political will and administrative will are required to be made operational. It seems that in the march of industrialisation, Maharashtra is forgetting its poor people who feed big cities and big towns. Time is ripe to take a re-look of the implementation of land reform measures along with making minor legislative amendments here and there. The Revenue Administration is to be given top priority, which was given in seventies. If the development schemes are not implemented or made operational, the land acquired should be returned to the tribals or at least unused or excess land should be returned to them. Panchayat Bodies are to be geared up and they should be co-opted in the process of land distribution and even in recording of sharecroppers. The tribals and poor cultivators in Vidarbha and Marathwada regions should be given institutional finance, *i.e.* bank loan for cultivation on concessional rates so that they may have not to commit suicide. Large number of suicides by farmers speak poorly of performance of land reforms in the State. Let this blot be removed and Maharashtra should lead in the field of Land Reform as in the past.

REFERENCES

1. Dr. Agrawal, P.K. (2000): *Issues in Land Reforms*, Rajiv Gandhi Foundation, New Delhi, p.44.
2. *Ibid*, pp. 45-46.
3. *Annual Report (2006-07)*: Government of India, Ministry of Rural Development-Annexure-XLIX, p. 258.
4. *Ibid*, Annexure-XLVII, p. 257.
5. *Ibid*, Annexure-XLVII, p. 256.
6. Dr. Agrawal, P.K. (1993), *Land Reforms in India*, MD Publications, New Delhi, p. 231.

8

Institutional Road Blocks to Land Reforms in Bihar

So called intellectuals jokingly say that everything is a roadblock in Bihar. It is not told about Jharkhand which has separated from Bihar. It may not be cent-per-cent true but there is some truth in the statement. Bihar should not take it as a criticism but should do thorough introspection. There is plenty of scope to improve things in the area of land reforms in the State. If the records of rights are updated in Bihar and are published, many of the genuine grounds of Naxalism in Bihar can be obliterated.

The status of main component of land reforms in Bihar including Jharkhand, i.e. vesting of ceiling surplus land and its distribution among the beneficiaries is, as follows as, on 30th September, 2006 (in acres)[1]

Area declared surplus	*Area taken possession*	*Area distributed to individual beneficiaries*	*Total no. of beneficiaries*
4,15,447	3,90,752	3,06,964	3,79,528

S.C. Beneficiaries		*S.T. Beneficiaries*		*Other Beneficiaries*	
No.	*Area*	*No.*	*Area*	*No.*	*Area*
2,34,861	1,02,045	43,050	39,978	1,01,617	84,941

Distribution of Bhoodan Land upto November, 2005:

	Area (in acres)	
Donated	*Distributed*	*Balance*
3,57,000	2,01,000	1,56,000

Distribution of Government Wastelands

Area distributed as in July 1997	*(Government of India Figures)*
13,21,000	

The problems were many. The information about the total land including in benami names with the ex-zamindars is not statistically available. Besides Zamindars succeeded in keeping 14 per cent of their estate in the form of khas possession which nobody could touch. As per an estimate of the Revenue Department of the Government of Bihar, the total land in khas possession of the ex-zamindars would be to the tune of 15 lakh acres.

In addition there was a bulk of disputed land. With various unscrupulous methods, such as *benamadari,* collusion with revenue officials and politicians, coupled with their social status and power, the ex-zamindars of Bihar succeeded, by and large, in protecting their class interests. The examples are there for everybody to see. The ex-zamindars of Darbhanga, Hathwa, Dumraon and Ramgarh still own large tracts of lands. Even tenure holders under them, like Raghubans Narain Singh of Kursela, happen to be big landowners. Maul Babu who once prided himself on being a modest *raiyat* of Raj Darbhanga, now possesses around 18,000 acres of land and an air strip !

It is clear that Bihar is much lagging behind in vesting of surplus land. In West Bengal, 13,98,139 acres of land has vested to the State though the total area of West Bengal is half of Bihar (Bihar 1,73,877 sq km, West Bengal 88,752 sq km) Bihar—population is 8.29 crore (2001 census), West Bengal—is 8 crore.

In Bihar Scheduled Tribe population as per 2001 census is 78,45,000 which is 10 per cent of India. In West Bengal 5,36,912 tribals got land as pattadar whereas in Bihar only 43,050 tribals got government land. This is the quantum of problem in Bihar and Jharkhand which are witnessing large scale extremists' activities. On the other hand, out of 86,291 cases filed for restoration of alienated land of tribals, only about 50 per cent cases, i.e. 44,634 have gone in favour of the tribals. This is palpably injustice to the tribals.[2]

However, there is still lot of scope to distribute remaining government land and 1.56 lakh acres of Bhoodan land which can be distributed among the tribals as priority apart from Government waste land which is yet to be distributed. Even consolidation of land holdings of 96.05 lakh acres of land was tilted in favour of land owners.[3] Therefore, it was stopped from 1992. It is not understandable why the consolidation operation has again been started Bihar w.e.f. 15-3-2004 without streamlining revenue administration.

The second biggest bottleneck in land reforms measure is non-recognition of sharecroppers in Bihar. As per report of Government of India as in September, 2006 total number of tenants conferred ownership rights were not reported. West Bengal achieved magical feat by recording 15 lakh Borgaders or sharecroppers without conferring ownership right on them. They only share 50 per cent share of produce if the owner gives plough, cattle, seeds, manures, fertilizers and other inputs. If the sharecropper provides all inputs for cultivation, he would get 75 per cent share of produce. The latter is only on paper but the right is there. If West Bengal can do it, why the adjoining State of Bihar cannot do it having the same system of land records and system of permanent settlement. Only little more initiative and political will are required for this purpose.

The landowners are tactfully utilising judicial proceedings to deny rights to the poor cultivators and are taking undue advantage of the corrupt and demoralised revenue machinery. They even go to West Bengal and take same order of stay or injunction on the pretext of title suit and prolong suits for years. As a result, the poor cultivators lay down their arms and hearts and leave everything on destiny. For past few years, they have now started taking recourse of naxalite elements who protect them from undue exploitation and injustice and take revenge from the zamindars by way of armed attacks for their annihilation. The landowners have also organised themselves. Therefore, it is no longer one way running over the others. It is only violence which comes on surface in which police and administration are dragged as law and order maintenance agency. Then, the movement of left wing extremists (LWE) will get diverted towards the police force and their main focus is lost. It is violence, murder and forceful occupations of land all-round and no permanent solutions come forth. The lands which were once forcibly taken possession by the LWE, are recaptured by the landowner with the help of their army or police force as the law of land is in their favour. Thus, correction and updation of land records become very crucial in Bihar for launching land reform measures. Let us examine how best the old and outdated records-of-rights in Bihar can be updated.

Updation of Land Records

Combining Khanapuri with Attestation and Disposal of Objections

Khanapuri (filling up the records) is the most critical stage in the survey operations. The rest of the stages involve correction of the database created. The matter of creating record should not be left to the amins. From the initial stage, the revenue officer or Naib Tehsildar can be associated with this work so that at later stages of attestation and objections, there may not be many objections. At local stage, there should be transparency. Even the representative of PRIs, should be given notice to be present. The objection should be decided at the Khanapuri attestation stage and only objections after final publication should be invited. Three stages objections thus should be reduced to two only or even one.

Adherence to the Time Frame

The total time envisaged is of two years at the maximum for survey operation in a medium sized district. Adequate number of teams should be formed even from other districts. Any operation running beyond time frame would necessarily will have lot of complications for cost, quality and corruption will creep in. Time is a critical factor and incentives and disincentives have to be linked in order to achieve the requisite efficiency. Even some trained personnel in survey from open market may be recruited on daily wage or contract basis subject to panel disincentives for wrong or faulty recording.

Final Publication

The final publication of records should be made available in the form of Khatian to the interest holder on whatever high fee that may be decided. After a time of 60 days, the objections should be closed and final records of rights may be entered in revenue records on computers after disposal of all objections on due hearing after giving proper opportunity of hearing to the objectors and passing reasoned orders. With the incorporations of these modifications the records of rights should be finalised and kept in CD or disc of computer.

Training of Survey Personnel

There is no substitute of field survey. Unless field survey is done periodically say after every 10 years or 15 years, the computers cannot themselves correct records. Even correction of record of one landholder cannot do because overall boundary of the village has to be tilted. This takes time. For this stupendous work, survey knowing or trained personnel are required who are in scarcity. Survey institutes are closing down one by one because the revenue department is a low cost department and they can't sustain financially now-a-days. Government should come in a big way to open survey institutes or survey training in ITIs or Polytechnic Colleges in India. The survey work should be made little more interesting and scientific. Survey of India has expertise and is experimenting with new technologies like aerial survey but they are not able to give final records of rights as required or used by the public in general from time immemorial.

Now, the survey personnel have to be trained in computerization of records and digitisation of maps. Then there will be constant correction of records by the some agency who will be well conversant with the field situation. Experiments of West Bengal combining management revenue functionaries and survey functionaries has not also been successful due to public pressure on management functions like correction of records, hearing of cases, mutation and conversion, As a result, the work of survey and preparation of record of rights terribly suffers. Collector in District Land &, Land Reforms Office should be strictly instructed not to employ survey and settlement staff and officers for other administrative works including elections.

Requirement of Additional Staff and Officers

The survey and settlement wing is inadequately staffed. In West Bengal, there are 30,000 employees and officers whereas in Bihar, there will not be more than 10,000 staff and officers. Government of India is providing liberal grants for the purpose but the State Government has to carry on the burden with its own resources. But this is worth. This is the basic responsibility of the State Government which they should discharge if they have to stay in seat of power otherwise disgruntled public led by the extremists will run over their ivory towers.

Digitisation of Maps

The biggest challenge of digitisation of maps has been met and a software has been developed after toil and continuous meditation for about 15 years. In West Bengal, successfully maps are being digitised to the accuracy of more than 99 per cent. This will solve problem of delay of number of years in printing of maps which are integrated parts of records of rights. State like Bihar can employ National Informatic Centre (NIC) of Government of India for this purpose with success.

Ideal Records as Reality

Andhra Pradesh has shown that the registration wing of government can be linked with the record or revenue or land reform wing. No registration should be done unless the records are seen as correct on computer. After registration the records can be simultaneously corrected. Thus, there will be automatic system of updation of records of rights. The fees for mutation and conversion can be duly charged at the common service centre like in Madhya Pradesh, Andhra Pradesh, West Bengal and Karnataka.

Once the maps are digitised, the raiyat can be given his records-of-rights along with map of plot boundaries with respect to the village. This will be the best and the final records of rights which will have no lacuna or gap. This record of rights will have all good qualities of permanent settlement in the Eastern India and North India and record with map of plot in Raiyatwari settlement in South India. The 'recording of rights' operation should be conducted in the mission approach on the pattern of 'Operation Barga' in West Bengal.

I am sure that Government of Bihar will venture upon this mechanism of correction and updation of records of rights with or without the assistance of Government of India.

Other Suggestions

Legal Measures

Under Section 44 of the present Bihar Land Ceiling Act, it should be obligatory for the State Government to prepare and publish a record of rights. Therefore, instead of the word 'may', the word 'shall' should be substituted in that section. This will provide a legal basis for annual updating of records which should be done on regular basis.

The provision of consultation with landlord for subletting the land should be done away with because it practically amounts to giving the landlord the right to change his tenants. The laws relating to land reforms should be codified in one single statute.

The implementation of the Maintenance of Land Records Act, 1973 should be taken up in the right earnest in blocks affected by ceiling legislation.

The names of encroachers should not be recorded.

Administrative Measures

A separate machinery for implementing land reforms should be set up and selected officers may be put on the job.

There should be regular training of officers in order to equip them with the requisite knowledge of the laws, rules, regulations and various instructions issued by the government from time to time.

Executive instructions should be reiterated so that the Police Officers should be bound to follow the orders of the revenue authorities in these matters and assert their authority in the interests of the allottees of the surplus land and the bataidars or share-croppers.

Construction of the office-cum-residences for lower revenue functionaries in the *tolas* of the weaker sections of society, will instill greater confidence and bring justice to their doorstep.

The provision of Section 71(a) of the Chhota Nagpur Tenancy Act (CNT Act) should be enforced strictly so that lands belonging to the members of the tribal community may be restored to them.

The number of appeals and revisions should be restricted to just one in order to avoid vexatious litigation.

Field visit by the original court should be made a mandatory provision in all restoration cases. Restoration register along with supporting records should be maintained at *Halka/Anchal*/sub-divisional level.

A time limit should be prescribed for all recording operations, say one year.

A 'rakma-milan' with the previous survey should be rigidly adhered to so that the alienation of tribal land is not regularised.

The recording officer should not be allowed to open *khatas* in respect of such lands in the name of non-tribals which have been recorded in the name of tribals in the previous survey.

Annual computation sheets (rent-rols) should be regularly prepared and updated.

Officer who have already done their district tenure, should be posted as settlement officers in these areas.

There should be special squad at the disposal of the Deputy Commissioner/District Magistrate for giving possession of land to the tribals and the landless.

Second Phase

Following steps are suggested:

(a) Abolition of absentee land ownership
(b) Enforcement of minimum standards of personal cultivation.
(c) Identification and recording of share-croppers/bataidars on the patterns of West Bengal's 'Operation Barga'.
(d) Effective implementation of ceiling laws including scrutinising about 84 land owners in the State who own more than 500 acres of land.
(e) Equitable distribution of surplus land among the landless specially those belonging to the Scheduled Castes and Scheduled Tribes.
(f) Proper implementation of rural development schemes and supportive facilities such as rural employment schemes, water harvesting schemes, minor irrigation, soil conservation and social forestry schemes.
(g) The land tribunals should be made to work effectively in Bihar.

Bandyopadhyay Commission on Land Reforms[4]

Government of Bihar had set up a three-men commission chaired by Shri D. Bandyopadhyay who had spearheaded barga recording operation in West Bengal. It is learnt that the Commission has given its report which *inter alia* contains recommendations on strengthening administration of land revenue set-up, updation and computerisation of land records and recording of informal tenants or sharecroppers. The Government is still examining the report as usual. Various commissions and committees are set-up with pious declarations but their reports or recommendations are not implemented with that seriousness. The same bureaucrats again examine these reports and put-up to their political executives who place before the Cabinet. This process goes on and on. The people's leader like Lalu Prasad did not implement land reforms measures in his 15 years' regime in Bihar. It is less expected that any other Chief Minister will do it. If Shri Nitish Kumar does it, he deserves kudos for his courage and statesmanship. History will remember him.

REFERENCES

1. *Annual Report*, Government of India, Ministry of Rural Development, 2006-07 pages 255, 256 & 257.
2. *Ibid.*, p. 260.
3. *Ibid.*, p. 259.
4. Internet.

9

Naxalite Movement and Land Reforms in Jharkhand

If one State can be said to be fully afflicted with Naxalism, it is the newly formed State from the erstwhile united Bihar. The solution regarding Naxalite problem in Bihar will *mutatis mutandis* will apply to Jharkhand State. In fact, most of the problems of Jharkhand have been inherited by the nascent State from Bihar.

Following are generally accepted suggestions on implementation of land reforms in Jharkhand which is an important tool to tackle Naxalite problem:

1. All party consensuses should be arrived at for speeding up the implementation process of land reforms at the village level before the situation goes beyond redemption.
2. Infrastructure should be strengthened.
3. Farmer's pass book be issued.
4. There should be regular arrangement of training of administrative personnel, concurrent evaluation of the quality of implementation and carrying out research is also recognized.
5. Correct and up-to-date records of rights are crucial for the implementation of land reforms. Therefore, wherever the records are incorrect and not up-to-date, necessary steps should be taken to rectify and update them.
6. For hill areas which have not been cadastrally surveyed so far, a special programme for a cadastral survey will have to be initiated.

7. Apart from the normal survey and settlement operations, which may continue where they are already under way, a record of tenants, including sharecroppers and others in cultivating possession of the land, and having presumptive evidentiary value should be prepared for all the villages matter the course of a year and the records should be maintained by annual revision. This can be done by way of digitisation of village maps through computers and integrating the village map with the individual plot of record-of-segment of each rayat and updation of land records by engaging private vendors on computers where latest changes by way of mutation and conversion of lands should be invariably incorporated.
8. A crash programme of recording tenants or bataidars should be undertaken on the pattern of recording of bargadars in West Bengal.
9. The tenant who is not tilling the land himself should be given an option, within a specified time, whether he would continue to cultivate the land himself or leave.
10. Benami transfers must be declared illegal, and such transfers made in the past should be annulled and the land be vested in the government. There should be some specific provision in the tenancy laws to precisely define and describe benami transactions.
11. The existing ceiling laws should be translated into the vernacular using simple language so that all concerned have a clear understanding of the implication of the laws. Awareness, particularly amongst the beneficiaries, should be created by disseminating correct information through the audio-visual mass media.
12. Ledgers of landholdings district-wise and taluk-wise need to be prepared by the method of card indexing for effective implementation of ceiling laws.
13. Lists of big rural families should be drawn up at the sub-divisional level and vigorous application of the laws be initiated.
14. To restore confidence among the tribals, the pending cases of all those who have been illegally dispossessed or evicted

should be disposed of expeditiously by summary trials in a time-bound programme. If necessary, additional special officers may also be deputed for the purpose.

15. Cases which have been suppressed due to collusion with the staff as laid down in the Act should be followed up. If necessary, additional staff may be given. The onus of proving any right over the land which a non-tribal claims, must be that of the claimant.
16. The Tribal Welfare Department staff should be posted in each *halka* and may be utilized to identify cases of alienation and indebtedness. The welfare staff should also pursue the cases of restoration and collusive title suits and take the follow-up action to give effect to the court's decision in case of tribal.
17. People's participation in land reform measures can be ensured through a committee constituted by nominated/elected representatives from amongst the members of the Scheduled Tribes living in that area or through Sub-Committees of Panchayat Samitis. Such committees should be formed at the *halka* and/or block level for the sole purpose of implementing the aforesaid measures and should have the active support of land reforms department.
18. The classification of land in Jharkhand should be reduced to three (against the existing six):

    - irrigated,
    - unirrigated, and
    - inferior quality of land, e.g. a unproductive, hilly, mountainous, sandy etc.

    The ceiling for these three categories of land can be 15, 22.5 and 30 acres respectively. However, to provide incentive to farmers to improve productivity, classification of land may not be changed when private irrigation is introduced. Provisions in any case exist for refixation of ceiling if public irrigation is introduced.
19. The West Bengal Land Reforms Act, 1955 as amended up to 1972, besides providing ceiling for a 'Family' unit, puts a limit for a sole surviving adult unmarried person to half of a

family unit. An amendment on the West Bengal lines would facilitate effective implementation in Jharkhand.

20. The exemption granted in favour of sugar mills should be withdrawn.
21. There should be regular training of officers in order to equip them with the requisite knowledge of the laws, rules, regulations and various instructions issued by the government from time to time relating to land reforms. They should also be properly and adequately equipped with one necessary skills and attitudes required for the job.
22. Section 40 should be suitably amended to prohibit any transfer of land by member of the STs to a non-tribal.
23. A time-limit should be prescribed for every settlement operation, departmental proceedings should be initiated against officers not conforming to these schedules, and punishment imposed.
24. The survey officials should not be allowed to open *khatas* in respect of such lands in the name of non-tribals which have been recorded in the name of tribal in the previous survey.
25. The government should take a lead in establishing bank/ consumption loan or in the financing scheme for the tribals in the area at the rate of not more than four per cent on the lines of the Gramin Bank Scheme in Bangladesh and the mobile banks in Pakistan.
26. There should be a major thrust on small and medium irrigation projects in these areas which are ideally suited in terms of employment potential and for the management of the cost-benefit ratio. The water resources thus created should be utilized for intensive vegetable cultivation, pisciculture etc.

10

Strategy to Tackle Naxalism in West Bengal Through Land Reforms

If there is imbalance in the society, violence is its natural consequence. An eruption of violence in the society is no longer considered a social malaise. It is appropriation of the rights of the weak by the powerful, which could be set right with the use of force. The farmers are the class, which is the worst deprived class in the world. In this category, tillers of land who cultivate the land personally are the worst affected because their labour is exploited by the landowners and the society equally. If the poor and the deprived farmers are not given their due share, they will have no other alternative except to resort to use of physical force or unruly behaviour.

In India the rural population is above 70 per cent and they are mostly engaged in agriculture. Therefore, any violent movement will emerge from rural population of farmers and cultivators and not from labourers as envisaged by Karl Marx. Marx himself advised the proletariat to take to arms only when all other means have been exhausted. Land reform measures can to a large extent keep the balance between the have and have-nots in the rural areas. Most of the property in India is also locked in lands. Therefore, it is only land reform, which can provide balance in the society specially in India.

1. Origin of the Naxalism

It has been proved beyond doubt that one of the repercussions of non-implementation of land reforms was the growth of 'Naxalite' movement. The surfacing of the naxalite movement in 1966 in West Bengal and its positive ending by the Left Front Government in West

Bengal by implementing land reform measures has proved this case in point very clearly. The studies have shown that one of the reasons of rising terrorist violence in Punjab was due to the widening gap between the rich and the poor former in addition to growing unemployment and disenchantment of the urban youths in the system of Government. The youths who would have otherwise worked in their farms, were searching for jobs in urban areas because they thought that their land could be cultivated by landless people in their villages and they were authorized to take the produce without tilling their lands. The compulsion of 'personal cultivation' or 'land to the tiller' under land reform will attract Punjab rural youths to their farms. As a result, further agricultural production will rise in Punjab.

"The Naxalite movement was an important movement that covered 80 million landless people including 30 million tribals. It was consciously given a political and a militant character and arose out of a sense of discontentment and disillusionment against the CPI (M)'s inability and other factors to implement the land reform even after forming the United-Front Government in West Bengal in 1976. The Naxalites or the C.P.I. (M-L) introduced a distinct style of peasant warfare, with its distinct ideology and strategy. This movement more than any other, shook the national sense. Its tremors are still heard in Andhra Pradesh, Madhya Pradesh, Chhattisgarh, Jharkhand and Bihar under different titles."

2. Status of Left Wing Extremism[2]

There are many Left Wing Extremist groups operating in the country with lot of underground and over-ground cadres and supporters.

While aiming to establish a classless society based on egalitarian principles and revolutionary struggles, resorting to violence remains the major tactics of most of major LWE groups. The CPM-People's War Group (53%) and Maoist Communist Centre (MCC) (30%) continue spearhead LWE violence respectively.

The basic thrust of the different outfits is to focus attention on the grievances of the people, inequities suffered by large segments of the population, release of victims of exploitation from the tentacles of the landlords, etc. and to inculcate 'class' responsibilities among the economically and socially deprived sections. In pursuance of these objectives, the groups have not only mobilized the people but have also ensured that distributive justice is available in a rough and ready manner. The peoples' courts organized by these groups to expropriate surplus land from the landlords to be distributed to the landless, dispense criminal justice, settle disputes and punish offenders. Thus, 'Jan Adalats' constitute a cornerstone of their efforts to win over the masses, particularly in the rural areas. Besides, they indulge in extortion from businessmen, contractors, traders, government officers etc. and resort to murders and kidnappings to eliminate interference by agents of the established administration and defiant class enemies.

Various LWE groups have their presence in different parts of the country, notably the heartland states including Andhra Pradesh, Bihar, Jharkhand, Madhya Pradesh, Chhattisgarh, Maharashtra, West Bengal etc. The CPML-PWG is well entrenched in almost all districts of AP, several districts of central and south Bihar, Jharkhand, southern districts of MP, Chhattisgarh and Orissa and a few eastern districts of Maharashtra and three districts of West Bengal. The most of extremism affected districts have gone to the newly created State of Chhattisgarh. It also has a presence in a few districts of Karnataka and Tamil Nadu.

The movement did not bring any immediate results in West Bengal and was short-lived but had far reaching implications and became a force behind numerous peasant struggles in different areas of West Bengal, Bihar, Jharkhand (by tribals), Chhattisgarh (by tribals), Andhra Pradesh and Punjab. However, the Left Front Government led by CPI (M) in its three successive terms starting from 1977 salvaged the situation by recording about fourteen lakh more share-croppers known as bargadar under "Barga operation" programme. This was consolidated by proper distribution of surplus lands to the landless and by providing bank credits. For example, up to 1978, in 6 years total 74,000 people got crop-finance whereas in the year 1976 alone 59,000 got crop-fincance.

Thus, the Communist Government in West Bengal has consolidated its position, which is envied by even Central Government and other state governments. The Naxalite movement has again resurfaced in West Bangal as implementation of Land reforms measures has slowed down.

3. The West Bengal Scenario[3]

In West Bengal, the implementation of land reform under the Left rule from 1977 has stabilized the rural society, e.g. the average size of land holding was .99 in 1976-77, which has come down to

.82 hectares in 2000-01. The land held by marginal farmers has increased. In 1976-77, the land held by marginal farmers was 14.18 lakh hectares whereas in 2000-01 it has grown up to 27.59 hectares. Similarly the land held by small farmers has also grown up from 14.9 lakh hectares to 16.07 lakh hectares, whereas the lands held by semi-medium and medium farmers have been reduced to less than 50 per cent, whereas in case of large farmers the total available land is negligible, i.e. 2.19 lakhs hectares. Similarly there is an increase in cultivated land by SC & ST marginal farmers. The total land operated by SC marginal farmers in 1995-96 was 5.33 lakh hectares whereas in 2000-01 it became 6.59 lakh hectares. It was 1.85 lakh hectares for ST marginal farmers in 1995-96 whereas it increased to 2.07 lakh hectares in 2000-01, whereas in case of large ST farmers, it has become 0 from 530 hectares in 1995-96. Similarly, considerable reduction in area cultivated by semi-medium and medium farmers belonging to SC & ST farmers is observed. Cases of SC & STs show that the land reform measures have really benefited the lowest strata of the society socially and economically. Even the ownership of land in case of SC & ST marginal farmers has increased. In 1995-96, 81 per cent SCs were holding land whereas in 2000-01, 85.4 per cent SC marginal farmers were land owners. In case of ST, 77.17 per cent marginal farmers were there, whereas in 2000-01, 80.42 per cent marginal ST were the land holders. The number of large holdings from the category of semi-medium and medium consequently have been considerably reduced. In fact the ST large farmers have become nil. It shows that there is a peaceful revolution. This has also been reflected in increase of area cultivated by SCs & STs. In 1995-96, 48.67 per cent area was cultivated by the SCs whereas in 2000-01 the area cultivated was 60.11 per cent of arable land. So also in 1995-96, 47.4 per cent. ST population of marginal farmers cultivated land whereas in 2000-01, 52.33 per cent of STs marginal farmers cultivated the land. Thus, land reform measures have created the basic stability in the rural society of West Bengal. As a result the naxalite movement cannot have their permanent setting in West Bengal. However, there are definite movements in the State by the extremists for the following factors:

1. Discrimination by the Panchayat bodies in distribution of fruits of rural development schemes.

2. Neglect of the area being far-flung from the main stream of development.
3. Increase of awareness of rights among the neglected rural population specially STs.
4. Lack of education and lack of health facilities in these areas as compared to other areas.
5. Non-effective participation by the ST representatives because of their simplicity in the functioning in grassroots level decision making bodies regarding rural development schemes specially Panchayats.

4. Tenancy Distribution of Land Situation in West Bengal[4]

The West Bengal is the only state in the country, which has recorded about 15 lakh bargadar on about 11.1 lakh acres of land. There is hardly any recording of share croppers in other states. They just want to overlook the issue showing that there are actually no share croppers, which is not a fact on the ground. Haryana had 18.22 per cent land under tenancy in 1981-82 whereas West Bengal had only 12.34 per cent land under tenancy and Haryana has not recorded any share-cropper. Similarly, total land in U.P. was 10.24 per cent under tenancy as per NSS 1981-82 figures whereas the recording of share croppers is negligible. There is no problem if there is no tenancy like in Gujarat (1.9%), Kerala (2.05%). Average number of tenant in a village in West Bengal is 50, whereas in U.P. it is 14 and in Tamil Nadu it is 20. Frequency of change of plot is almost negligible in West Bengal 97.09 per cent tenants do not change plots whereas in U.P. 47 per cent tenants do not change plots. Tamil Nadu is another State which shows 95.97 per cent stability of plots by tenants. In U.P. the STs are not shown under tenancy whereas in West Bengal 20.3 per cent STs are tenants. It means from tenancy point of view also there is stability in rural West Bengal. On the other hand, unrecorded tenants were noticed in the villages of Bihar as 95.36 per cent, U.P. 87.29 per cent and Haryana 57.8 per cent.

5. Distribution of Surplus Vested Land

West Bengal is the leader in the country in respect of distribution of vested land. The State has distributed almost 22 per cent of the total surplus land distributed in the country to almost 53 per cent of the total beneficiaries in the country. The total beneficiaries of land distribution, i.e. patta holders are 29 lakh on an area of 10.23 lakh acres as per reports published by Government of India, Ministry of Rural Development. Similarly land has been distributed to about 3.16 lakh poor families for homestead purpose involving a quantum of 18,989 acres of land. Perusing above, we find that land reform provides basic stability in the State.

6. Land Reform and Productivity

It is a wrong conception that land reform is anti-productivity. In fact increase of productivity is the ultimate aim of the land reform measures. The West Bengal is an example. Due to land reform, the productivity has increased manifold and the State has now become self-sufficient in food production. The recent study by the Food and Agricultural Organization of the United Nations has found that small land holdings given by Government is creating confidence in rural masses.

"In the later phases of the land reform, the administrators began allocating the vested land in smaller parcels. Given the fact that large numbers of landless are owning even a very small parcel of land, this implementation of policy made good sense.

Most interviewees who commented on the relative effectiveness of the land redistribution stated that those who had received agricultural land had realized significant livelihood improvements as a result. There were, however, some exceptions. One farmer who had not himself received land reported that households in his village who had received land had not realized significant benefits because they lacked implements and thus were not able to put the land to good use. The same farmer claimed that some of those beneficiaries had mortgaged their land away to larger farmers. A farmer in another village who had received vested land reported that while the former owner had produced three crops per year, he was only able to produce one crop per year."[5]

Two farmers interviewed had received homestead plots. The homestead plots allocated were extremely small, typically 0.04 acres (about 1700 square feet) or less. Even such tiny plots, we observed that these interviewees and other who had received tiny household plots were growing vegetable or had planted fruit trees for household consumption (Rural Development Institutes, Washington, USA).

7. Strategy to Solve Problem of Naxalism in West Bengal

When I joined as Land Reforms Commissioner, I identified the blocks affected by naxalism in the State. After that, it was assessed how much Government surplus land was available for distribution in these blocks. Then, Block Land and Land Reforms Officers of these blocks were called in a meeting at the State headquarters along with respective Sub-Divisional and District Land and Land Reforms Officers.

During the meeting, the plan of action was drafted to distribute most of the remaining Government vested lands to the really deserving landless beneficiaries irrespective of party colour or affiliation. It was pointed out that the joint field verification of land along with the panchayat functionaries takes time. To tackle this problem, instructions were given to do field verification by Government, machinery only with amin and revenue inspector at the gram panchayat level. The list of proposed beneficiaries was also traditionally submitted by the panchayat functionaries. It was also changed as BPL lists were readily available at block and gram panchayat level. Out of those, landless persons were to be identified first. Priority was given to ST and SC landless BPL families or persons.

A time bound programme was chalked out and Director of Land Records & Surveys was asked to monitor the progress of work. Officers from Directorate of Land Records & Surveys were also deputed in three affected districts of West Medinipur, Bankura and Purulia. They were asked to visit those three districts and affected blocks and guide the field functionaries to expedite preparation of case records for final decision by the Land Sub-Committee (Bhumi "O" Ban Sthayee Samity) of the Panchayat Samity. Final gearing up was done by fixing the patta distribution camps at selected places where dignitaries or VIPs would attend the programmes of distribution of land. The first such camp in the worst affected blocks was attended by LRC himself. This energized local level machinery. This also expedited the decision making by panchayat bodies and sub-divisional officers have not been attaching so much importance to the job.

One patta distribution camp was even attended by the Chief Minister himself. Other Ministers including Minister of Land & Land

Reforms of the Government, of West Bengal attended patta distribution programmes. Senior officers attended the programmes where Ministers were not available. This generated confidence among, tribals and other man who were feeling neglected due to apathy of their panchayat representatives who were again very simple people. They could not overcome obstacles created by the middle class bureaucracy armed with feudal rules and regulations in the rural development works. It was ensured that the deserving persons get pattas. This generated confidence and support in the masses residing in far-flung areas of the State who have became supporters of Naxalism. They came in great numbers in these camps. Wherever, lands were not available, Government implemented another land distribution scheme by purchasing lands from the open market with State Government funds. Rest of the things were done by departmental funds of Public Works Department and 12th Finance Commission to construct roads in these inaccessible areas.

The correct message also reached to the local rural development administration including panchayat that they have to function without fear and favour. The Government's political will also was very clearly demonstrated by the top government functionaries and ministers attending to land reforms programmes.

8. Land Reform vis-à-vis Naxalism

There has been considerable dilution in the ideological purity of the left wing extremist movement and a noticeable criminalisation of its cadres at the grassroots level. As a result, many land-owners organizations have come into existence to militarily oppose them. And some of these violent groups have large support base including that of high castes in Bihar. Several factors have helped to sustain the LWE movement, some of which are on account of administrative lacunae. These include *inter alia* shortcomings and delays in the criminal justice system, absence of rural policing, absence of a satisfactory mechanism for instant justice in the rural areas, policy changes introduced as a result of change in government at the state level and lack of a political direction in some cases. All these factors only assist the naxalite cause and prompt the rural poor to gravitate towards the movement. A much more comprehensive and holistic approach needs to be adopted to tackle the problem of left wing extremism. Lack of land reforms, declining standards in the political/

administrative/judicial system and the perceived failure of the democratic process in some areas to provide an adequate channel for the people to meet their grievances are basic issues without tackling which the left wing extremist philosophy will find increasing acceptance in several parts of the country. Thus, implementation of social legislation including land reforms, restoration of tribal lands distribution of surplus land, minimum wages and schemes to tackle rural indebtedness need to be taken up on a priority. However, the task of providing an appropriate climate for these agencies to function will simultaneously have to be accomplished by the police.

9. Conclusion

It is found that in Bihar or Jharkhand that apart from above facts, the non-maintenance of proper land records is the main cause for frequent skirmishes between the landowners and landless persons. Similarly in Andhra Pradesh, the tenants or sharecroppers are neglected. The ceiling limits are also more generous in Andhra Pradesh which should be brought at par with other states. In part of MP and Chhattisgarh, the loopholes including recording of their names and rights of tenants should be recognized in tenancy laws. Loopholes in laws should be plugged or done away with. In Orissa, the sharecroppers should be recognized as tenants and ceiling surplus land should be distributed among the deserving beneficiaries and they should be put in possession of those lands. They should also be provided with institutional financial support to stand on their legs away from the money lenders or the land owners who will exploit them by giving loans.

Foregoing discussions show that distribution of small parcels of land is not anti-land reform. If land reform is not implemented as effective tool to counter the Naxalism, it will re-surface time and again and will continue to cause heavy violence including loss of life more than even the terrorist violence. The Left Front extremists easily guide or misguide the simple villagers and cultivators who have been suffering and have been neglected for about 62 years after independence. The feeling of discrimination in them have become more pronounced due to increasing awareness under influence of media and due to Information Technology. No longer the bureaucracy or the popular government can 'take shelter or alibi to delay the implementation of land reforms under garb of 'political will'. If 'political will' is not formed now, it will have to be formed under compulsion of violence of Naxalism but not without threatening basic framework of the democratic society. It is the time to wake up and implement the measures of land reforms in all sincerity and earnestness.

REFERENCES

1. Agrawal, Dr. P.K.: *Land Reforms in India, Constitutional and Legal Approach, (with special reference to U.P.)*, Published by M.D. Publications Pvt. Ltd., Daryaganj, New Delhi-110002, 1993, p. 582.
2. *Issues in Land Reforms*, Published by Rajiv Gandhi Institute Foundation, Jawahar Bhawan, Dr. Rajendra Prasad Road, New Delhi-110001, 2000, p. 12.
3. *Agricultural Census Report—2000-01 for State of West Bengal*, (Summary), Published by Land and Land Reforms Department & Directorate of Agriculture, Government of West Bengal, December 2005, pp. 28.
4. Iyer, Prof. K. Gopal: *Land Reforms in India*: Vol. I, Published by Land Reforms Unit, Lal Bahadur Shastri National Academy of Administration, Mussoorie, 1989-90, pp. 157.
5. Hamstad, Tim Brown Jennifer: *Land Reform Law and Implementation in West Bengal: Lessons and Recommendations*, Published by Rural Development Institute, Seattle, Washington 98105, U.S.A., December 2001, pp. 65.

11

Need to Implement Radical Land Reforms in Andhra Pradesh

State of Andhra Pradesh tops the list of Naxalite violence in the country. The figures are as follows;

	2003		2004		2005		2006	
	Incidents	*Deaths*	*Incidents*	*Deaths*	*Incidents*	*Deaths*	*Incidents*	*Deaths*
Andhra Pradesh	577	140	310	74	535	208	163	43
India	1597	515	1533	566	1608	677	1272	610

Only during, 2006-07, new States of Chhattisgarh and Jharkhand are overtaking Andhra Pradesh.[1]

Andhra Pradesh used to be one of the better organised states from land reform point of view after independence. There is good political party organization as well as good revenue set-up. Therefore, we shall examine in details as to what has gone wrong.

A Comprehensive Law on the Ceiling on Agricultural Land Holdings was enacted and brought into force in Andhra Pradesh in 1975. At that time, it was, estimated that over one million acres of distributable surplus land would be available. But it was noticed that the State Government could take over only 0.54 million acres. What was more significant was that 0.258 million acres got caught in the throes of court litigations at different stages. Every declarant who could afford it, moved the court. Often enough the verdicts favoured them. In the course of these ponderous litigations, several appeals which the Government decided to file could not be filed and where matters were carried to the Supreme Court, they found themselves in a queue of appeals and revisions which would take years to resolve.

In Andhra Pradesh "standard holdings" range is from acres 10 to 27 wet and 35 to 54 dry. No scientific study has gone into the determination of a "standard holding".

The State has enough problems to contend in regard to agricultural land ceiling schemes. If the State Government manages to bring to some conclusion the litigation pending in courts, in Andhra Pradesh alone substantial extent of land will be available for distribution.

Another bane of the land reforms legislation has been the concealment of surplus lands by the declarants. Unfortunately the Act does not provide for a "review" of the closed cases when any concealment is detected. Attempt has been made to correct this infirmity through legislative action. It is also proposed to provide for voluntary declaration by land-owners, if they had concealed any surplus land. Such declaration would save them from the punitive actions provided in the Act.

Today, the position is that most tenancies in Andhra area are based on oral contracts. Barring in a minority of cases, the land records are scarcely a guiding factor in determining as to who the tenant is. The Protected Tenancy Act was introduced in Telengana area in 1950. But for 6 years previous to it, Government ensured that the occupation of the lands by the tenants was properly recorded in the land records which eventually became the basis on which the tenants' rights and his legitimacy were established. For historical reasons, it was not so in the Andhra area.

In Andhra Pradesh, re-survey was conducted as early as in 1920 or even before this in Andhra and sporadically between 1880-1920 in Telengana area. The land holdings have undergone copious changes ever since due to regular civil action and as a result of land reforms and tenancy legislations.

The State Government having been fully conscious of the strong emotional attachment of the tribals to the landed properties, have accorded utmost importance to deal with the problem of alienation of tribal lands in the Scheduled Areas. Special Regulations were made in exercise of the special legislative powers conferred under Fifth Schedule to the Constitution of India. The Regulations provide for the prevention of alienation of tribals land and on the other hand, they provide restoration of the illegally alienated lands.

The A.P. Scheduled Areas Land Transfer Regulation, 1959 which was amended in 1970, 1971 and 1978 is in force in the Scheduled Areas of the State. These Regulations were preceded by the local laws of the Madras province and Ex. Hyderabad State.

The Regulations prohibit several forms of transfer of land such as sale, lease, gift, mortagage, exchange etc., in favour of non-tribals. Whenever a transfer of land is made in the scheduled areas, it should be only in favour of a tribal or registered Cooperative Society consisting of only tribals. To support this measure, the Regulations also prohibit registration of transfer deeds unless the transfer is in favour of only a tribal or an exclusive tribal society.

A special machinery has been created to implement the Regulations effectively and to evict the non-tribals in illegal occupation of tribal lands and also to restore such lands to tribals. The regulations also seek to punish such non-tribals who acquire lands in contravention of the Regulations or who continue to remain in occupation of the lands even after they are evicted by the authorities with rigorous imprisonment for a period upto one year. The Regulations of this State are unique in the country inasmuch as they prohibit transfer of not only tribal lands to non-tribals by also those of non-tribals unless they are transferred to tribals or their exclusive Cooperative Societies. This measure ensures prevention of the alienation of lands which the non-tribals iilegally acquired from tribals in violation of the legal provisions. The Regulations do not affect the legitimate family partitions. Similarly, inheritance by succession is also not affected on account of Regulations.

Recognising the position that the indebtedness of tribals is one of the important reasons contributing to the problem of land alienation, the Government has brought out Debt Relief Regulations and Money Lending Regulations for redeeming the tribals from the indebtedness and to control and regulate Private Money Lending.

Besides, the State Government has also recognised the need for the survey and updating of land records in the Scheduled Areas effectively combating the problem of tribal land alienation. Three special survey divisions with full complement of the staff have been established for undertaking this task in parts of the Scheduled Areas where the problem is more acute.

In Andhra Pradesh, there are different provisions of land reform provisions applicable to different regions. In Andhra area, the old Act of 1950 was repealed and a new Act, A.P. (Andhra Area) Tenancy Act, 1956 was enacted. Similarly, tenancy reform in Telengana is guided by the Tenancy and Agricultural Lands (Validation) Act, 1961. The Telengana Act recognizes temporary leasing for six years which can be again renewed for the same period. A family holding in Telengana area varies between 4 to 60 acres.

The Andhra Pradesh Land Reforms Ceiling on Agricultural Holdings Act, 1973 prescribes ceiling limit. The ceiling area of the family unit was fixed as equivalent to one standard holding with a maximum of 2 standard holding for a family unit in excess of 5. In 1977 the Act was amended which allowed one additional standard holding for each major son. Nearly 4.45 lakh declarations were filed in the State but only 13.53 per cent declarations were decided as surplus and remaining 86.4 per cent were decided as non-surplus. The area declared as surplus is 5.25 lakh acres of which 93.76 per cent was dry land and only 6.24 per cent was wet land. Out of above, 3.8 lakh acres of land was assigned for agricultural purpose and 0.02 lakh acres were allotted for house sites. Thus, there was ineffectiveness of land ceiling programme in the State. Sometimes, provisions relating to 'personal cultivation' have been misused by the landlords to deprive of the poor lessees or tenants-in-possession.

It is learnt that the State is trying to have a relook to rejuvenate land reforms set-up under the pro-active leadership of the Chief Minister. At least, pending cases could be decided and possession to assignees of vested land would be given and updated land records will be handed over to each person.

Until 1966-67 rising in Srikakulam in Andhra Pradesh, the general belief was that rural India has always been mass of the sleeping villagers acquiescing in every form of injustice.

The Telengana Movement was aimed at restructuring agrarian social relations through direct action against the Government. The Government was thus, obliged to embark upon a radical land reform policy to wean the peasants away from militancy. The Telengana region has a high proportion of tenancy due to the prevalence of pervasive absentee landlordism.

The first round of land ceiling in AP in 1961 was abysmal failure. Only about 7400 acre land became available and very little land could actually be distributed to the poor against the estimated target of 30 lakh areas of land.

The second round of land ceilings legislation in 1973 was somewhat better. Against the estimated surplus of 20 lakh acres by 1992, about 8 lakh acres is were distributed, although much of this was dry land of inferior quality.

Problems

In Andhra Pradesh, the informal tenancy persists even in Telengana area where leasing is not permitted. The landless tenants are in a bad shape. The land taken on lease, by them keeps them at below subsistence level. The landowners frequently change their plots. They are mostly sharecroppers. They meet the entire cost of cultivation and receive less than 50 per cent share of produce.

The following anomalies still persist:

(i) The administrative machinery to identify and detect informal tenancy hardly exists,
(ii) The provision of conferring the status of occupancy tenants to sharecropper/tenants-at-will is under neglect,
(iii) The right of continuous resumption without any time limit, provision of surrender, and loose definition of 'Personal Cultivation' continue to be the loopholes in the tenancy provisions of the State,
(iv) Lack of acquisition of optimum quantum of surplus land (3,64,168 out of 1,38,46,740 hectares),
(v) Distribution of poor quality of land partly Government based land. The average allotment—1.4 to 1.7 acres, mostly dry land is insufficient to establish a self-sufficient holding, not to speak of any regular marketable surplus,
(vi) The domination of big farmers like politicians and merchants,
(vii) Exemption of cash plantation from ceiling laws.

Solutions

(i) The ceiling laws are very generous and they should be brought at par with other States as per the guidelines laid down by the Government of India,

(ii) Restriction of right of transfer of land in Telengana by the tenants for institutional credit is depriving of the cultivators of land,
(iii) Training of Revenue Officers,
(iv) Formation of new land tribunals,
(v) Functioning of Taluka level review committee relating to land reforms,
(vi) Updation of land records in the State,
(vii) Disposal of returns/cases relating to ceiling surplus land should be done on the basis of operation made,
(viii) Ensuring institutional credit to the assignees of government vested land,
(ix) The greatest drawback of the Act is that it does not envisage suo-motu taking up of cases. The special officer can at best play the role of an adjudicator when moved and cannot take up cases himself for protection of even registered tenants,
(x) The definition of 'Personal Cultivation' is vague,
(xi) The Tenancy Act should recognize oral agreements,
(xii) The burden of proof should rest on the landowner not only in the context of fixation of Fair Rent but also in respect of all other matters like 'Personal Cultivation',
(xiii) Tenancy reform can be implemented only through Revenue Department and all disputes relating to such matters should be adjudicated by competent revenue official. The jurisdiction of the judicial official should be restricted,
(xiv) The right of resumption seriously affects security of tenure. It should be abolished,
(xv) The rent is still on the high side. It should be fixed at 1/5 of gross produce.

The glaring ineffectiveness of land ceiling measures is borne out from the fact that only 13.53 per cent declarations were decided as surplus and remaining 86.47 per cent were decided as non-surplus. The area declared as surplus is 5.25 lakh acres of which 93.76 per cent was dry land and only 6.24 per cent was wet land. In several cases, assignment has been done on papers. Physical possession has not been handed over to the assignees. Further, the assigned lands have not been demarcated on ground levels in many cases. In spite of irrigation potentialities created over course of time, the land records continue to show it as dry land.

"The ineffectiveness of land ceiling programme in the State tends to be further corroborated from the following facts. The empirical study in the villages show that 30 per cent of the area allotted was completely uncultivable and 67 per cent of the allotted land was unirrigated. The average extent of land allotted was not economically viable. This suggests that land ceiling programme in Andhra Pradesh was a failure. Besides this, of the total extent of land distributed in the surveyed villages only 6.91 per cent was allotted to Scheduled Castes and 32.79 per cent was allotted to Scheduled Tribes. The State ceiling rules prescribed that at least half of the declared surplus should be allotted to Scheduled Castes and Scheduled Tribes. In surveyed villages, the allotment of land to these two categories falls short by at least 10.40 per cent of the prescribed requirement. The distribution of land is further tilted against Scheduled Tribes in particular. The uncultivable land, in one of the villages, to the extent of 54.55 hec. was allotted to 30 Scheduled Tribes which amounted to 1.82 hec. per Scheduled Tribe beneficiary."[2]

The cumulative progress of implementation of land ceilings laws for the quarter ending December 2007 is as follows:[3]

(*Area in Acres*)

Returns			*Area Declared Surplus*	*Area Taken Possession*	*Area Distributed to individual beneficiaries*	*Total No. of Beneficiaries*	*SC/ST Beneficiaries*			
Filed	*Disposed*	*Pending*					*No.*	*Area*	*No.*	*Area*
1	2	3	4	5	6	7	8	9	10	11
447103	417279	29824	837840	652282	593944	532078	205126	229656	85758	120277

Other Beneficiaries		*Area Declared Surplus But Not Distributed*	*Total No. of Cases And Area Involved In Litigation*		*Revenue Courts*		*High Courts*		*Supreme Courts*	
No.	*Area*		*Area Involved*	*No. of cases*	*Area*	*No.*	*Area*	*No.*	*Area*	*No.*
12	13	14	15	16	17	18	19	20	21	22
195019	243933	243896	131570	2193	86694	1111	35933	874	8943	208

Area Not Available for Distribution			*Total Area Not Available For Distribution*	*Net Area Available For Distribution*
Reserved/Transferred for Public Purpose	*Unfit for Cultivation*	*Misc. Reasons*		
23	24	25	26	27
16717	13673	14859	176819	67077

In Andhra 43.93 lakh areas of waste land and 1.10 lakh acres of Bhoodan land out of total 2.52 lakh acres of Bhoodan land have been distributed. There is lot of scope of distribution of 1.42 lakh and Bhoodan land,[4] lot of waste land and 67,077 acres of land available under the ceiling laws.[5] There is lot of scope of further vesting of surplus land to Government, because 29,824 returns are still pending for disposal. As per an estimate and as per statement in the Assembly during the A.P. Land Reforms (Ceiling on Agricultural Holdings) Act, 1973, about 20 lakhs acres of land would be surplus whereas at present only 8,37,840 acres of land could be declared surplus indicating an achievement of 40 per cent. Out of the precious surplus land, 2,43,896 acres land has yet to be distributed. This has 1,31,570 acres of land which is involved in litigation. Revenue Courts alone account for pendency of 86,694 acres of land. The Government of Andhra Pradesh or Department of Revenue rather than blaming the High Courts or Supreme Court, should have introspection and gear up its quasi-Judicial machinery of revenue courts and fix up their responsibility for non-disposal of cases or delay in disposal of cases. However, most of the land determined as surplus is dry, which under the given climatic condition implies low and insecure yields. Thus, the average land allotted to each beneficiary is too small to offer full employment or livelihood for a family four or five persons. Most of the distributed land is in need of irrigation, levelling and other developmental activities. The Central Government has planned to assist these new small land holders either by special schemes or by integration into existing schemes. George and Rao (1979) have made a pilot study in two villages in Nalgonda district. According to them, the new cultivators, who are beneficiaries of the reform, have invested in their land and developed it, though the quality is poor. They have met all costs earned a surplus and built up their assets. Thus, the new land reform beneficiaries are solid base for increase in production because they cultivate their holdings with a higher intensity of labour per hectare. However, there is altogether different story regarding allocation of the government wasteland. Field investigations in Andhra Pradesh for example, indicate that perhaps as much as 30 per cent of the reported beneficiaries do not have both legal and physical possession of the allocated land. The gaps between the reported numbers and secure land rights occur for a variety of reasons, including:

(i) assignment of land is on paper only, and the beneficiaries are not in physical possession;
(ii) more powerful have evicted the beneficiaries from their land; and
(iii) in numerous cases, especially Telengana where large compact blocks have been assigned to the poor, the beneficiaries have not received their individual parcels of land because the survey subdivision work is incomplete.[6]

Andhra Pradesh's recent efforts to address the 'gap' in allocation of government, land provide a model for other states to consider. Andhra Pradesh's IKP project identifies often with the help of the community-based organisations-specific local opportunities or developmental schemes or assistance for enhancing the poor's rights to government land. The joint efforts of the revenue department, IKP and numerous State officials and local communities or panchayat bodies have put secure-rights to at least lakh of acres of government land into the hands of the rural people. Government of Andhra Pradesh recognised the good work done by the CPI (Maoist) in October 2004 when they agreed to a cease fire and promised to consider in the meantime the Naxalities' main demand for distribution of land among the landless. The State government also agreed to consider the landless or poor cultivations for allotment of government surplus land who were put in forcible possession by the Naxalites. There should be no anti-attitude to it. Even in West Bengal, the first priority in land allotment goes to the person in possession provided he is otherwise eligible. This is just to keep peace in rural India because ownership is 9/10th of possession. In West Bengal, the CPI (M) and other parties identify the excess land of the ex-jamindars, jotdars or the land-owners through their own technical wing and then put its landless people or marginal farmers into the possession of surplus land lying either uncultivated, or in benami names or is in excess of ceiling limit. Then, the priority lists are made at the block level or panchayat samity in consultation with the local pradhan and then get resolution passed to distribute these surplus land among the eligible beneficiaries. If Naxalites adopt the same technique or procedure, what hell can fall upon the government machinery? They are just assisting the government machinery to make preliminary lists of the eligible beneficiaries. One should not oppose a sound proposal/offer, if it has come from the Naxalite camps[6] 'Opposition for opposition' sake ultimately pays nothing.

Tenancy Reform

Total number of tenants recorded in Andhra Pradesh as in September 2006 are 1.07 lakh on an area of 5.95 lakh acres. The latest research studies[7] indicate that the informal/concealed tenancy in the coastal Andhra ranges from 15 per cent of the 30 per cent of the total owned area.

Thus, oral tenancy requires to be recognized in AP and the period of lease in case of sharecroppers should be extended at least during his lifetime and no longer.

Tribal Land

Andhra Pradesh has a very long record of legislation for the protection of Tribal Land. There are large tracts of tribal lands which are still under the occupation of the non-tribals. For example, as in March 2004 the status on alienation and restoration of Tribal Lands in Andhra Pradesh is as follows:

1. No. of cases filed in the Court 65875
2. Area 287776 (acres)
3. Cases disposed of by the court 58212
4. Area 256452 (acres)
5. Cases rejected 31737
6. Area involved 150227 (acres)
7. Cases decided in favour of tribals 26475
8. Area 106225 (acres)
9. Cases in which land was restored to tribals 23383
10. Area 94312 (acres)

(*Source*: Annual Report, 2004-05, Ministry of Rural Development, Government of India, p. 213).

"Thus, only one-third of the total area alienated has been restored to them. Besides, they are subjected to displacement from thousands of acres due to various development projects and evictions by forest department on the plea of encroachment of forestland. The Samta Judgement and the Panchayat Extension Act of 1996 are silver linings in this respect which should be utilized by the peasant organizations in protecting the land rights of the tribals."[8]

Updation of Land Records—A New Approach

Andhra Pradesh is spearheading campaign to update land records along with Karnataka and West Bengal. The Government of Andhra Pradesh have taken up a novel project called Bhu Bharati with an object to establish a comprehensive system of land administration based on secured titles and title registration, leveraging the available technology. This project also aims at legal reforms, process re-engineering and administrative restructuring. Andhra Pradesh has drafted a Bill entitled the Andhra Pradesh Land Titling Act, 2008.

The statement of Objects and Reasons of the above Act reads as follows:

"In India, records relating to immovable property transactions are dealt with in the form of documents and such documents are got registered under Registration Act, 1908. In the document registration system, title verification is not done. With India's rapid movement into the technological age, there is every need to ensure maximum utilization of land as a resource, by introducing title registration system, which gives scope for growth in land market with reduced litigation in courts.

In order to improve the system of land administration, and to ensure, security of titles to the property holders, the State of Andhra Pradesh seeks to enact a novel legislation for putting in place a mechanism for a Land Information System and an Authority to manage the same, with the following broad objectives:

- To provide for creation and maintenance of record of all immovable properties in the State of Andhra Pradesh, so as to serve as conclusive record of titles.

- To provide for title registration system.
- To provide for a mechanism for ensuring that land records data in the State of Andhra Pradesh is captured and maintained in digital form and in an integrated manner.
- To ensure that the information pertaining to the records maintained by the Andhra Pradesh Land Authority is protected from any unauthorized access and provide for the establishment of the efficient security system for such purpose.
- To provide for a special adjudicatory authority for the efficient and speedy resolution of disputes arising out of the operation of this legislation."[9]

This is a good initiative undertaken by the Directorate of Survey, Settlements and Land Records under the consistent and long leadership by Shri Vinod Agrawal, IAS, Commissioner. This is possible in Andhra Pradesh because there is already an infrastructure of Common Service Centre (CSC) existing throughout the State where all services converge and are available to citizens. Andhra Pradesh is the first State perhaps in the country which could integrate registration with change of land records through process of mutation and conversion. In other states, it will take long time due to interdepartmental quibbling as registration and maintenance of land records are with two different departments. As soon as, it is done, better it is. The Central Government has given such a guideline. But states do take their own time to implement even the best of policies enunciated by the Central Government.

The suggestions to improve upon the maintenance of proposed land records and titling system are as follows:

1. Registration should be linked with the incorporation of the same in the record of rights. Record of rights may be prepared according to the possession or rather verification of each and every plot of the concerned 'mouza' supported by a deed of transfer or inheritance or partition or exchange etc.
2. Together with the titling in the record of rights, there should be a noting in the possession column of the record of rights in order to the alteration in the mode of cultivation, for example, by a bargadar/share-cropper.

3. The Land Titling Appellate Tribunal should be above Land Authority and this Tribunal may consist of a chairman who will be a sitting or retired judge of High Court and other judicial members along with senior administrative members very much conversant with the various land laws of the State. The persons aggrieved of the judgement of such Tribunal, may prefer an appeal to the Division Bench of High Court formed for the purpose.
4. There should be a family ceiling for determination of ceiling area in case of every raiyat. Persons aggrieved by the decision should go to the newly proposed Land Titling Appellate Tribunal.
5. The excess land so determined may be distributed to the landless/homeless people in the area concerned. The Panchayat functionaries along with the Revenue Officials who are conversant with the geographical position and socio-economic condition of the concerned Mouza/Village should be delivered the power to determine as to who would be selected to be issued patta in his/her favour. Joint pattas may be issued in the names of husband and wife.
6. Special provisions should be made for incorporation of the names of the bargadars and pattadars as suggested above.
7. A corporation in order to advance funds to a recorded bargadar or a landless person may be formed for the benefit of the landless people and bargadars belonging to the low rung of the society. If any, such person intends to sell out land such corporation may provide finance to such person for purchase of such land according to the assessed marked value of the land to be sold for the purpose. In this case Section 2lC of the West Bengal Land Reforms Act, 1955 may be consulted.
8. The Government of Andhra Pradesh may like to place the fact of digitized maps in the Act and digitized map along with the records-of-right will be given to the individual raiyats as record-of-rights which will have proper boundaries of the plot with the adjoining plots. Thus this type of record of right will be the best record of right in the country. It should be mandatory that after 10 years, there should be compulsory updation of records of rights by the State.

9. The Bargadars and Pattadars may be given financial support annually in the form of credit or subsidy by the bank and by the State Government for cultivation of crop. This may find place in the proposed Act.
10. In case the Government does not find suitable government surplus land for allotment to the landless persons, the Government may purchase the land from the willing persons on the market value and may allot the land to the landless person up to 15 decimal of land so that this small piece of land may support him for his livelihood and will save him from starvation. This may be done on the pattern of similar scheme in West Bengal.

Conclusion

1. Remaining *banjar* land in tribal areas should be surveyed on time bound fashion and should be distributed among the tribals.
2. Land ceiling exemptions for temple lands, charitable trusts, plantations should be withdrawan unless they agree to come directly under the Government.
3. "Absentee landlordism" specially in coastal Andhra and Telengana Region should be discouraged and definition of personal cultivation should be incorporated in the A.P. Act on the pattern of definition of 'personal cultivation' in Section 2(8) of the W.B. Land Reforms Act, 1956, which reads as follows: "Personal Cultivation" means cultivation by a person of his own land on his own account—
   (a) by his own labour, or
   (b) by the labour of any member of his family, or
   (c) by servants or labourers on wages payable in cash or kind not being as a share of the produce or both; provided that such person or member of his family resides for the greater part of the year in the locality where the land is situated and the principal source of his income is produce of such land.
4. Encroachments from government lands should be removed and surplus lands should be distributed among the landless or poor cultivators.

5. Priority should be given in distribution of government vested land to those eligible persons who are already in possession of land and are cultivating the same.
6. Exemption for 'brackish water poramboke' and 'acqua farms' should be withdrawn and retrieved land should be distributed to among agricultural labourers and fishermen unless they make cooperative society of these workers and earmark their land as owner in that society.
7. The tribal lands illegally transferred should be restored to the tribals.
8. Informal sharecropping or tenancy should be recorded only upto the life time of the sharecropper unlike in West Bengal which is heritable. Thus, 15 per cent to 30 per cent of total owned lands can be recorded under tenancy without ownership only for right of cultivation by the tenant. If some of these suggestions are implemented in true spirit in a time bound fashion, Andhra Pradesh will come out of morass of Naxalism soon.

REFERENCES

1. Government of India, Ministry of Home Affairs : *Annual Report 2007-08*, North Block Secretariat, New Delhi.
2. Iyer, Prof. K. Gopal: *Report on Empirical Study on Land Reforms in India*, p. 97, published by LBS National Academy of Administration, Mussoorie.
3. Government of India, Department of Land Reforms : *Quarterly Progress Report* (Cumulative) on implementation of Land Ceiling Laws for the Quarter ending December, 2009.
4. Government of India, Ministry of Rural Development : *Annual Report 2006-07*, p. 256.
5. *Ibid.* 3.
6. Bergmann, Theodor: *Agrarian Reform*, p.126, published by Agricole Publishing Academy, New Delhi-24, 1984.
7. *Ibid.* 4: p. 258.
8. Iyer, K. Gopal: Paper on "Land Reforms and State Repression" presented in the Hyderabad Convention entitled 'Status of Land Reforms in A.P. and the Need to Implement Radical Land Reforms'.
9. Tim Hamstad, T. Haque, Robin Nelson: Improving Land Access for India's Rural Poor, p. 54 *EPW*, March 8, 2008.

12

Great Strides of Land Reforms in Tamil Nadu

Tamil Nadu has 6.24 crore population as per 2001 census. Out of above population, Scheduled Castes are 1.19 crore (19%), whereas Scheduled Tribes are negligible 6.51 lakh. It has 1,30,058 sq. km. area which is $1^1/_2$ times of West Bengal area of 88,752 sq. km and less than half of Bihar. Thus, South Indian States, are well positioned as far as area is concerned. The total cultivated area in Tamil Nadu was 5.88 million hectares in 2004-05. The principal crops include paddy, millets and pulses. This is a low rainfall State. Therefore less area is irrigated and waste land is more. The State is well administered and has a good track record. The governments of different political parties come and go. The people have craze for movie stars, yet they have basic goodness of hard work, loyalty and sincerity. As a result, peace generally prevails and there are chances of success of any programme run by government including implementation of land reforms if undertaken sincerely by the government.

In Tamil Nadu, with a view to introducing major agrarian reforms, various Acts abolishing intermediaries between the Government and the ryots like Zamindars, Inamdars, etc. have been passed as early as in 1948. There are at present no tenure intermediaries in Tamil Nadu except a few cases which are still pending before the courts.

A number of tenancy laws have been passed providing protection of tenants from eviction, fixing fair rent payable by them and providing for registration of names of persons cultivating lands belonging to land owners and Public Trusts in the State. At present no land can be resumed by the land owners other than those belonging to armed forces except on the orders of the Court for non-payment of rent.

There were about 4,94,000 registered tenants cultivating lands belonging to individuals and Public Trusts on an extent of about 6,84,500 acres. There may be some unregistered tenants also. The question of conferring ownership rights on these tenants was examined by the government.

The State Land Ceiling Law came into force in 1962. At present, the ceiling area for a family of five members is 15 standard acres.

Out of the 1.75 lakh acres of surplus lands acquired by the State Government, about 1.37 lakh acres had been distributed to the landless agricultural labourers. Most of them belong to Scheduled Castes and Scheduled Tribes. State Government distributed pattas for lands for nearly 5,000 landless agricultural labourers of whom more than 3,600 belonged to Scheduled Castes. At present, the allottees were eligible to get Rs. 2,500 per hectare for the reclamation of the land.

Implementation of land reforms has been delayed due to protracted litigation and issue of stay orders, it was felt that the establishment of a special tribunal will speed up the matters. The State Government has took steps for the setting up of a Land Tribunal. The necessary statutory formalities have been completed and the Tribunal itself is constituted. Appeals pending before the High Court are transferred to this Tribunal for quicker disposal. The Tribunal consists of Judical and Administrative members.

Tamil Nadu is the first State to pass a legislation as early as 1971 to protect the rural landless poor who are in occupation of the dwelling units constructed in private lands. 1.81 lakh rural agricultural labourers and rural artisans were given ownership rights for their homesteads. A recent improvement of the above Act provides for the extension of the eligibility to those in occupation as on 1st April, 1990. It may be added here that the Government is also issuing house site pattas to the poor at the rate of about 3 lakh sites per year.

Tamil Nadu has got a very large number of small farmers and marginal farmers and many landless agricultural labourers are being assigned small extents of land under various schemes.

The Government is also taking the co-operation of the social workers in the rural areas for proper implementation of the land reform laws. Finally, this Government has also initiated steps to reorient the attitudes of the revenue and police officials in the matter of protection of the rights of a rural poor *vis-à-vis* the land rich.

The population of Scheduled Tribes in this State is small and scattered. As per 1981 census, the population of Scheduled Tribes was 5.20 lakh which constitutes 1.07 per cent in the total population of this State. Although the population of Tribals is very small, the problems they are experiencing are exactly the same as the problems in other parts of India. The problems are, total social, economic and educational backwardness on the one hand and exploitation by money lenders both by way of usurious rates of interests and through illegal land alienation on the other. At present there is provision in the Revenue Standing Orders to prevent alienation of Government lands assigned to Scheduled Tribes.

Latest Position of Land Ceiling

The latest available status of vesting and distribution of ceiling surplus land is as following as in December 2007 (GOI Report)[1]

1.	Area declared Surplus	2,68,006 acres
2.	Area distributed	1,89,428 acres
3.	Total No. of Beneficiaries	1,49,952
4.	S.C. Beneficiaries	66,290
5.	S.T. Beneficiaries	12,047
6.	Other Beneficiaries	83,426
7.	Distribution of Waste Land	2,89,000 acres[2]
8.	Land distributed as in November, 1992	21,000 acres[3]

Thus, there is gradual improvement in vesting of ceiling surplus land and its distribution thereafter. However, much more is still required to be done and big landowners still dominate rural scene.

The Tamil Nadu Land Reforms (Fixation of Ceiling on Land) Act, 1961 is the principal Act governing land ceiling in Tamil Nadu. This Act reduced the ceiling on agricultural land of 15 standard acres as amended in 1970 from 30 standard acres in the case of every family consisting of not more than five member under Section 5(1) (a) of the Act.

Standard acre is equivalent to 2 to 4 acres of dry land.

An additional 5 standard acre for every member of the family is provided.

For institution, following exemptions are provided:

Recognised college 40 acres, High School or any other school 20 acres, Student's Hostel 25 standard acres, Polytechnic institution 25 acres, Agricultural school 25 acres, Orphanage 25 acres.

However, under Section 5(1) (d), the public trust of a charitable nature in existence on 1st March, 1972 will be provided 5 acres apart from above institutions. The institution is treated as owner of the land. Then it may claim full exemption.

Further 1970 Act, reduced the number of exemptions and considerably tightened the loopholes, which very few state governments do after enforcing initial enactment.

However, in the new Act, the provision of appeal to the Land Tribunal was provided at five stages. That was sufficient for the landlords and courts to defeat the spirit of the Act to a large extent.

Delays in assignment of land after declaration of surplus, have been inordinate. This has also caused additioned litigation.

A peculiar problem, again in Than javur district, is the existence of vast tracts of temple land almost 56,455 hectares which is outside the scope of ceiling.

The exemption upto 10 acres as *stridhan* is also anti-land reform measure. The land is for the tiller and not to rehabilatee people so that overall production of foodgrains may increase for pattadars ensuring food security in the society.

Land allotted to Scheduled Castes, were less than to other castes and it was of inferior quality. Therefore, lot of land is lying waste, wherever land assigned to others was of good quality, beneficiaries got lot of support. Institutional support through loans and subsidy and government support to reclaim waste land can do wonders, in putting the land reform beneficiaries or pattadars.

Suggestions

Section 73 of the Act 1961, provided more exemptions, than required. Now the public trust can be exempted under Section 37(B), on condition specified specially for the purpose of establishing any educational institution or hospital.

Thus, change is quite an improvement over earlier provision of exemption where "Public Trust" or even private trusts were exempted from the ceiling without any question.

Other Suggestions are as follows

(a) It is nice that Land Tribunals are now presided over by revenue officers and not by judicial officers who go only by dry provisions of law and cannot appreciate ground condition of poor man in the village.

(b) A watch dog mechanism must be created possibly within the judiciary itself, to prevent transgression by Civil Courts into areas where their jurisdiction has been specifically barred.

(c) All transfers made in anticipation of the imposition of ceiling law should be reviewed carefully and those found to be *mala fide* should be invalidated.

(d) The number of exemptions from ceiling should be reduced. The 'Stridhan' exemption and for additional member of family beyond 5 (five) should be reduced from 10 and 5 to 3 acres. Other loopholes should be plugged.

(e) A major drive should be undertaken to unearth benami landlords.

(f) The schemes to create awareness among marginal farmers and to provide financial support to the pattadars should be geared up.

Status of Tenancy

In Tamil Nadu upto September 2007, 4,98,000 lakh sharecroppers or tenants have been recorded on 6,95,000 lakh acres of land. As per a survey by I.A.S. probationers of the L.B.S. National Academy of Administration, 70.5 per cent tenants have been recorded. As per NSS Survey, 26th & 37th Round, percentage of operated area leased in 1971-72 was 13.07 per cent whereas it came down to 10.24 in 1981-82. In Tamil Nadu, the pure tenants may be around 51.68 per cent and owner-cum-tenant are 48.32 per cent as per report of IAS probationers.[4] The maximum percentage of recorded tanants was in the district of Tenjore (32.17%), Tiruneveli (15.84%), Tiruchirapalli (13.92%), Madurai (8.47%) and North Arcot (7.20%). The recorded tenants were more in the wet pockets and less in dry pockets. Another striking feature was that registered tenants were both on temple and landlords lands.[5]

This was possible because of militant struggles on issues of tenancy reforms in the state during the 1950s and the 1960s. It resulted in the enactment of legislation or Tenancy Reforms including the record of Tenancy Rights Act, 1969.

Another epoch making legislation was the Madras Public Trusts Act, 1961. The Madras Public Trusts (Regulation of Administration of Agricultural Lands) Act, 1961 provides *inter alia* for regulating the administration, either by personal cultivation or by lease (upto 5 standard acres), of agricultural land held by public trusts and for regulating the relation of public trusts and the cultivating tenants.

The Public Trust include any temple, math, mosque, church or other place of public religious worship.

This is a very wide definition apart from the trust dedicated for charitable purpose or educational institutions.

It is provided under Section 5 that no tenant shall personally cultivate land in excess of twenty standard acres.

No public trust can evict a cultivating tenants except under Sections 7, 15 and 19 of the Act. Section 7 provides ground of eviction if the cultivating tenant has total land under cultivation above ceiling limits, Secondly, if the cultivating tenant does not pay rent within a month after such rent becomes due or does not cultivate the land personally.

The rent is payable in kind or on market value on the date of deposit.

The fair rent payable by the tenant under Section 24 of the Act is defined as 40 per cent or 35 per cent of the normal gross produce in the case of wet land. In any other class of land, $37\frac{1}{3}$ per cent of the normal gross produce or its value in money is payable. Where contract provides for payment of lower fair rent, the contract rent shall be payable.

The Acts on Tenancy or sharecroppers are crystal clear and unambiguous unlike in any other state. Any land man can understand the whole gamut of tenancy as sharecropping by going through the status on tenancy. The definition in section 2(b) of the Madras Public Trust Act, 1961 lays down:

> "Cultivating tenant" means a person who contributes his own physical labour or that of the member of his family in the cultivation of any land belonging to another, under a tenancy agreement express or implied, and includes any such person, who continues in possession of the land after the determination of the tenancy agreement on the heirs of such person but shall not include a mere intermediary or his heirs."

Following further steps can be taken in the field of tenancy or sharecropping in Tamil Nadu:

(1) A special drive should be undertaken on the pattern of "Operation Barga" to unearth concealed tenancy and confer on them the status of "Occupancy Tenancy" for lifetime or less as determined by the State Legislatures.

(2) The "Fair Rent" payable by the tenant should be limited to 1/4 of the gross produce which may be payable in cash or in kind.

(3) Any person who is continuously working with the same landowner as a sharecropper/tenant/tenant at will for a period of three years, he should be conferred the status of "Occupancy Tenant" as per tradition in Tamil Nadu.

(4) The "Occupancy Tenant" may be conferred ownership right on the lands of religious institutions, charitable institutions or trust if he has been working for more than 20 years and the institutions or trust is paid compensation by the government on behalf of the tenant.

(5) *Suo motu* action on periodical basis need to be taken than by the land revenue or survey and settlement set-up to record the cultivating tenants a part of their updation of records of rights which is their solemn duty.

(6) The panchayat bodies (PRIs), recognised peasant organisations, tenant organisation/agricultural labour organisations, should be allowed to represent tenants or sharecroppers for enforcement of their rights, e.g. protection from illegal eviction, confirming occupancy ownership rights etc.

Thus in spite of numerous problems and litigation, tenancy played an important role by helping aspiring entrepreneurial farmers to move right from the ranks of the agricultural labourers to owner cultivators. It provides a smooth and gradual transfer of the ownership rights of vast tracts of lands once held by the absentee owner to the actual cultivators through legal means of sales and gifts, with an undisturbed process of production taken care of by the intermittent period of tenancy. It could, thus avoid the unwanted methods of land transfers through forced sales, illegal occupations, land grabbings etc.

Tamil Nadu is a vibrant State as far as protection of interest of the poor cultivators is concerned. It is hoped that they will continue to take the rural folk with the government machinery by implementing religious and social reforms among them which can keep them away from drinking and indebtedness. This is one noble measure by State of Tamil Nadu which needs to be emulated by other states in India.

On the other hand, the government will ensure institutional financing to the assignees of government vested lands and the sharecroppers. Even government will launch a scheme to purchase lands to settle with the poorest of the poor landless persons upto 16 decimal of land.

The future of Land Reform in Tamil Nadu looks bright among dark clouds prevailing in many other states in the country.

REFERENCES

1. Government of India, Department of Land Reforms: *Quarterly Progress Report* (cumulative) on Implementation of Ceiling Laws for the Quarter ending December, 2007.
2. Government of India, Ministry of Rural Development: *Annual Report 2006-07*, p. 257.
3. *Ibid.*, p. 256.
4. L.B.S. Academy of Administration, Mussoorie, Government of India: *Land Reforms in India – an Empirical Study, 1989-90*, Vol. I, p. 10.
5. *Ibid.*, p. 15.

13

Changes in Forests Management as Part of Land Reform Measures in Madhya Pradesh

Madhya Pradesh had about 6 crore population as per 2001 census. The Scheduled Tribe population is 1.22 crore which is 20.3 per cent of the state's population and Scheduled Caste population is 15.17 per cent. Madhya Pradesh is rich in forests. Tribals and forests are inseparable. Most of the tribals are habitated in forest area or in the fringes of the forests. There are 14 forest rich districts which are inhabited by almost 80 per cent of the tribal population. Madhya Pradesh has 20 per cent of the total forest cover in the country.

The districts which are mostly affected by the Naxalites activities are also forest rich district like Balaghat, Mandla. Mandla district has famous Kanha National Park. Similarly, some portion of Jabalpur district covering forest rich area is also affected by the Naxal activities. The villages covered by naxalites are located in dense forest areas where the communication and transportation facilities are very poor. The Gond and Baiga people of these villages used to go for bamboo cutting and other work to Chand district of Maharashtra and Bastar district of now Chhattisgarh where they came in touch with the Naxalites who were active there. Secondly, the economy of the tribal areas cannot be thought of without forests. Therefore, in Madhya Pradesh having left over influence of Naxalism, we shall examine the Naxalism *vis-à-vis* forest management and how can forest management be made supportive to the tribal economy which will also be consistent with the preservation and maintenance of forests.

The Social Forestry failed in Madhya Pradesh so also farm forestry. However, Joint Forest Management (JFM) was to some extent successful with its 'care and share philosophy'. Fulfilment of livelihood needs of the poor and the tribals are the preconditions for the sustainability of natural resources. Therefore, the tribals will like and encourage 'trees of poor' which are essentially employment generating trees, as they require labour for gathering and collection, as opposed to trees which are clear-felled and either fill up government coffers or the bellies of the rich or forest mafia. The tribals worship such trees which help to sustain their livelihood needs. Therefore, in Madhya Pradesh land reform will have another component of forest. This will more or less be also applicable in other Naxalitie areas which are forest and tribal dominated. This is borne by the fact that over 60 per cent of the country's forest cover is found in 187 tribal districts of India where less than 8 per cent of national population lives.[1]

Rather than going into theoretical aspect of tribal *vis-à-vis* forest, let us examine how the recently passed "the Scheduled Tribes and other Traditional Forest Dwellers (Recognition of Forest Rights) Act, 2006 by Parliament can change the outlook of the tribals towards development. The Act was a long time need. It was implemented in bits and pieces in various parts of the country through executive order but a consolidated Act was not passed. This may be termed as Magna Carta in the field of forest management towards the interest of the tribals if the Act is implemented fast and in true spirit.

The Act aims "to recognize and vest the forest rights and occupation in forest land in forest dwelling Scheduled Tribes and other traditional forest dwellers who have been residing in such forests for generations but whose rights could not be recorded..."

In the Preamble of the Act, the State has accepted that "their forest rights on ancestral lands and their habitat were not adequately recognized in the consolidation of State forests during the colonial period as well as in independent India resulting in historical injustice to the forest dwelling Scheduled Tribes and other traditional forest dwellers who are integral to the very survival sustainability of the forest ecosystem."

Tribals have emotional, psychological and cultural attachments with the forest and they always live in the forest so also naxalites. On the other hand, for non-tribal forest dwellers, forest related livelihood activities are the last resort. However, the Act cannot discriminate. The Act in most of the States is being administered by the Tribal Department or the Backward Class Welfare Department who are working for the tribals and other backward classes like Scheduled Castes.

The following problems are coming in the way of implementation of the provisions of the Act before the tribals can be handed over records-of-rights for lands in forests or fringes of the forests:

(1) The tribals do not have proper caste certificates. Issuance of caste or tribe certificate is a herculean job which is not possible for the simple and illiterate tribal to get from the respective sub-divisional officer.

(2) The revenue machinery is not prepared to take up the responsibility of such a stupendous job of survey of all tribal areas near forests, the demarcation of land of each tribal or dweller and prepare a record-of-rights for each individual raiyat or owner.

(3) The forest officials without whose co-operation the Act, can not take off are not mentally prepared to accept primary position accorded to the tribals whom they used to treat like thieves or trespassers in the forests.

(4) In some of the areas Gram Sabhas are not constituted or convened. Then how can the cases be cleared, remains to be answered.

(5) The Act is silent against lot of charges/prosecutions pending against the tribals under the Forest Conservation Act of 1980 and the Indian Forest Act of 1927 with retrospective effect.

There is no provision in the Act of 2006 that cases under the Forest Conservation Act of 1980 against the forest dwelling Scheduled Tribes for accessing minor forest produce would be dropped or closed. There are thousands of such cases pending and hundreds of plough and cattle remain impounded by the forest department officials. These cases are to be dropped or withdrawn by the Government.

There were 2,57,226 forest cases pending against 1,62,692 tribals between 1953 to 30th June, 2004 under Sections 26, 33 and 41 of the Indian Forest Act, 1927 pertaining primarily to illegal felling of trees for domestic use and ferrying of wood by bullock carts in Chhattisgarh as on 8 November, 2005 and 2531 such cases in Orissa as on I0th March, 2005. Thus, incidents of the high-handedness is more in the State of Chhattisgarh. As a result, proportionate influence of the Naxalism is more in the State of Chhattisgarh. If the administration terms its majority population as accused person or criminal, they will have to behave accordingly whatever guise it may be.

The same problems were projected on 25th June, 2008 in a seminar convened by the Ekta Parishad attended *inter alia* by Chief Minister Shri Shivraj Singh Chauhan, Principal Secretary, Scheduled Tribes Welfare Department, Principal Secretary, Forest Department and other service officers. It was alleged that the forest officials are not accepting the applications, because the tribals have been encroaching upon the forest lands for a long time.[2] Thus, the Act has yet to be popularized through vide publicity and training so that the even lowest level functionaries recognize the legal position.

There were large scale transfers of tribal lands to the non-tribals. Even Forest Department got transferred about 1 lakh acres of tribal land through Tribal Agriculture Societies. In districts of Gwalior and Morena, lot of Bhoodan lands have been transferred.

The Status of Alienation and Restoration of Tribal Land

As per Government of India's report, Department of Land Resources, Ministry of Rural Development, the position as in September 2008 is as below including Chhattisgarh[3]:

No. of cases filed in Court—53806 Area 1,58,398 acres	Cases disposed of by the Court—29596 Area 97,123 acres
Cases rejected—29596 Area 97,123 acres	Cases in which land was restored to tribals not available
Cases pending in Court—24210 Area 61,275 acres	

The number of cases pending are huge involving 97,123 acres. These are revenue courts or officers under the Tribal Department. A special drive and fixing up of responsibility for non-disposal or delay in disposal can ease out the situation. Cases rejected against the tribals should be examined by superior officer or group of superior officers. Responsibility should be fixed for rejection or disposal of cases against the poor tribals. Appeals or review in suitable cases should be filed. The Revenue Courts should follow the dictum of the latest amendment in the Code of Civil Procedure (Order XVII Rule 1) whereas not more than three adjournments should be granted in any case. Rules should be made by the Government of MP so as not to allow more than three adjournments in a case of restoration of land to the tribal. More officers should be deputed for this purpose exclusively. The courts should also ensure that the tribals are given possession of the land simultaneously and the other person is paid due compensation on behalf of the government as the tribal is below poverty line. Legal aid lawyers should be provided to the tribal. Firstly, the advocates should not be allowed to appear in any revenue or land reform cases through a provision in the ceiling Act as is, prevalent in few states like West Bengal and has been upheld by the Supreme Court on more than one occasions. In superfluous cases, even tribal applicant should be asked to pay heavy costs to the opponent party.

As regards Bhoodan lands 31,000 acres of land is still to be distributed in addition to 92,000 acres of land ceiling surplus land which is good quality cultivable agriculture land.[4]

Madhya Pradesh government has hardly done anything on the front of distribution of government waste lands and is one of the lowest in the country through the State has the largest geographical area in the country. Only 134178[5] acres of lands has been distributed by September, 2006 which is 18.53 per cent of the total land 308000 sq. km. Government of MP should awake and do the needful to distribute government wasteland among the landless persons giving priority to the tribals.

Suggestions

1. The tribal land is alienated through transfers or transfers by concealing material facts which are not allowed and should be prohibited by way of new amendment in the relevant Act or Acts.
2. Transfer of tribal land by the competent authorities mistakenly or by obtaining the permission by fraud should be allowed to be reviewed or through revision as *suo motu* case or on application by the tribals or on his behalf by the official of Scheduled Tribe Department or by or on behalf of the gram panchayat or panchayat samity.
3. In scheduled areas having 50 per cent or more than 50 per cent Scheduled Tribe population, the industry using local resources and land, should not hold more than 50 per cent

shares. The government should hold more than 50 per cent share or holding in the company so that long term interests of the tribals can be safeguarded and they do not become foreigners in their own village.

4. The provision of conversion or diversion of agricultural land for non-agricultural purposes must be done strictly before the transfer or land acquisition so that tribals get partial advantage of enhancement of rate of land on this basis.
5. The land records should be updated in tribal pockets on priority basis and gram panchayats may be authorized to appear on behalf of the tribal to certify occupation if the tribal raiyats or landholder doesn't appear during K.B. operation or later on during hearing before the survey and settlement authorities.
6. The Bhoodan lands, government waste land, Gaon Sabha lands/poramboka lands have been encroached upon by the powerful landowners. They should be evicted and such lands should be distributed to the tribals and other weaker sections of the society.
7. The unirrigated or otherwise banjar lands distributed to the tribal beneficiaries should be provided with irrigation facilities or the land should be reclaimed or developed under various schemes of the Rural Development Ministry like 100 days labour employment scheme known as NAREGA or various schemes under Integrated Tribal Development Programme (ITDP) where lot of surplus funds go back to Government of India as unutilized. The popularly known as 100 days employment scheme has the biggest contribution to increase the daily wages in tribal areas which were starting from Rs. 35 per day. Thus, government schemes have salutary contribution which should be exploited and these schemes should be properly and honest implemented.
8. As regards implementation of the Scheduled Tribes and Other Traditional Forest Dwellers (Recognition of Forest Rights) Act, 2006 now known as STORFA, the implementation is tardy. It is a stupendous task. The same revenue machinery has to take the leadership. The forest officials cannot have change in their mindset by admitting a basic change in the

relationship of the community and the forest. The tribals in forest fringes are not only merely the users of the forest but are also the protector albeit in association with the State. Thus, the gaps in the main Act are to be filled in by clearly spelling out their revised role in the Rules in keeping with the spirit of the new provisions. The Act should not stumble just because Gram Sabhas are not constituted or there are other new hindrances created. The problem should be overcome by way of envisaging foolproof administrative procedures or constituting committees having representatives from the Panchayati Raj Institutions (PRIs) specially from the panchayat samity level or gram panchayat.

9. The Gram Sabha is vague. It should be Gram Panchayat of the Gram Sabha. Secondly, effective functional committee is at panchayat samity level which is missed in the Act. This gap should be filled in.
10. The ownership of Minor Forest Produce has been unequally provided in PESA in 1996 and also in STORFA. This proposition has been pursued variously in different States ever since the consensus reached in State Ministers Conference in 1976 as a part of Tribal Sub Plan strategy.
11. The remaining tribal lands alienated should be restored on war footing through drive or operation like administrative mechanism. It is hoped that the Naxalism will be fully brought under control if foregoing analysis regarding tribal lands is taken into consideration and adequate measures are taken to plug loopholes in land laws specially relating to tribals.

REFERENCES

1. Saxena, N.C.: Forests and the People: Policy Issues in Madhya Pradesh, p. 337, *Land Reforms in India*, Ed. By P.K. Jha, Sage Publications, New Delhi, year 1993, pp. 427.
2. *Dainik Jagran*: A Hindi Daily newspaper published from Bhopal, dt. 26th June, 2008.
3. *Annual Report (2006-07)*: Government of India, Ministry of Rural Development, p. 260.
4. *Ibid*., p. 256.
5. *Ibid*., p. 255.

14

Problems of Implementation of Land Reforms in Chhattisgarh

Chhattisgarh is a newly formed State carved out of erstwhile Madhya Pradesh consisting of seven districts, namely Bilaspur, Raipur, Durg, Rajnandgaon, Raigarh, Sarguja and Bastar.

More than 80 per cent of Chhattisgarh's population live in its villages and only 12 per cent of the region's agricultural land is irrigated. The little irrigation facility that exists is limited only to the plain region. Hardly any irrigation is there in extremists' affected district of Bastar and industrialisation has managed to engage only about 16 lakh persons in urban centres out of total population of 1.76 crore as per 2001 census.

Thus, land reform is the central issue in Chhattisgarh which will encompass following components:

(i) Distribution of land to the landless under Land Ceiling Acts and ensuring possession of lands to the allottees of the Government vested land.
(ii) Land alienation.
(iii) Non-recording of sharecroppers or bataidar.
(iv) Land buying/grabbing spree of new landlords and exploitation of underground water by them.

The *Chhattisgarh Mukti Morcha* (CMM) under *Comrade Shankar Guha Niyogi* cultivated surplus land in Pithora, Basna, Saraipali areas of Raipur District. After the well-planned and consptied murder of *Guha Niyogi* by the vested interests, the movement went into the hands of the extremists.

The tribals have faith in local moneylenders and not in banks and cooperative institutes. Since they have been rendered further vulnerable to exploitation because of their innate cultural ethics of honesty and morality and their concern for the present instead for the future. The alienation of land by the tribals to the non-tribals for various reasons added to their woes. The Collector permitted alienation of agricultural land under the sham classification of non-agriculture land. Secondly, Collector did not apply adequate force to restore their lands. The quantum of illegal *(benami)* land alienation from tribals to non-tribals is like that part of the iceberg that remains under the surface of water.

The fundamental cause of tribal land to protect the tribals can be successful unless it is complemented by measures to meet their genuine credit needs for cultivation including those for consumption and to protect them from usury. Secondly, the tribal having non-tribal lands are equally vulnerable to exploitation. The judicial redress is not available to them unless they seek joint redress or go-through legal aid system.

After orders passed in favour of tribals, non-tribals should be forcibly evicted from the lands and administration should ensure peaceful and effective possession of lands to the tribals. There should be irrefutable presumption that the lands shall belong to the original tribals unless it is obtained as per provisions of law with the permission of the Collector.

The present legal measures to protect tribals from exploitation by money-lenders should be made more stringent and proactive. Even cooperative society or government body should come into the shoes of the tribals to take the burden of loan and ensure him delivery of land free from all encumbrances.

As per survey in 1992 of NSS, the total area leased in came to only 7 per cent of the area owned by all households. Thus, like MP, Chhattisgarh is a low tenancy State. However, there is 25 per cent of the total area under lease. Moreover, the village-level study of *LBSNAA reports* that sharecropping accounts for over 75 per cent of tenants and 65 per cent of the area leased in.

There are three dominant patterns of sharecropping arrangements, which vary in incidence across regions:

(1) In 30 per cent of the cases, the sharecropper has to bear the entire cost of cultivation and gets only half the share of the gross produce.
(2) In 14 per cent of the cases, the share cropper bears the entire cost of production and gets 75 per cent of the gross produce.
(3) In 56 per cent of the cases, the landowner and the sharecropper share the cost and the gross produce equally.

The stagnation in agricultural productivity is of concern in the extremists' affected areas. It shows that the productivity per landowner in the agricultural sector has not increased. There is need for more investment in the agricultural sector though the size of farm has reduced and number of marginal and small farms has increased. This is possible only through institutional financing of pattadars and share-croppers though not recorded even. Out of all divisions, Bilaspur Division having Bastar District *(undivided)* has 75 per cent poverty as compared to 60 per cent in the State. The district is now divided into three districts, namely Bastar, Dantewla and Kanker. The rainfall is also not adequate. It is in few strong spells and therefore, run off and evaporation are more. As a result in the absence of protective irrigation, the rice crop is highly prone to agricultural drought. A location specify strategy for extremists' affected areas has to be developed in Chhattisgarh. Total Watershed Planning *(TWP)* is one of the solutions. It will stabilise the natural resource base so as to facilitate its equitable and long-term use. The preservation of the natural base and ecology of these areas is the priority area for action.

Land Records not Updated

The land records regarding facts of cultivation are not updated for years. As a result, the farmers are denied access to credit, electricity or agricultural inputs and deprived of benefits of various anti-poverty programmes. The Panchayati Raj Institutions (PRIs) have to be more effective and assertive in collaboration with the local non-governmental or governmental bodies. If the vested interests in bureaucracy or elsewhere threaten them, they should face them with perseverance and sustainability. PRIs should ensure that they control Common Property Resourses (CPR) like *naala* (drains), ponds, common grazing areas, outskirts of reserved forests, barren and degraded forests and even forest produce which cannot be used otherwise by the forest officials of the Forest Department. However, as per the latest initiative of the Government, tribals living in forest areas will be given lands and they will be entitled to use forest produce without any fear or discrimination.

However, the state must not abandon its crucial role in protecting cause of land reforms in these backward regions simply by handing over its pious responsibilities to PRIs and NGOs.

Programme of *Adhikar Abhiyan*

The united M.P. administration started an innovative scheme known as *Adhikar Abhiyan.* It was to ensure the restoration of land to the dispossessed Bhumi swamis. This ensured delivery of physical possession to patta-holders and punishment of the vested interests who resisted in this process. In U.P., it was also implemented successfully. But these campaigns are terminated before they are completed. It is to be kept in mind that land reforms like this process is a continuous one. The tribals cannot resist temptation to alienate land or mortgage the same because of their pressing personal, family or social obligations. If such processes are implemented on a certain intervals, then the villagers will find it financial folly to mortgage the land of the tribals and the tribals on the other hand will take shelter of the government or semi-government institutions, like banks, cooperative societies and others who will at least not exploit them to that extent.

Salwa Judum[1]

Official version of the *Salwa Judum* portrays it a people's struggle against the excesses of Naxalism. Villagers go in processing to other villages and convince them to join. Many were attracted to join by the promise of payment of Rs.1,500 (One thousand and Five hundred) only per month, the weapon and the hope of getting permanent employment in the police force. But due to retaliatory action by the Maoists, and mismanagement on the part of police administration, nearly 46,000 people were living in camps in artificial conditions which the villagers do not like. They were to be settled in 581 new villages near road side but the scheme could not get off the ground. Both sides claim civilian deaths. Government officers list 268 (two hundred and sixty eight) civilians killed (including some 50 SPOs) and 706 injured by the Maoists since June 2005, the Maoists have released a partial list of 116 civilians killed by the Salwa Judum till March 2006. In addition 72 (seventy two) police personnel and 30 (thirty) Naxalites had died.

The leader of the Salwa Judum, Mahendra Karma told that it is the 'citizens' initiative' on the pattern. *'Bhumkal'*, the rebellion against the British, because the Maoists had singularly opposed modern development.

The Maoists claim to include 60 lakh people in their 'organisation sweep' of their Dandakaranya "guerrilla zone" (comprising Godchiroli, Bhandara, Bala Ghata, Rajnandgaon, undivided Bastar and Malkangiri). Maoist literature claims that they have engaged considerably in development work over the last 20 years. For instance, in South Bastar and Godchiroli, they have established 135 (One hundred and Thirty Five) people's clinics, started 6 (six) primary schools, 10 (ten) night schools, built 25 (twenty five) huts for government teachers to persuade them to attend schools regularly, set up 10 (ten) village libraries, 81 (eighty one) tanks, 4 lakh fish seedlings, bullock carts built in 10 (ten) villages, diesel pump sets introduced in 9 (nine) villages, 268 (two hundred and sixty eight) cattle detention yards built, 5 (five) rice mills introduced, people trained in forest protection, cooperative paddy bank set up and agricultural cooperatives created in 220 (two hundred and twenty) villages.

However, in the drive to establish their own *'Janata Sarkar'*, the Maoists have resisted even genuine government initiatives. The Maoists are dependent on contractors for funds and the contractors are dependant on Maoists to work in their areas or get contracts.

Whatever may be the reality, the *Salwa Judum* campaigning brings out the fact that the Maoists' movement is not beyond public scrutiny. If they fail or go astray, another countervailing movement will arise and resist in their own courtyard. Thus, the Maoists have to be very cautious. Had they attended only implementation of land reforms, their movement could have gone unchallenged. The government machinery is better equipped in doing developmental works and have unlimited recourses. This is high time that the government implements land reforms measures without further delay in Chhattisgarh where the Maoists have lost focus of their main aim. However, in the democratic system like ours, violence neither by the Maoists nor by the Salwa Judum can be justified. A third path has to be carved out and that will be carved out sooner or later.

REFERENCE

1. Sunder, Nandi: Bastar, Maoism and Salwa Judum, *E.P.W.*, July 2006, pp. 3187-3192, Vol. XLI, No. 29, ed. C. Rammanohar Reddy, Hitkari House, 284, Shahid Bhagat Singh Road, Mumbai-400 001.

15

Land Reforms to Counter Feudalism in Rajasthan

Rajasthan is traditionally a State of Rajas, Rajawades and Maharajas. The people of Rajasthan specially in rural area have intrinsic loyalty and reverence towards their existing and ex-feudal lords. It is, therefore, essential to break the stronghold of the feudal landlords in the countryside.

Rajasthan's land scenario is governed by following Acts or Statutes:

1. The Rajasthan Land Reforms and Resumption of Jagir Act, 1952.
2. The Rajasthan Zamindar and Biswedari Abolition Act, 1959.
3. Rajasthan Agricultural Rents Control Act, 1953 & 1983.
4. The Rajasthan Tenancy Act, 1955 (RTA).

After the abolition and resumption of all non-religious and religious jagirs along with zamindaris and the biswedaries were allowed upto maximum limit of 500 acres land for cultivation. In all 2.99 lakh jagirs covering an area of 77,110 sq. miles were resumed. Similarly, 9.33 lakh zamindaris and biswedaries were also resumed and compensation amount to over fifty crore rupees was paid to them.

The ceiling laws were brought into force as late as from 15th December, 1963. The law relating to ceiling was incorporated in the Rajasthan Tenancy Act, 1955 by introducing Chapter III-B and not by a separate law on ceiling on agricultural holding.

The latest position as reported in Quarterly Report of Department of Land Resources, Ministry of Rural Development upto December 2007 is as follows:[1]

(i)	Area declared surplus	6,15,177 acres
(ii)	Area taken possession	5,71,146 acres
(iii)	Area distributed	4,65,517 acres
(iv)	Total number of beneficiaries	83,617 acres
	SC—30,340, ST—12,047	
(v)	Surplus area not distributed	1,49,660 acres
(vi)	Area involved in Revenue Courts in 704 cases	50,246 acres
(vii)	Area locked in High Court 211 cases	21,094 acres
(viii)	Reserved for Public purpose	63,891 acres

Thus, it is clear that there is lackluster approach to land reforms in Rajasthan because of following reasons:

(a) The land declared surplus is much less than required.
(b) There was delay in taking over possession of land which caused heavy toll on land to the extent of 44,031 acres.
(c) The number of beneficiaries covered is much less though there is lot of demand and the number of landless persons is very large specially Scheduled Castes and Scheduled Tribes.
(d) The total land involved in revenue courts is largest in the country, i.e. 50,246 acres. It means that there should be reorganisation of revenue courts. Like in West Bengal, Board of Revenue may be abolished and Land Tribunal may be set up so that appeals may not go to the High Court.
(e) The quantum of land reserved for public purpose is very large. The major amount of the land should also put to distribution among the landless persons or the persons who are otherwise eligible to get government surplus land.

Steps Suggested

(a) The lands locked under judicial process should be taken out.
(b) The surplus lands diverted to the Forest Department instead of its allotment to the weaker sections should be unearthed and put to distribution among the landless SC and ST persons who have been cultivating or are occupying these lands.

(c) Most of land owners owing more than 50 acres of land have not filed returns. Their lands including benami lands should be identified and surplus land should be declared and vested in government. An effective administrative drive be undertaken to identify concealed lands.

(d) The sale or mortgage of lands by allottee should not be allowed and these lands should be taken back and settled with other equally deserving persons.

(e) The average extent of land allotted for beneficiaries is 5.77 acres which is one of the highest in the country. It should be reduced considerably so that more beneficiaries could be covered.

(f) The names of the allottees of vested lands should be entered into the revenue records.

(g) Reclamation and development of allotted land at government cost and linking them effectively with the anti-poverty programmes be undertaken.

(h) Voluntary and activist organizations though very few are existing in Rajasthan, should be associated with the implementation of the land ceiling programme.

(i) The exemption given to religious and charitable institutions be abolished.

(j) The existing definition of 'Family' be amended to include husband, wife and all their children irrespective of their age.

Status of Tenancy or Sharecropping

Sharecropping is the major form of tenancy in all the districts except in the districts of Nagaur and Kota. In the district of Nagaur 80 per cent had leased in on fixed kind rent terms and in the district of Kota 75 per cent had leased in on fixed cash rent terms.

There is main system of sharecropping, i.e. sharing of cost and crop between the land owner and sharecropper.

Second type of major sharecropping is one where the sharecropper meets the entire cost of cultivation and receives only 50 per cent share of the gross produce. This is exploitative.

In third type of exploitative tenancy, the sharecropper meets the entire cost of cultivation and receives two-third share of gross produce.

The ideal form of tenancy in very few case is also existing where the sharecropper knows his rights well. In these cases, the landowners bear the entire cost of cultivation and he gets three-fourth of the gross produce.

The leasing out of land was common to all landlords, big and small. The small landowners leased out due to paucity of means of production like cattle and plough. Other types are absentee landlords or they considered tilling of land personally below their dignity.

The security of tenure is not assured to tenant or sharecropper which can be allowed.

(i) If he is allowed to work with the some landowners, for any length of time.
(ii) If the legal provisions permit the right of recording the tenancy which should be permitted forthwith either by law or rules or executive instructions.
(iii) As per Government of India's report, so far recorded tenants[2] in Rajasthan are only 18000 upto September 2006 Administrative steps are to be taken to enter their names in the khasra, i.e. revenue record.

Conclusions

(1) The abolition of the intermediary system after Independence conferred heritable and transferable rights to tenants. Around 42 lakh persons were declared *khatedar* tenants and were brought into direct relationship with the state. Further, as a result of implementation of the RTA, 1955, nearly 1.38 lakh tenants and subtenants were made owners or *khatedar* tenants in respect of 7.91 lakh acres of land in the state. The benefit, however, was mostly confined to the hereditary tenants. The tenants-at-will and share croppers were evicted outright resulting in considerable increase in the number of agricultural labourers between 1960-61 and 1970-71. The Agricultural Census also shows that during 1970-71 and 1980-81 about 5.26 per cent and 4.31 per cent respectively of the operated area in the state were leased-in which was cultivated by nearly 15 per cent of the cultivating households and all of them were tenants-at-will. In the context of tenancy

this is not at all an insignificant figure. The study of 318 tenants conducted by IAS probationers in the state between September 1989 and May 1991 established that still 8 per cent of the total operated area was leased-in and 12 per cent of the cultivating households were tenant households.[3] Tenancy reforms thus continues to be a crucial issue in the land reform programme in the state.

(2) Though 75 per cent were owner-cum-tenants and only 25 per cent were pure tenants yet the study revealed that the tenants belonging to both the categories were basically either at or below the subsistence level. Of course, some of the owner-cum-tenants as also some pure tenants were above subsistence level. But that in no way negated the continued relevance of ensuring security of tenure, payment of fair rent etc. to rectify the situation in the interest of the larger section of the peasantry.

(3) Sharecropping was the major form of tenancy. Five main patterns of sharecropping were observed depending on the terms of lease. The largest group of sharecroppers (108) fill into the pattern of equal sharing of crop and inputs with the landlord. The next largest group (73) is that of sharecroppers who meet the entire cost of cultivation and receive 50 per cent of the gross produce.

(4) The tenancy reform legislation in the state prescribes the payment of 25 per cent of gross produce as rent where the landowners meets the entire input cost: in all other cases, the rent is fixed at one-sixth of the gross produce. The payment of rent in excess of what is statutorily fixed in each of the cropsharing patterns mentioned earlier was true for all the cases that were studied. The excess paid ranged from 17 per cent to 33 per cent over the statutory norm; the major number of cases fell into the 25 per cent excess payment category.

The administrative apathy in implementing the statutory norms of rent payment is absolute.

There is also lack of organization of beneficiaries to take up their rights. In such a situation the only alternative appears to be to gear up the administrative machinery to implement the statutory provisions so as to safeguard the interests of the sharecroppers.

Apart from the payment of exploitative rents, the sharecroppers also faced acute problems of security of tenure. The tenancy reforms legislation of the state permits leasing for a period of five years. Sharecroppers were subjected to frequent changes of plots mostly within two years and some within five years. Certain other policies of the state government have also increased the problem of security of tenure for sharecroppers. Instructions were issued by the state government in 1974 not to enter the names of actual cultivators in the record of rights. In its absence, the sharecropper is unable to provide evidence of his working as a tenant. These instructions are against the basic principle of recording of rights and the state thus emerges as the major violator of the fundamental rights of cultivators. This anomaly needs to be corrected forthwith especially as the study has shown that the age range of sharecroppers is 20 to 60 years and amongst whom a substantial proportion are in the age group of 40 to 60 years. If the tenancy rights are not ensured to tenants in the higher age group, they will be deprived of such rights in their lifetime. Further, there is no provision in the tenancy reforms legislation of the state to confer occupancy rights to the tenants-at-will/sharecroppers. It is suggested that provision on the lines of the Assam tenancy legislation may be enacted which confers occupancy right to a tenant on the completion of working as a tenant for a period of three years.

The leasing out was undertaken by all categories of landowners, namely, small, medium and big. The reasons for leasing out, however, varied.

Immediate Tasks

On the basis of the foregoing analysis, the following important tasks for tenancy reforms in Rajasthan have been identified:

(1) The patwaris should be directed to record the names of the tenants in the Khasra and the order of 1974 issued by the State government should be withdrawn.

(2) Tenants including the sharecropper, fixed cash rent and fixed kind rent tenants should be recognized legally.

(3) The leasing-in should be permitted without time limit. The existing provision of limiting leasing for a period of five years goes against the interests of the tenants.
(4) There should be provision similar to that enacted in Assam of confirmation of occupancy rights on non-occupancy tenants on the completion of working as a tenant continuously for three years.
(5) There should be security against eviction.
(6) The fair rent provision contained in the tenancy reform legislation in the state needs to be implemented thoroughly.
(7) Voluntary/activist organizations should be actively associated with the identification of concealed tenants, procedure of conferment of recording of rights and ensuring payment of fair rent.
(8) A campaign of recording the tenants on the line of Operation Barga of West Bengal should be undertaken in the state.

Suggestions

(1) It is encouraging that as a result of land reforms, measures whatever taken so far, the number as well as area under very large holdings have declined and holdings between 1 ha to 2 ha and 2 ha to 4 ha constitute the largest land holding group in the State. The most conspicuous increase in number is recorded by the marginal holding, i.e. holding below 1 ha. Interestingly, the area under marginal holdings has increased from 0.32 ha in 1961-62 to 0.43 ha in 1982. But that is not enough. As per 2001 Census Rajasthan has 96.99 lakh Scheduled Castes and 70.98 lakh Scheduled Tribes. Out of these only 30,340 SCs and 12047 STs have been allocated government vested lands. There is lot of scope to distribute land to more landless or marginal farm errs belonging to Scheduled Tribes and Scheduled Castes apart from to landless of other castes or communities. Thus a lot is still required to be done in Rajasthan. So far only the tip of iceberg has been touched.
(2) More areas are coming under common area of the Indira Gandhi Nahar Pariyojana (IGNP). Thus the land owner who

are getting their fertile and irrigated lands assessed as non-irrigated should be caught and punished.

(3) The ranks of agricultural labourers is swelling in Rajasthan. Many marginal and small farmers are also joining the ranks as wages are high. It means that the agriculture is not a profitable venture. There are lot of inputs required for agriculture which are not available to the sharecroppers, marginal and small farmers. Thus institutional crop farming and support are immediately required on a wide scale. On the other hand big landowners are ruling the scene in all respects. Now Rajasthan is irregularly getting unpredicted rainfalls. Therefore, there is a need of relook into the land reform related aspects of agricultural production in Rajasthan. The thrust of land reforms in state like Rajasthan should be to make small and marginal holding economically viable. It is essential to gear up the institutions of credit, marketing, extension and research to meet the requirements of small holding.

(4) Freezing of lease market has done more harm to the poorman than good. With a proper recording of tenants and large number of sharecroppers estimated to be 5.72 lakh households on 12.90 lakh hectares, the production base can increase when the sharecroppers will be entitled to bank loan by showing their recorded names in the records of rights of the government. At present as per Gervernment of India report only 18000 tenants were recorded initially. Thus, there is lot to be done in the field of just recording the sharecroppers without giving them ownership right or even heritable right of cultivation.

Unless foregoing steps are taken urgently in Rajasthan, the seemingly peaceful baloon may burst any day throwing its splash up to the country's capital Delhi. The tourism or industry sectors can not sustain a state. The state requires its basic equity through redistribution of landed properties so that there is social equilibrium in the society. How much will the poor folk wait on the mercy of their ex-Raja, Maharaja, Zamindars or landlords? Already simmering discontent has started through caste war. If this is diverted to economic issues, i.e. the issues of hunger, the sustainable development will take place. It is a fact that the landowning class in Rajasthan also dominate all political parties, yet leadership can emerge from amongst the young generation of Rajas and Maharajas who have studied abroad and have modern and democratic bent of mind. I leave it to the leadership of upper and middle-class in Rajasthan to take reins of land reforms in their powerful hands in the State.

REFERENCES

1. *Quarterly Progress Report* (Cumulative) on Implementation of Land Ceiling Laws (Distribution of ceiling surplus land) for the Quarter ending December, 2007 published by the Department of Land Resources, Ministry of Rural Development, Government of India, Nirman Bhawan Annexe, New Delhi, 2008.
2. Government of India, Ministry of Rural Development: *Annual Report 2006-07*, p. 258
3. *Land Reforms in India: An Empirical Study 1989-90*, Vol. I, L.B.S. National Academy of Administration, Mussoorie, 1990, p. 55.

16

Institutional Financing and Political Will as Essential Components of Land Reforms in Karnataka

Karnataka is a proud Information Technology giant State in India. Unfortunately it is the latest entrant to the Naxalite fold as per Government of India's report. During 2005, there were 8 Naxalite incidents causing 6 deaths[1] whereas the same trend is continuing. Let us examine where Karnataka has not done well which is causing concern to the rural landless poor or the sharecroppers.

1. Deficiencies in Distribution of Land in Karnataka

The eligibility for the grant of land for agricultural purpose is:

(a) the person must have attained the age of 18;
(b) his gross annual income should not exceed Rs. 4,800 as per Amendment Act, 2003;
(c) he should either be a *bona fide* agriculturist cultivating land personally or have a *bona fide* intention of utilizing land for personal cultivation; and
(d) he should not be a sufficient landholder.

However, in case of the ex-servicemen and soldier, land may be granted if the gross annual income of the applicant does not exceed Rs. 12,000.

The extent of land granted to any person should not exceed the prescribed limit, including land already held by him.

However, following reservation of land for distribution leaves no discretion with the local authority or panchayat body to deviate in deserving cases:

(a) ex-servicemen and soldiers	10 per cent
(b) person belonging to the SCs & STs	50 per cent
(c) backward tribes	5 per cent
(d) political sufferers	10 per cent
(e) others	25 per cent

The salutary principle in land distribution is that the land should be given to the one who cultivates the land personally so that production increases. Land is not donation or gift. It is for landless people who are capable enough physically to cultivate land and have been habitually, traditionally or practically doing the job of cultivation. Allotment of land to ex-servicemen and political sufferers is now out of context. The priority list for distribution of land should be ideally laid down as follows like in West Bengal:

(i) *First priority*: Landless Scheduled Tribe.
(ii) *Second priority*: Landless Schedule Caste.
(iii) The ceiling for allotment of land should be one acre. Persons who already hold less then one acre of land may, however, be given land to an extent which is equal to the difference between one acre and the land already held by them.
(iv) In case of a sharecropper or tenant, half of the land cultivated by him as a sharecropper is taken into account in computing this total land upto 1 acre.
(v) The sthayee samiti or sub-committee on land of the Panchayat Samiti at the block or taluka level may advise local revenue official in the matter of allotment.
(vi) No settlement of land is made with a person who is employed in a business, trade, undertaking's service or industrial occupation etc.

Thus, general cultivators will come under consideration after BPL category, STs and SCs one considered first for allotment of land. These BPL category list of persons is readymade available at each panchayat level and can be used to drawn up priority list for allotment.

First preference is to be given to the person in possession of land but only upto one acre of land. In that case, he will get priority even over and above Scheduled Tribe and Schedule Caste cultivators or agricultural labourers or the landless persons, because disturbance in possession may lead to a war between the two poor persons which is not the aim of the land reform measures.

However, limit for allotment for homestead should be 0.0339 ha which comes to about 8 decimal and is sufficient for a house along with cattle and kitchen garden. The deed of settlement known as patta is issued in the name of the Governor and the land is not transferable but is heritable. The name of wife is also written jointly in West Bengal in view of gender justice. Possession is given simultaneously because land without possession has no meaning.

As the allotment of land and delivery of possession cut links of the allottee with the land owner who is also his money lender, the financial institution like banks, cooperative societies or service-cooperatives should immediately step in, otherwise he will again mortgage the land to the erstwhile landowner.

A survey by IAS probationers of the L.B.S. National Academy of Administration brings out following fallacies in land distribution in Karnataka:

(a) The norms of allotment in about half of the quantum of land allotted have been violated.
(b) The package of economic assistance along with land allotment was lacking.
(c) The encroachment of land mainly in Bangalore district has been done by the powerful and ineligible persons.[2]

Thus, this is high time that injustice done to the underprivileged persons should be undone and they should be given government surplus land.

They should in a big way be assisted for crop finance loan on concessional rate of interest and government subsidy or schemes to reclaim and develop their barren or waste land through various water harvesting schemes etc.

It was surprising to note that as in December 2007 about 1,15,765 acres of land is not distributed out of total area of 2,41,710 acres of land which is the poorest performance among all States (as per GOI report).[3] Even before taking over possession, lot of land got involved in litigation. This shows utter callousness. The vesting of land and taking over possession are simultaneous processes. At least paper possession is taken by the government which is also provided generally in most of the land reforms legislations. One fails to understand what State Government of Karnataka has been doing with 45,343 acres of land pending in 1,505 cases at the High Court which is the highest in the country. Even in Revenue Courts, 15,682 acres of land is locked. Karnataka is the first State to set up the Land Tribunal which should be an alternative to the High Court. One fails to understand why the cases from High Court were not transferred to the Karnataka Land Tribunal. It is not understood why 38,008 acres of land is not being distributed which is held up for miscellaneous reasons. Failure of the State Government in this most important field of land reform gives ample reason why the Naxalism is raising its head in otherwise peace loving, proadministration and prosperous State of Karnataka.

Karnataka has done well in promoting distribution of homestead plots as per study conducted by the Rural Development Institute, New York, U.S.A. These homestead plots upto 15/16 decimal have been successfully used for vegetable and fruit cultivation and partly evergreen cultivation. These plots at least save the beneficiaries from starvation and put stability in their minds. This scheme is known as Ashraya scheme and even panchayats are purchasing land from free markets and are distributing among the deserving landless persons successfully. The homestead cum garden plot of at least 2178 sq. feet and upto 6544 sq. feet deserve serious consideration and these are to be dovetailed with the Indira Avas Yojana of the Ministry of Rural Development, Government of India.

Karnataka has also done well by distribution of 13.72 lakh acre[4] government waste land which requires to be developed further through various government schemes or liberal financial grants or loans.

Tenancy Reforms

Karnataka is in line with a least seven other States in India which have banned land tenancy. After conferment of ownership on about 6 lakh tenants[5], the State has been sitting on its laurels that it has done whatever was required for the tenant or the sharecroppers. But, in fact, informal tenancy exists all over the State. The tenancy that persists in the field is concealed/oral and the names of tenants are not entered in the revenue records. In 1981-82, 6.04 per cent of the operated area was leased-in in the State despite legal abolition of tenancy. The average area leased-in by the tenant was 4.76 acre.

The study by IAS probationers[6] shows that of all tenants, 62.5 per cent have leased in on sharecropping terms, 22.9 per cent on fixed cash rent terms, and 14.6 per cent on fixed rent terms in kind. Similarly, of the total area leased in 59.6 per cent is under sharecropping, 21.6 per cent under fixed rent terms in kind, and 18.8 per cent under fixed cash rent terms. The profile of the tenants reveals the following:

(a) Most of the pure tenants live below subsistence level, only a small portion having reached subsistence level.
(b) The proportion of tenants living at above subsistence level is much higher among the owner-cum-tenants, some of whom fall in the category of rich peasants.
(c) In view of low economic status of tenants, and also because most of them are concealed tenants, the question of tenancy reforms is an important one for all of them except those in the rich peasant category.
(d) The tenant owners are drawn from all the castes.

In a survey of agriculturists in Karnataka in 2000, the Rural Development Institute, Bangalore[7] found:

1. 45 per cent of the respondents answering definitively state that tenancy prohibitions should be lifted;
2. 94 per cent of respondents answering definitively state that existing tenancy restrictions harm the landless;
3. 38 per cent respondents answering definitively report that at least one farmer in their village keeps land fallow rather than renting it out because renting may lead to the loss of such land.

Benefits of Relaxation

Overwhelming majority of the expert opinions and people support change of the existing tenancy prohibition policy in Karnataka into one regulating it instead of banning it. Such regulating law will have, as revealed in other states, more beneficial effects, the significant ones being:

1. Removal of tenancy ban makes more lands available for landless poor to cultivate, at least as tenants;
2. Relaxation of prohibition allows lease of land for more productive use, diversification of agriculture and contract farming;
3. Tenancy regulation provides tenure security to cultivators and regulates rentals and brings in transparency;
4. Tenure security enables tenants to borrow credit, obtain input subsidies and other extension services easily;
5. Tenancy relaxation eliminates land left fallow for fear of losing it;
6. Permission to lease out eliminates unavoidable social conflict, insecurity of losing land as collateral security and social status symbol;
7. Equity issues can be addressed by reasonably fixing rental levels and providing tenure security to cultivators;
8. Ceiling limits on total holdings both for tenants and owners or partly as one and partly as other may be regulated to ensure equitable distribution of land which will meet demands of equity;
9. Tenancy regulation along with reasonable ceiling limit would render farming economically viable; and
10. Having achieved removal of exploitative intermediaries, zamindar, jagirdars and inamdars, tenancy prohibition is no longer necessary. On the other hand, there is need to regulate commercial type of leases by companies to prevent "new baniyas" converting farmers into "new serfs".

The informal tenants or sharecroppers on the basis of Barga Operation of West Bengal can be recorded as follows:

(i) Composite squads of the land revenue machinery and settlement department should be made led by Revenue Officer or Kanungo.

(ii) The squad will work in specified pockets where concentration of tenants as per report of panchayats and District Land Reforms Officer or settlement officer is more.

(iii) The Panchayat or members of local political party will collect applications in bulk.

(iv) Then the squad should go and hold evening meeting where in a mauja or group of villages the recording of sharecroppers will take place and explain the procedure so that the tenants and landowners may attend recording process without fear of favour.

(v) After hearing both sides, *parcha* or record of recording will be handed over to the sharecropper along with the details of plots, he cultivates in an impartial and objective manner.

(vi) These squads will be legally empowered by the Government through suitable notification or notifications.

Contract Farming

In Karnataka, the contract farming has some good dividends specially in the field of exports of coffee, spices, fresh fruits, flower, cashew, vegetables, gherkins and raisins.

Some of the even marginalized farmers who were hungry of money have made tons of money by adopting above types of crops and selling them through the corporate or agri-export zones. Gherkins alone has got Rs. 140 to 150 crore export markets every year. Rose Onions were exported from the state during 2005-06 for Rs. 50 crore[8] and Karnataka, have captured world markets like IT from Bangalore. The total area covered and the farmers involved in contract farming in Karnataka is still less then one per cent. In the meantime, the corporate have started seeking to lease out their lands which should not be permitted creating new brand of zamindars and landlords. No comment can be offered at present. The experiment is to be kept under watch for some more years. If the benefits reach directly to the farmers in a substantial quantum, then the contract farming can be further promoted by relaxation of ceiling laws and tenancy laws on those farmers. It is still demanded from the corporates that they may involve farmers whose lands they have acquired not as daily labourers but as shareholders or individual owners in the form of cooperative farming or the registered society etc. If Naxalism spreads due to contract farming, then the contract farming will have to be discontinued.

Updation of Land-records

Karnataka is the leader in the field and has been awarded by Government of India in this regard. Thus Karnataka has good revenue set-up and the machinery is quite-motivated. It is estimated that all records of rights alongwith maps of plots of individual raiyats or owners have been computerized in Karnataka and people can have most up-to-dated records of rights near to the cent-per-cent accuracy. Thus, it is clear that Karnataka can venture successfully to bring about all types of land reforms to tackle problem of Naxalism in the State.

Suggestions

1. The balance ceiling surplus and government waste land should be distributed without further delay giving top priority to the Scheduled Tribes specially in the Naxalite affected areas/talukas of the State.
2. The priority list for the land reform beneficiaries needs on suitable amendment, Land is for those who cultivate land personally.
3. The existing tenancy prohibition policy should be changed into the tenancy regulation policy.
4. Informed tenants or sharecroppers should be recorded in Karnataka on the pattern of Barga Operation in West Bengal and involvement of the Land Tribunal should be only as the final appellate tribunal.
5. The scheme for distribution of homestead-cum-kitchen garden plots requires further encouragement and patronage by Government and panchayats.
6. Extensive schemes should be implemented for reclaiming and developing government land also by dovetailing various rural development schemes.
7. Efforts should be made to link up transfer of lands through registration with updation of land records through normal processes of mutation and conversion. Karnataka should attempt to give map of plots along with the records of rights or copy of *khatian* with respect to village boundary and adjoining plot configuration as is being experimented in West

Bengal. This will combine best points of both rayatwari system in south and permanent settlement system in rest of the country.

It is hoped that the good network of revenue and settlement administration will soon tide over temporary show of discontent in the form of Naxalism. The resurgent revenue administration led by requisite 'political will' will be able to contain the Naxalism in the State.

REFERENCES

1. Government of India, Ministry of Home Affairs: *Annual Report, 2007-08*, Annexure V, p. 143
2. L.B.S. National Academy of Administration, Mussoorie: *Land Reforms in India, An Empirical Study, 1989-90*. Vol. I, pp. 75-76, 113 to 117.
3. Government of India, Department of Land Resources: *Quarterly Progress Report* (cumulative) on Implementation of Land Ceiling Laws, for the quarter ending December, 2007.
4. Government of India, Ministry of Rural Development: *Annual Report, 2006-07*, Department of Land Resources, Annexure-XLVIII, p. 257.
5. *Ibid*: Annexure-XLIX.
6. *Ibid* 2: Table S T-I, p. 7.
7. Jaamdar, S.M.: Contract Farming in Karnataka, Its Implications for Policy in *Contract Farming and Tenancy Reforms* ed., R.S. Deshpande, Concept Publishing Company, New Delhi-110 059, p. 152.
8. *Ibid*: p. 144.

17

A Lot To Do towards Land Reforms in Gujarat

Like the peasant movements of Telengana and Tebhaga, Gujarat also witnessed the revolt by the Koli Kshatriyas and tribals of north and eastern Gujarat against the exploiters. They tried to take their land back. They grabbed land from Bame and Parsi landlords and harvested the standing crop. Yet, due to police action in favour of landlords, the agitation died out.

For the first time, the Land Ceiling Act was introduced in 1960 which came into force in September 1961 after formation of Gujarat State. The Act was amended in 1974 which further lowered the limit of the ceiling. But the Act largely remained on paper. The big farmers, from the upper castes divided their land in the names of their families including minor children. Sometimes, they transferred land in the names of distant relatives or loyal servants to evade their ceiling limit. The government received only 74,877 hectares till 1982, out of which possession was taken of 38,995 hectares. From that 20,804 hectares of lands were distributed to 16,541 beneficiaries. Most of their surplus land was of inferior quality, thus defeating the purpose of law.

As per report of Department of Land Resources, Ministry of Rural Development, Government of India, the position of distribution of ceiling surplus land in Gujarat is as follows as in December 2007.[1]

(i) Area declared surplus	2,37,644 acres
(ii) Area taken possession	1,78,906 acres
(iii) Area distributed to beneficiaries	1,61,805 acres
(iv) Total number of beneficiaries	36,051

Scheduled Caste beneficiaries are only 17,083 against total S.C. population, in the state as per 2001 census which is 35.93 lakh and against S.T. population as per 2001 census of 74.81 lakh, only 14,628 tribals have been allotted government ceiling surplus land. This is unsatisfactory state of affairs because this is supposed to be the best cultivable land.

However, good work has been done by distributing 13.81 lakh acres[2] of government waste lands upto September 1991 and 27,000 acres[3] of Bhoodan land out of total 34,000 acres upto March 2006.

The most surprising figure shown is 70,454 acres as area available for distribution but net area available for distribution is 5387. Second more surprising figure is area involved in litigation[4] is 62,950 acres in 1112 cases whereas the account given in various courts is far short than the areas involved in following courts:

(a) Revenue Courts	6980 acres
(b) High Courts	24660 acres
(c) Supreme Court	7464 acres

If this land can be found out, another land reform drive for distribution can be successfully undertaken in Gujarat.

In fact, the deprived classes of people like the Kolis and the Dalits did not get any significant advantage of reform. The Land Ceiling Act which adversely affected rich Patidar farmers largely remained on paper.

Under the Revised Ceiling Act, a number of existing exemptions were withdrawn while some of them were altered. Exemptions for land held by religious trusts were completely withdrawn. But for panjrapole or goushala, exemption for trusts was allowed. This is being equally misused.

One of the major drawbacks in allotment of land was that about 48.5 per cent of the land taken possession, had been allotted to beneficiaries and a considerable extent of land (47.4%) had been allotted to organisations which was a violation of the norms of allotment. All the lands declared surplus should have been allotted to the landless beneficiaries in order of priorities among Scheduled Tribes, Scheduled Castes and others, depending on their poverty.

Naturally, people below poverty line *inter se* will get first priority if he is also a landless one. Thus definite norms of allotment should be followed and lands should be allotted to the tillers of the land only who will put all his physical and mental labour for increase of productivity in the state.

Sometimes, efforts were made to give financial assistance to the assignees of government vested land but these were stray efforts. The institutional financing or crop, financing of the land reform beneficiaries should be one of the top priority government scheme in cooperation with Banks and other financial institutions or cooperatives. Good work has been done in Gujarat to restore tribals lands.

Implementation of Tenancy Reforms Legislation

Under the Bomaby Tenancy and Agricultural Lands Act, a total of 12,32,742 persons became occupants with regard to 10,02,004 hectares of land by February 1988.

As per report published by Government of India, Department of Land Resources, 12.76 lakh tenants have been conferred ownership on 25.92 lakh acres of land as in April 2006.[5]

Thus, a good work has been done by Gujarat pertaining to the abolition of tenures and conferment of occupancy rights as on the tillers day.

This was by way of constitution of record of rights team. It was headed by a mamladar and included 10 deputy mamladars and 10 circle inspectors which discovered concealed tenancies and updated the record of rights.

But, lot of work is still to be done. As per NSS 37th record, 2 per cent of the total operated area during 1981-82 has additionally gone away from the tenants. This is due to concealment of tenancy.[6]

Both, sharecropping and fixed cash rents were the prevalent forms 86.4 per cent of the sharecroppers received half the share of the gross produce which was the most predominant pattern, around 4.5 per cent of them received two-thirds of the gross produce and 9.1 per cent among them only received three-fourths share of the gross produce. The major reason for the high incidence of concealed tenancy in the district of Jamnagar and Junagarh was neo-absentee landlordism. The landlords were engaged in non-agricultural occupations in cities and some were also in the countries of Africa. A majority of the leasing out was undertaken by middle and large farmers.

Encroachments of Government Land

At least half of the government land is being cultivated. It is another story that the dominant and powerful landowners encroach more of government land. Even then, half of the area of government land (CPR) is still available for distribution. This is being utilised at present for grazing purpose. However, the gram panchayat which is the custodian of this land is unable to prevent encroachment. This calls for active policy intervention with strong political will and definite administrative support.

Extensive survey of such lands should be undertaken and these lands should earmarked which are fit for distribution among the landless and marginal farmers. Panchayati Raj Institutions (PRIs) should be duly empowered for their proper maintenance, regeneration and preventing encroachment. Area under forestry or social forestry should be regenerated. A package programme for reclamation and development of land allotted to the beneficiaries may be undertaken after integrating it with anti-poverty programmes. The ban on allotment should be lifted and if eligible cultivators is in possession of such land, he should be allotted this land as pattadar.

Position of Alienation of Tribal Land

Gujarat has done very well to restore back the alienated land to the tribals. The position as in September 2006 is as follows:[7]

(a) No. of cases filed in court	20704
(b) Area involved	1,87,636 acres
(c) Cases decided in favour of tribals	19320
(d) Area involved	1,77,751 acres
(e) Cases rejected	497
(f) Land involved	3,342 acres

This is the best performance. Yet, there is lot to be done for the tribals in Gujarat. Gujarat has large tribal pockets. It is hoped that due implementation of the Scheduled Tribes and Other Traditional Forest Dwellers (Recognition of Forest Rights) Act, 2006 will do the rest job by filling the gaps left. Gujarat is administrative sound state. It has surplus revenue and can employ more staff and officers without the Central assistance. It is hoped that the poorest of the poor and the deprived tribal communities like Dangi will be duly taken care of under the new Forest Act of 2006.

Land Reforms Through People's Movements[8]

Apparently peaceful state of Gujarat has a rich history of people's movements for implementation of land reforms.

The Dongs district has 98 per cent of forest and has about 92 per cent of adivasis. They are Bhils, Kumbis and Vaslis, Kotwaliyas, Kuthidars, Garmoust and Chandaries.

Land in Dongs is almost distributed but the holdings are small and uneconomic. The stoppage of harassment by forest officials and Talathis will improve their situation. The reverse encroachment by Forest Department will also be stopped forthwith. Thus the Bhil Rajas will not have to again rise in revolt against their own government which they did against the imperial rule of the Britishers.

The struggle of adivasis of south Gujarat for implementation of land reforms legislation is known as Pardi Ghasia Satyagrah. It followed Gandhian method for asserting their rights. Pardi is the name of the area where battle was fought. It is a taluka in Valsad district. The struggle engulfed surrounding talukas, Dharampur, Umargaon and Valsad. Their leader was Iswarbhai Desai who taught the basics of satyagraha to the adivasis. Pardi area is also less developed in terms of infrastructure network.

Pardi Taluka was owned by 100 big landlords who grew grass to feed Bombay fodder markets. Thus, adivasis is got work for a month or two and starved for 8 to 10 months in a year. So the movement spread like the wildfire and ultimately landowners, had to handover 14,000 acres of land to government to distribute among the landless adivasis.

The Pardi Satyagrah "spread to Bhiloda Taluka of Saber Kantha district under the auspices of the Kisan Sabha in the eastern belt of Gujarat. Ultimately orders were passed in 1972 to register lands in the names of those who had been tilling lands until 1967. Later on DISHA and the EKLAVYA Sangathan spearheaded the movement. Ultimately government of Gujarat issued Government Rules for regularization of authorized and unauthorised cultivation of forest lands, which has now got the sanction under the new Act of 2006. Therefore, we may not go into further movements in 1994, 1995.

Now all eyes are set to see that the STORFA is implemented with utmost sincerity and with zeal and spirit.

Struggle and Rehabilitation of Project Affected People

The first ever movement against big dam started against the Sardar Sarovar Project in Gujarat. This was under the banner of "Narmada Bachao Andolan" (NBA). The movement attracted national attention and national connivance through in Gujarat, it could not succeed due to literal relocation and rehabilitation (R&R). Though it is debatable whether NBA was justified in view of larger benefits for the state in view of greater production in future ensuring food security in times to come, yet the NBA has compelled to the administration to be serious about relocation and rehabilitation and not treating it as an eye wash or formality. The Sardar Sarovar Project provided land for land base relocation package which allows at least 5 acres of agricultural land to 4578 families from 19 submerging villages of Gujarat, in 125 new sites. Naturally, oustees try to have double cropping and more intensive marketing. Thus, the oustees have also to be supported financially to cultivate fruitfully for at least 10 years so as to adjust in the new environment.

As a result, the Sardar Sarovar Project also suffered losses in few lakh crores of rupees yet it is worth as it has awakened the Indian administration from its slumber, which culminated in 2007 policy of Resettlement and Rehabilitation by Government of India for that the PAPs, had to travel to the national capital Delhi many times in processions to ensure that the Centre Government realises their problems. The echo of NBO was later on heard in setting up industries starting from Singoor and Nandigram in West Bengal.

Conclusions

We can arrive at the following action points after foregoing analysis:

(1) Land ceiling laws require to be implemented freshly implemented after their reviews districtwise. Lot of additional ceiling land will be further available for distribution among the landless and poor cultivators. *Suo motu* cases should be started to bring the landowners in the ceiling net. The benami lands of all the landowners should be unearthed and

government surplus land should be kept ready for poor persons even for project affected persons in future as land is going to be scarce and acquisition of land is going to be further more difficult for all governments.

2. The land concealed from distribution should be immediately put to distribution. Reconciliation and survey of such lands should be made. Responsibility should be fixed of revenue officials who had so far kept the poor people deprived of such government land by manipulating revenue records in connivance with the unscrupulous landowners. A drive mechanism should be adopted for this purpose.
3. The Land Revenues Department should be strengthened by way of recruitment of more people and taking away jobs like disaster or relief from it rather land reform should be added as one of its declared priority job.
4. The tenancy should be recognised and tenants should be recorded on the pattern of large operation in West Bengal or through the strengthened or rejuvenated land revenue machinery through selected personnel known for their efficiency and integrity as normal updation of records of rights in the State.
5. Extensive survey should be taken up on government lands or CPR. The appropriate feasible and viable technologies should be adopted to make the waste lands. Suitable species should be planted on these lands specially gaucher lands which will be fast growing and fit in with the local soil and climate. Encroachments from the government lands by ineligible persons should ruthlessly removed and the lands so recovered should be distributed among the local eligible landless persons priority being given to the Scheduled Tribes and Scheduled Castes.
6. Gujarat was the first State to have powerful PRIs. The panchayat bodies specially at the block level, i.e. panchayat samitis should be strengthened so that they become the effective vehicle to carry the land reforms upto the last person in the village or in forest.
7. The provisions of the STOFRA and the Government of India Policy of Resettlement and Rehabilitation should be

implemented. However, Gujarat can make better provisions for relocation or rehabilitation as the policy only lays down the minimum standards.

I am sure that the forward looking, revenue surplus and well administered state of Gujarat will join the bandwagon of land reforms so that the volcano of the poor in rural Gujarat doesn't erupt destroying or prohibiting its industrial progress and advances.

REFERENCES

1. Government of India, Department of Land Resources: *Quarterly Progress Report* (Cumulative) an implementation of Land Ceiling laws for the quarter ending December, 2007.
2. Government of India, Ministry of Rural Development: *Annual Report 2006-07*, Annexure XLVIII, p. 257.
3. *Ibid*: Annexure XLVII. p. 256.
4. *Ibid.*, 1.
5. *Ibid.*, 2: p. 258, Annexure XLIX.
6. LBS National Academy of Administration, Mussoorie: *Empirical Study*, year 1989-90, Vol. I, Table ST-1, p.7.
7. *Ibid.*, 2: Annexure LI, p. 260.
8. Desai, Kiran, "Land Reforms through People's Movements" in *Land Reforms in India, Performance and Challenges in Gujarat and Maharashtra* (ed) by Shah, Ghanshyam, Sah, D.C., Sage Publications, New Delhi, pp. 319-336.

18

Need for Protection of Land Rights of Tribals in Orissa

Orissa was known as Kalinga in ancient days. Now, it is widely known as the land of Lord Jagannath. It has 3.7 crore population as per 2001 Census (approx). It has 81.45 lakh Schedule Tribe population which is 22.13 per cent of the total population which is much more than the national average of 8.2 per cent of Schedule Tribe population in the country. About 75 per cent of people in Orissa depend on agriculture. 80 per cent of these 75 per cent people are marginal farmers having less than 5 acres of land.

Therefore, any land reform measure to be undertaken in Orissa will have to take into account the poor tribals. Second problem in Orissa is large scale displacement of the people due to mining projects, plantations, proposed setting up of large industries and richer farmers occupying lands of large number of poor people. As per estimate by the Ekta Parishad, an NGO, about 1.5 lakh people have been driven away from their lands and forests.[1]

It is also a fact that the tribal belts of Andhra Pradesh, Orissa, Chhattisgarh and Jharkhand even in West Bengal where the Naxalites are most active, are also among the areas in the country that have the lowest development indicators. There have been maximum deaths due to hunger in Orissa in districts like Kashipur, Lanjigarh and Kalahandi. Kalahandi is synonymous with deaths due to hunger in the country. Of course, their level of health, literacy and housing is much lower than their counterparts in Orissa and in other parts of the country.

It is commonly acknowledged fact that the Scheduled Castes now even termed as dalits and tribals are the two most disadvantaged sections of the Indian society. The increasing presence of Naxalites in areas dominated by adivasis has geographical reason, viz. that is hills and forests of Central India or earlier known as Dandakaranya are well suited to the methods of roaming guerilla warfare. But it also has a historical reason, namely that the adivasis have gained least and lost most from 60 years of political independence. There were local leaders from the tribals but after modern education or rising above their own clan equal or higher than general class, they got alienated from their own tribal clan. Secondly, being tradition bound, less literate or educated and having simple life style, the tribals did not even exert their rights at the panchayat levels where they could easily extract lot of benefits or gains of the development process. The present development process is demand based. Unless the baby cries, none cares for it. None goes to the doorstep of a person who is in need of help. The needy has to go for help. This will take number of years to change style of working of development process in India. As a result, the tribals are left behind in the race of development though lot of funds flow for them. They live on their destiny or some *so-called* champion of their welfare.

Status of Implementation of Land Reforms in Orissa

Implementation of land ceiling laws upto December, 2007[2]

(*Area in Acres*)

Returns			Area declared Surplus	Area Taken Possession	Area Distributed to Individual Beneficieries	Total No. of Beneficiaries	SC/ST Beneficiaries			
							SC Beneficiaries		ST Beneficiaries	
Filed	Disposed	Pending					No.	Area	No.	Area
1	2	3	4	5	6	7	8	9	10	11
60335	60076	259	189979	171463	159546	142959	48866	51136	53060	66303

Other Beneficiaries		Area Declared Surplus But Not Distributed	Total No. Cases and Area involved in Litigation		Revenue Courts		High Courts		Supreme Courts	
No.	Area		Area Involved	No. of Cases	Area	No.	Area	No.	Area	No.
12	13	14	15	16	17	18	19	20	21	22
41033	42094	29784	15051	288	7137	169	7014	116	123	3

Area Not Available For Distribution				
Reserved/Transferred For Public Purpose	*Unfit For Cultivation*	*Misc. Reasons*	*Total Area Not Available for Distribution*	*Net Area Available For Distribution*
23	24	25	26	27
5025	2539	10061	27524	1889

Bhoodan Land

(*Area in Lack Acres*)

Area		
Donated	*Distributed*	*Balance*
6.39	5.80	0.59

Government Waste Land

Area Distributed in Lakh Acres	*Number of Beneficiaries*
7.34	NR

Alienation and Restoration of Tribal Lands

(*Area in Acres*)

No. of cases filed in the Courts	*Area*	*Cases Disposed of by the Courts*	*Area*	*Cases Rejected*	*Area*	*Cases Decided In favour of Tribals*	*Area*	*Cases in which land was restored to Tribals*	*Area*	*Cases Pending in Courts*	*Area*
1	2	3	4	5	6	7	8	9	10	11	12
105491	104742	104644	103556	43213	46677	61431	56879	61364	56854	847	1186

The track record of distribution of ceiling surplus land of Orissa Government seems to be satisfactory. However, one fails to understand why 5025 acres land has been reserved for public purpose which is not in any other state. Secondly, 10,061 acres of land has not been distributed due to miscellaneous reasons or due to undisclosed reasons. Even land unfit for distribution, viz. 2539 acres can be put for distribution. If the beneficiaries return or reject the land, then only it should be treated as unfit. This apart from 15051 acres of land locked in litigation, about 17,500 acres land can be additionally put to distribution in addition to other areas of land available for distribution under Bhoodan land and Government waste land.

It is learnt that thousand of acres of land is with Shri Jagannathji Religious & Charitable Trust spreading over in all districts. As this is a government managed trust, the cultivators of the land may be recorded as sharecroppers and they may be asked to give at least 25 per cent share to the Trust if the Trust provides no input for cultivation. But this land cannot be left uncared for. This should not in any case go into the hands of big landowners. The poor people are closer to God. Let them honestly cultivate land and offer due share to Lord Jagannath. The Trust will have to undertake extensive land reform measures.

The worrisome point is that the lands of tribal landowners is not vested to government. This cannot be the approach except in the North-Eastern State where community ownerships is recognized as far as land of the tribal raiyats is concerned. The Government of Orissa is in the mainstream of the national life. They may make an amendment that the surplus land of the tribal landowners can only be distributed among the tribal beneficiaries. It will serve both ways and will balance the traditional and modern outlook towards landlessness among the tribals. Secondly, the land locked in cases of restoration of tribal lands amounting to 847 acres should also be decided fast. Mostly the cultivable land of the Scheduled Castes and Scheduled Tribes are unrecorded. In many cases, land owned by the tribals is physically occupied and cultivated by non-tribals. Due to ignorance and lack of awareness of land laws, the tribals accept the claim over land of the local dominant non-tribals.

The next plank of land reform is conferment of right of cultivation or ownership on tenants.

In Orissa, 2.97 lakh tenants have been conferred ownership on 1.15 lakh acres of land, as in September 2006.[3] This figure can also be increased to a large extent as informal tenancy is in vogue in Orissa.

The Orissa Estate Abolition Act, 1951, aimed at abolition of all intermediary interests including mortgages and lessees of such lands. The Orissa Estate Abolition (Amendment) Act, 1972 was further enacted to extinguish outstanding estates.

But the implementation of land reform laws could not be successful due to sway of landowner class in the politics and in bureaucracy. As a result, the toiling masses in Orissa still migrate to many States in India as they do no have requisite quantum of land to hold on in their villages.

After observing the success of land reforms in the neighbouring State of West Bengal, the efforts were made by government from time to time after the change of leadership to record sharecroppers or to distribute land among the landless persons, but in the final analysis proper impact could not be seen.

Thus, State of Orissa requires thorough review of land reform laws so that they can be implemented by the enlightened bureaucracy. The panchayat institutions are also weak in Orissa. Unless, the rural landless persons or sharecroppers are organized, no fruitful results can come out. The panchayat bodies are also to be made truly representatives and should be protected from onslaught of the rural landowners.

It is of interest to note that in the districts of Koraput, Kalahandi, Bolangir and Sambhalpur, more quantum of land has been distributed than in coastal districts. The tribals or the rural poor could not take full advantage of the same because it was not followed by financial assistance for their cultivation which is a must at the initial stage of allotment otherwise the beneficiaries will be tempted to lease out those lands again, due to their distress or inability to tide over the transitional vacuum of credit with them.

In Orissa, raiyati rights have been conferred on more that 1.6 lakh temporary lessees.

In the three tribal districts, i.e. Kalahandi, Koraput and Phulbani, the incidence of tenancy seems to be low. The tribal tenants particularly Halas were treated as annual farm servants by landowners. The administrative machinery seems unconcerned about the gross violation of Fair Rent Provision in the statute which provides for ¼th of the gross produce. The NSS data observes 7.84 per cent of the operated area was under tenancy during 1981-82. Orissa has prohibited future leases but in practice, it appears that informal tenancy persists. The informal tenants need to be conferred status of occupancy tenants and ownership subsequently.

Tenancy Reforms

1. 'Sharecroppers' should be recognized as 'tenants' in the State tenancy legislation.
2. The Implementation of Fair Rent is tardy and ineffective. It should be vigorous and potent.

3. A special drive should be undertaken to unearth informal tenancy and implementation of Fair Rent.
4. 'Sharecroppers' should be recorded first and then they should prohibited to change the plots as the sharecroppers now and then.

Land Ceiling Situation in Orissa

There is a need for a much closer scrutiny of the returns filed by land owners, specially the need to have a good second look at the question whether landowners who ought to have filed returns under the present land ceiling laws have really done so.

Lot of privileged raiyats are evading dragnet of ceiling laws. These are cooperative societies and Lord Jagannath public trusts and public financial institutions. The poor cultivators, if allowed secured, permanent and heritable rights on such lands will offer much more product to Lord Jagannath as they are true devotees of Lord Jagannath.

For a family of five members a ceiling limit of 5 hectares for the best category of land with assured irrigation capable of raising at least two crops a year, 7.5 hectares for the next category with assured irrigation for at least one crop a year and 12 hectares for all other lands is suggested.

The village record is the most crucial tool for ensuring efficient implementation of either ceiling or tenancy laws. Hence, its proper maintenance is very necessary.

Taking into account the observations on various loopholes in the existing law, it is clear that the best of the bureaucracy supported by flawless law, but unaided by the organizations of rural workers cannot achieve any significant success.

In a large part of Koraput District, the sub-tenants and under-raiyats were not recorded under the first settlements operations of 1962-63. In view of this, it is only to be expected that an important area of OLR Act has been inoperative in the District for all practical purposes.

The allottees belong to the landless category and they have got 0.8 hectares of land. The land allotted is of dry category and the productivity is very poor. The development assistance could be dovetailed to make the land more suitable for agriculture. But this has not happened. Moreover most of tribal allottees have been doing pod cultivation for the lands allotted to them but that alone cannot sustain their livelihood.

> "In village Barafunds of District Kalahandi, the lands in some of the cases were not the physical possession of the allottees as they were under forcible occupation by farmers of the higher castes, some of who were also small farmers. In certain cases after the physical possession was given, the amount of land recorded was less than initially allotted."[4]

However, there was no perceptible change in social and economic status of the allottees of land because of their poverty and extremely bad quality of the land distributed to them.

The financial inputs through banks and other financial institutions can help them to improve their conditions.

The land records in Orissa require through updation for which Central Government has placed lot of funds with the Revenue Department, Government of Orissa. Most of the funds are unutilized. This is high time that land records are updated. As a result lot of concealed land will be surfaced and will be available to a large number of dalits and adivasis in Orissa.

The opposition to land acquisition in Orissa also requires a thorough insight. If it is motivated by some vested interests led by few NGOs, it should be overlooked by the government. However, genuine demands of people should be addressed by the popularly elected government. The tribals and dalits best know the cultivation. Therefore, their right of cultivation and right to land, which is very dear to them, should be attempted to be protected or preserved with best possible efforts by the government and the industries which will be coming up. The jobs should be offered to one member from each family. Thirdly, alternative land should be purchased for them. Fourthly, they should be paid compensation for land in a phased out manner so that at least for next ten (10) years, their livelihood is ensured. Other suggestions as per Government of India's the National Rehabilitation and Resettlement Policy, 2007 can be implemented.

I am sure that after implementation of foregoing suggestions, Orissa will usher into new era of land reforms which is long awaited.

REFERENCES

1. Ekta Parishad: Internet.
2. Government of India, Department of Land Resources: *Quarterly Progress Report* (Cumulative) on Implementation of Land Ceiling Laws for the Quarter ending December, 2007.
3. Government of India, Ministry of Rural Development: *Annual Report, 2006-07*, Annexure-XLIX, p. 258.
4. L.B.S. National Academy of Administration, Mussoorie: *Land Reforms in India: An Empirical Study*, 1989-90, Volume I, p. 128.

19

Implementation of Land Reforms in Kerala

Kerala has a population of about 3.18 crore as per 2001 census. It has 9.81 per cent Scheduled Caste people and only 1.14 per cent Scheduled Tribe people. Total geographical area of this beautiful State surrounded by sea and mangled with backwaters of sea is 38,863 sq. km.

About 50 per cent of Kerala's population depends on agriculture. There is gradual decline in area of rice cultivation from 22,000 ha. in VIIIth Five Year Plan period to 13,000 ha. in the Ninth Plan period. Everybody is concentrating on cash crops like coconut, rubber, pepper, cardamom, ginger, cocoa, cashew, arecanut, coffee, spices etc. Coconut itself covers 9 lakh ha. which is 41 per cent of the net cropped area and provides livelihood to over 3.5 million families. 83 per cent of area under the rubber in the country is in Kerala. So also Kerala is first in tourism industry. It employs about 8 lakh people.[1] Thus, the worry is to ensure minimum area for rice cultivation so that minimum food security can be ensured in the State irrespective of hassle of transport and communication or other hazards or emergencies which may occur at any place at any time.

Land Ceiling Situation in Kerala

The Kerala Land Reforms Act, 1963 is the pioneer Act for bringing about revolution in rural Kerala. It was mended several times to accommodate practical problems in the year 1969, 1971, 1972, 1976, 1978, 1981, 1989 (twice) and all Acts are included in the Ninth Schedule to the Constitution of India and they enjoy the shelter of the IX Schedule. The famous marathon case Kesavananda Bharati *vs.* State of Kerala (1973) 4 SCC was also in regard to the amendments by the Kerala Land Reforms Act, 1971 in which it was held that right to property is not a fundamental right but the essential features of the Constitution cannot be taken away by the legislature as in 25th Constitutional Amendment.

Let us examine how Kerala has performed on this front. As per Government of India's report, the performance of Kerala up to December 2007 is as below:[2]

(1) Area declared surplus	1,70,605 acres
(2) Area taken possession	99,195 acres
(3) Arca distributed	76,676 acres
(4) Total number of beneficiaries	1,65,149
(5) S.C. beneficiaries on 27,832 acres of land	68,240
(6) S.T. beneficiaries on 9,364 acres of land	9,718
(7) Other beneficiaries on 39,480 acres of land	87,191
(8) Surplus area not yet distributed	99,929 acres
(9) Area involved in litigation	49,714 acres

Thus, one can safely conclude that in spite of all tall claims, successive government of Kerala have not done satisfactory on account of distribution. There is no problem for them to distribute about 50,000 acres of land free from court cases. It is not understood why about 70,000 acres of land could not be taken possession of though under court cases, only 49,714 acres of land is involved. It shows deficiencies in laws and also in their implementation. These lands, if distributed can ensure ushering Kerala into another bloodless revolution in the State.

It is learnt that most of the surplus land involved in litigation is at High Court level. The Government has constituted special tribunals and their disposal figures is also encouraging yet their constitution changes as the government changes in the State. That is one of the reasons why High Court has taken up so many land cases under consideration. If Kerala constitutes special Tribunals on the pattern of Karnataka, lot of ills can be taken care of because after all any quasi-judicial forum has to be objective and impartial. At least it should look so.

However, whatever implementation has been done, that is fine. The entire class of rent receivers and intermediaries have been liquidated from the agrarian society of Kerala as a result of land reforms.

Although Kerala does not have zamindars in the real sense of the word, there are a large number of plantation owners who are ultra-rich and influence the socio-economic and political policies of the State. To make the land reforms in progressive Kerala more meaningful, the excess land or fallow land in the plantations must be brought under the provision of the Act gradually without stifling economic growth and to ensure minimum food security in Kerala which is not there at present.

Tenancy Reforms

It is an example of a State where tenancy reforms have been thoroughly implemented. Militant peasant movements and presence of necessary political will, were instrumental in achieving the desired objective. The land to the tiller policy has been nowhere as successfully carried out in the country as in Kerala. It provides a useful model to implement tenancy reforms effectively.

Very low incidence of tenancy was observed in the field survey. The data collected during the 1989-91 by the IAS probationers of the L.B.S. National Academy of Administration amply prove above.

The Kerala Land Reforms Act, 1963 which is one of the most radical pieces of Land Reform legislation is the result of militant peasant mobilisation. The NSS data of 17th Round indicates that the State has 15-30 per cent of operated area under tenancy during 1960-61.

The Act confers the right on the cultivating tenant to pay not more than the Fair Rent and to purchase the landlord's rights so as to become the full owner of the land. It permits the small landholder to resume half the extent of the holding in the tenant's possession. It bans the creation of future tenancies.

The position of tenants conferred ownership rights or rights of cultivation up to September 2006[3] is:

(a) No. of tenants	28.42 lakh
(b) Area accrued or recorded	14.50 lakh acres

Such a small State has done wonder in the field at par with Assam. While West Bengal affords a success model for continuous recording, the rights of bargadars or sharecroppers, Kerala has achieved the ultimate objective of land to the tillers.

Thus, the incidence of tenancy has come down only to 2.05 per cent. But tenancy cultivation is a fact and not a myth. Therefore, progressive government of Kerala should rather lift the ban on tenancy and arrange at least to record new sharecroppers who join the neo-rich farmers of Kerala enriched either due to cash crops like cashewnuts or flow of dollars from the Gulf or other countries.

Updation of Land Records and Revenue Administration

Kerala is lagging behind in these two fields. Only 83 per cent data entry work in computer has been done of land records so far. Secondly, the old revenue set-up requires over-haul which again will involve lot of investment and due administrative attention.

Marching with Time

The Kerala Land Reforms (Amendment) Act, 2002 was passed to put back traditional cashew industry, medicinal plants and vanilla plantation away from the ceiling net.

Similarly, the Kerala Land Reforms (Amendment) Act, 2005, provides that any person in possession of any land, not exceeding 4 hectares acquires the land by way of purchase or an payment of consideration, from any person holding land in excess of ceiling area during 1963 to 2005, shall be deemed to be tenant.

Thus, this provision has further given fillip to record more tenants as owners by way of legislative device.

Thus, Kerala is an example that the best land reforms steps should march with time and should not be dogmatic. The law which cannot or does not pay attention to needs or aspirations of people remains the piece of papers only. It also pulls back the society which is not the aim of any land reform legislation or measure. If the society advances, the land reform beneficiary gets a share in it. However, equitable distribution should always be kept uppermost in mind.

Land Reform vis-à-vis Economic Growth

The Kerala Land Utilization Order, 1967 deals with the problem of food security in Kerala. The State Government if satisfied that it is necessary or expedient to increase production of food crops in any area, Government may by notification in the Official Gazette direct every land holder of that area shall grow over such portion of his land and within such period such food crop or food crops as may be specified in addition to any crop he may have grown over such land. The Collector may by notice call upon the holder of any occupied waste or arable land which is not in cultivation and in the opinion of the collector is likely to be left fallow during the crop season to cultivate the land with paddy or other food crops within the period specified in the notice. If the holder of the land fails to comply with the directions in the notice, the Collector may direct and arrange for the sale by public auction of his right to cultivate the land in question for a specified period which shall ordinarily be three years. Out of the revenue realized by sale of right to cultivate the land, the revenue due on land and other dues to Government, if any, shall be first adjusted and the balance shall be made over to the holder of the land by way of compensation.

Further as per the Kerala Land Reforms Act, the land owned or held by the Government of Kerala or the Government of any other State in India or the Government or local authority or any authority which the government may in public interest exempt by notification in Gazette from the provisions of the Act. The land comprised mills, factories or workshops and which are necessary for the use of such mills, factories or workshops are also exempted from the ceiling provisions. The land belonging to or held by an industrial or commercial undertaking at the commencement of the Act and set apart for use for industrial or commercial purpose of the undertaking are also exempted from the ceiling provision provided the exemption under the clause shall cease to apply if such land is not actually used for the purpose for which it has been set apart, within such time as the District Collector may by notice to the undertaking specify in that behalf.

The extent of land acquired for other purposes are decided by Government.

Conclusion

It can be safely summarized that implementation of land reforms in Kerala is in the right direction. However, a lot is still to be achieved in the field of distribution of ceiling surplus land. Kerala has done also poorly by vesting only 1,000 acres under the Bhoodan movement but whole of the land has been happily distributed. So also in small State of Kerala (area-wise), 4.57 lakh acres of waste land has been distributed up to March 1992. However, further 2,179 ha. Government waste land has been distributed among the landless persons from April 2007 to February 2008. It is correct that within the ceiling surplus land pending for distribution, some quantum of land will be barren or unfit for cultivation. But there are numerous schemes of Central Government under which these lands along with the waste land can be reclaimed and developed.

It is hoped that the same will be done and Kerala will compete with West Bengal and Jammu & Kashmir to be the front ranker in overall performance in the field of land reforms in the country.

REFERENCES

1. *India 2008*, Government of India. Kerala, pp. 971-972, Publications Divisions, Ministry of I & B, Soochna Bhawan, CGO Complex, Lodhi Road, New Delhi-10 003, 2008, pp. 1179.
2. Government of India, Department of Land Resources: *Quarterly Progress Report* (cumulative) on Implementation of Land Ceiling Laws for the quarter ending, December, 2007.
3. Government of India, Ministry of Rural Development: *Annuali Report, 2006-07*, Annexure XLIX, p. 258.

20

Land Reforms in Punjab and Haryana

The land reform measures have not been properly implemented in Punjab and Haryana. It seems that land lobby is ruling the roost in these two agriculturally rich States. Firstly, the ceiling laws were given lot of ropes for the land owners to escape. Secondly, whatever was to be done by the revenue administration to analyse the returns filed and order for ceiling, has not been done so far. Thirdly, most of the large cases have gone to courts either revenue or judicial and are still pending on some pleas or other. Fourthly, in the garb of village common land, lot of surplus land is still in possession of jotedar and big landlords.

In place of implementation of tenancy laws or recognising sharecroppers, new concept of contract farming in agriculture is being floated.

The ceiling laws were enacted in two phases in Punjab and Haryana. In the first phase, the Punjab Security of Land Tenures (Amendment) Act, 1915 and the Punjab Security of Land Tenures Act, 1957 were enacted. In the second phase, the Punjab Land Reforms Act, 1972 and Haryana Ceiling on Land Holding Act, 1972 were passed.

The data relating to working of the ceiling laws in Punjab were collected between 1988 and May 1991 by I.A.S. Probationers.

Their finding is that the land size distribution of the surplus ceiling owners indicates that 50 per cent of the landowners had land less than 50 acres and the remaining 50 per cent had land more than 50 acres. This shows that some of the big landowners have also been netted within the ceiling limit but very large land owners with more than 100 acres have not been adequately captured within the ceiling net. This indicates that the administration machinery has not been effective enough. Most of the cases of land ceiling violation were instituted between 1971 and 1975 (77.3%) indicating that the implementation of old ceiling laws was lukewarm. By 1971-75 the big landowners had already made benami or clandestine transfers to evade the ceiling net or made other legal arrangements for avoidance of ceiling net. Out of the ceiling under old ceiling laws, 51,194 standard acres still remain under dispute in different courts. Similarly, under the 1972 Land Reforms Act of Punjab, over one lakh acres were declared surplus in the state, but hardly 1440 acres surplus land was distributed among 2,140 landless persons, while over 73 per cent of the land declared surplus remained under dispute in various courts.

In Haryana, until March 1989, the area declared surplus under the old Act was 350,991 hectares and under the new surplus ceiling Act of 1972, only 31,048 hectares.

It indicates as per table below that most of the efforts to identify surplus ceiling cases were made only between 1951 and 1960 and the period after 1960 has been weak implementation of the land ceiling Act in State. There is still a considerable extent of surplus land lying underground which needs to be unearthed through rigorous implementation of land ceiling laws.

The position of implementation of land ceiling laws ending in December 2007 is as follows:

	Punjab	Haryana
Net Area available for distribution	9593 acres	72 acres
Area involved under litigation	24,514 acres	4542 acres

In Punjab 40,000 acres of ceiling surplus land and 4,000 acres of Bhoodan land is still to be taken possession of. It is surprising that 11,009 acres land is locked in revenue courts. It shows that Revenue Department of Punjab is not land reform oriented. Secondly, in Punjab 1,03,409 acres of land has been distributed among 27,520 beneficiaries which should have been distributed among more number of beneficiaries. So also in Haryana 1,01,169 acres of land has been distributed among only 29,351 beneficiaries. SC beneficiaries in Punjab were only 11,138 against 28.85 per cent of SC population in Punjab. So also SC beneficiaries in Haryana were 12,687 against 19.35 per cent SC population as per 2001 census.

District-wise area Declared Surplus Under the old Ceiling Act as well as under the New Ceiling Act, 1972, in Haryana as in November 1987.

District	*Area Declared Surplus*			*Percentage of the State Total*	*Total Area Under Exemption*
	Old Act	*New Act*	*Total*		
Rohtak	15,687	962	16,649	4.36	55
Karnal	42,357	1,314	43,671	11.43	550
Ambala	8,994	1,521	10,520	2.75	1,624
Sonepat	11,385	565	11,950	3.38	7,997
Kurukshetra	28,456	2,356	30,812	8.07	22,953
Hissar	72,435	8,097	80,532	21.80	50,022
Gurgaon	6,352	482	6,834	1.79	1,658
Narnaul	4,051	725	4,776	1.25	2,418
Jind	10,614	3,543	14,157	3.71	3,577
Bhiwani	16,956	1,702	19,658	7.76	18,171
Sirsa	114,590	8,678	123,277	32.27	82,226
Faridabad	9,119	89	9,208	2.41	6,264
Total	**350,991**	**31,048**	**382,044**	**100.00**	**227,909**

The tactics adopted by the landowners to evade ceiling laws are generally followings:

(1) *Declaration of Land*: It was based on certificate from the revenue authorities and in connivance with them. As a result, double-cropped irrigated land could be made as single cropped unirrigated land.

(2) *Setting up of fake tenants*: As a result, the land was settled in favour of tenants by way of dwnisti (correction of the past records) and the land escaped the dragnet of ceiling.

(3) Showing children below 5 years as adults by producing fake certificates from some private schools or oath commissioners.

(4) Recourse of prolonged litigation.

There was an anti-ceiling provision in the 1972 Act which allowed transfers upto 20th July, 1952. As a result many lands were exempted from ceiling provisions. The allottees were not provided thoroughfare to go to their lands. Thus the landlords in Punjab and Haryana have been successfully circumventing the ceiling provisions through wrong classification of land in connivance with the officials.

Tenancy Scene

As per survey, by IAS probationers of the LBS Academy of Administration, the concealed tenancy is very high in Haryana as 73.7 per cent of the tenants were unrecorded tenants and only 26.3 per cent were recorded tenants. The average area leased in by pure tenants (8.13 acres) is more compared to the owner-cum-tenants (5.82 acres) and the area operated by them (8.13 acres) is also lower than that of the owner-cum-tenants (10.47 acres).

The in-depth study revealed that the patwari does not enter the names of the tenants as cultivator in *girdawari*. The tenants are also not well organised. The recorded tenants operate below 5 acres, i.e. 40.4 per cent as against 25.3 per cent in cases of unrecorded tenants. It means that people encourage unrecorded tenants. There is a unhappy tendency among recorded tenants to sublet their lands under tenancy which nullifies the object of tenancy. The tenancy is for cultivating the land personally or by members of the tenant's or sharecropper's family.

Generally fixed cash rent (58.7%) and sharecropping (65.7%) emerge as the forms of tenancy at the state level in Haryana. However the incidence of sharecropping is declining and fixed cash rent is generally ascending.

Village Common Land

Village common land in Punjab and Haryana is known as *shamilat deh* and *abadi deh*. Utilisation and regulation of common land in these states is regulated by the Punjab Village Common Lands Regulations Act, 1961.

There is a provision for putting panchayats in possessions of lands vested in them and ejectment of unauthorised occupants. The Collector has been empowered to cancel or vary lease of land vested in Panchayats in certain cases. One-third of these lands under section 5 of the Act can be distributed among ejected or landless tenants and landless persons or small landowners. But presently, this cultivable shamlat land is under encroachment of big and medium sized landowners who are politically powerful.

The provisions of the Punjab Village Common Lands Act have been openly violated, but no action has been taken so far by the government.

There is illegal selling of village shamlat land in Faridabad and Gurgaon districts, which are closer to New Delhi and are part of the National Capital Region of Delhi. These land mafia go to courts and none can defeat them with their battery of the top and intelligent lawyers of the Supreme Court. There operates a close nexus among builders, colonisers, realtors, bureaucrats and politicians. The builders did not stop at shamlat deh. They entered into a tacit agreement with villagers involving protected forest land on lines similar to *jumla malkan* connivance with the revenue machinery.

Contract Farming

In Punjab and Haryana, the small and marginal holdings have not become viable as there is highly commercialised and mechanised capital intensive farming. Even if surplus land is distributed among the poor, the land will shift to the medium and large owners through the land lease system. Similar is the reason for the decline in sharecropping. In view of cropping intensity, the time involved in the completion of a particular operation has been reduced, with which the sharecropper could not cope. Therefore, contract-farming has entered into the arena specially where there is no government procurement under MSP like vegetables, fruits, medicinal plants, pulses, oilseeds, fish production and minor crops. But now in Punjab, it has spread to rice and wheat crops as these have fast rotation varieties. The Punjab Agro Food Grain Corporation prepared a plan to promote contract farming in four lakh acres in the year 2003, nine lakh acres in 2004, 13 lakh acres in 2005, 18 lakh acres in 2006 and 25 lakh acres in 2007. Even in the year 2007, only 20,000 acres land was under vegetable crops.

The contract farming is not successful in Punjab and Haryana so far. It is wrong to say that ceiling laws are the impediments in the implementation of contract farming programme. Similarly, tenant's right to cultivate has to be protected at all costs. The lessor may develop the land properly on long term basis without any fear of handing over the land to somebody else and on the other hand the lessee will also lay aside the fear of losing ownership of the land. In India, the ownership of land is very dear to the farmers. Without the ownership, or sharecropping right intact or undisturbed, he would not give his best to the cause of productivity of land.

The following policy measures will bring improvement in the contract system in the state:

(1) For effective implementation of contract farming system, the Department of Agriculture and Horticulture, Punjab along with Punjab Agricultural University, Ludhiana should be consulted.

(2) The contract farming should be promoted after identification of the area specific for agricultural commodities on the basis of agro-climatic conditions for cost-effectiveness and quality production and also on the basis of compatibility of contract crop with the fellow crops.

(3) Plant material/seed should be selected based upon database (which should be presented to the scientists and farmers). If, however, the data does not exist, testing the material at Punjab Agricultural University, research stations before taking it to the farmers' fields, should generate the same.

(4) Good quality and certified seeds of recommended varieties and other requisite inputs including credit should be provided well in time before sowing. Cost of inputs should be lower than market rate to cut down the cost of production.

(5) Contract rates should be fixed in such a way that it takes into account the average rate for the last three years and at the same time not below the MSP.

(6) Legal validity to the contract agreement should be attached by incorporating all the five essential elements of contract farming, namely quantity, quality/grade, price, time and place of transaction of the produce. Copies of the agreement should be made available to both the contracting parties.

(7) For extending technical guidance to the farmers, the nodal agency should ensure the availability of sufficient and competent staff with the contracting agency to provide quality extension services to the contracting farmers.

(8) Farmers should be given compensation for the crop failure, if the poor quality of produce is due to the fault of the contracting company.

(9) There should be an assured procurement of the produce by the agency and produce should be procured in time. It should

also be ensured that purchase centres are near the production area.

(10) The nodal agency should act as enforcement agency and watchdog to safeguard the interest of both farmers and the contract agency and also to ensure implementation of the programme including processing, value addition and export of the contracted produce.

(11) For contractual farming, the farmer instead of land should be treated as a unit for charging any fee, if any.

(12) Some infrastructure should also be developed by the nodal agency to ease out the situation arising out of gluts and price decline.

(13) There should be effective dispute settlement mechanism.

(14) After the completion of the contract-farming scheme, there should be some mechanism to evaluate the performance for future improvements.

(15) No government agency should be directly involved in procurement of contracted crops; the contracting agency should put some financial stake in the contract. These should not charge cash for seeds and extension services given to the farmers. These costs should be deducted from the sale proceeds of the produce purchased by the contracting agencies.

(16) To cover the risk, crops under this system should be covered under crop insurance and premium may be shared.

(17) Farmers should be imparted knowledge in advance regarding the contract crop so that they can adjust their cropping pattern and follow proper package and practices for the crop.

Conclusion

I do not agree with the protagonist of contract farming in India like Mr. T. Haque, former chairman, Commissioner for Agricultural Costs and Prices, Government of India. It does not and has not contributed for diversified rural growth and poverty reduction in India. The farmers should be organized first. Their landownership should be protected at all costs. The right of personal cultivation by the sharecroppers also requires to be protected at all costs. The legal safeguards should be provided and should be inbuilt so that the private traders or corporations or companies, do not become a class of neo-zamindars in villages. They can organise farmers into cooperative or group farming and marketing on the pattern of agriculture in Egypt or Israel. The land leasing system has also contributed to concentration of land by favouring the medium and large cultivators who are owners of modern implements. The same can be said about the use of the village common land. The weakest part, in the implementation of land reforms in Punjab and Haryana, has been lack of distributive justice in landed property particularly in favour of the Scheduled Castes engaged in agriculture. This requires correction on priority.

REFERENCES

1. Dhaliwal, H.S. & Sidhu M.S.: "Contract Farming in Punjab" in *Contract Farming & Tenancy Reforms*, ed. by R.S. Deshpande, Centre for Rural Studies, L.B.S. National Academy of Administration, Mussoorie. pp. 139-40.
2. Iyer, K. Gopal: *Land Reforms in Punjab & Haryana: An Empirical Study, Land Reforms in India*, Vol. 6, ed. by Sucha Singh Gill, Sage Publications New Delhi, p. 57.
3. Kaul, Neety Advocate: *Land Laws in Punjab & Haryana*, Chawla Publications (P) Ltd., Sector-17B, Chandigarh-60017. 2007, p. 484.

21

Achievements of Land Reforms in Jammu & Kashmir

Jammu & Kashmir is the head of India. It has about 1 crore population as per 2001 Census. Scheduled Castes and Scheduled Tribes constitute 7.59 per cent and 8.2 per cent of population respectively. It has 2,22,236 sq. km. geographical area. It includes areas illegally occupied by Pakistan and China and has large barren tract of Ladakh. Jammu & Kashmir State has mountains and semi-mountainous plains. Naturally, Jammu area is more productive as far as food crops are concerned.

About 80 per cent population of the State depends on agriculture. Paddy, wheat and maize are the major crops. The State produces fruits worth Rs.2,000 crore annually including export of walnuts worth Rs.120 crore.

In spite of terrorism in Jammu & Kashmir basic good work in the field was done just after its merger in the Indian Union under the leadership of Sheikh Abdullah. The people of Jammu & Kashmir shall feel very grateful to that personality and hope that they will have another leader like him so that the State may usher in the final phase of land reforms.

Jammu & Kashmir was among the first States in the country to introduce and implement radical and far reaching land reforms under the Big Landed Estates Abolition Act, 1950. A remarkable feature of this enactment was that no compensation was paid to the landlords. Under this law, the tiller was made the owner of the land while the landlord was permitted to retain a maximum of 182 Kanals (Approximately 22 ½ acres) of land.

Under the subsequent Agrarian Reforms Act of 1976, the rights in a holding of land of any person not cultivating it personally were extinguished and vested in the State. The ceiling of holding in all other cases was reduced from 22½ acres to 12½ 'standard acres' which could be higher than 12½ acres depending on different categories of land of low quality and as low as 8 acres in the case of the best quality irrigated land.

With this enactment, landlordism stood abolished, though this was made subject to the payment of a small levy by the prospective new owner to the previous owner. The Act was implemented within a period of five years and it made available 4.5 lakh acres of land for distribution among the tillers and the landless.

In the area of tenancy reforms, there is already a provision that land owner, from the Defence Services, widows, minors, physically disabled or insane persons or those incapacitated due to old age or infirmity and owners under detention or in prison shall be deemed to be personally cultivating the land even when the land is cultivated by an agent of such a person through servants or hired labourers.

There is also a law banning transfer of land to non-agriculturists and providing for resumption of land by ex-proprietors for personal cultivation within the overall reduced ceiling of 2½ standard acres. The religious institutions are also covered under the Agrarian Reforms Law which ensures that the tenants of lands belonging to such institutions, as also their successors, remain undisturbed.

As regards distribution of surplus land, the law in the State provides for giving of surplus land of tillers and ex-owners, refugees of 1947 having less than 2.50 acres and landless agricultural labourers, in that order of priority. Within these categories, priority is given to persons serving in Defence Forces, Gujjars, Bakerwals and Scheduled Castes.

Government is also undertaking settlement operations to update land records to serve as the data base for developmental strategy in the areas of Agriculture, Irrigation and Rural Development. Simultaneously, work relating to consolidation of holding is being resumed, especially in the areas where Agrarian Reforms Law has been enforced.

Let us further examine in details how the implementation of land ceiling legislation and distribution of surplus land has made an impact in the State. The State has initially achieved 100 per cent mark when out of 59.43 ha. estimated surplus land per land owner, 58.68 ha. per land owner has been finally declared surplus per landowner.

The abolition of jagirs, muafis and mukarries in April 1948 was the first step taken in direction of agrarian reforms after the installation of popular government in 1947. The jagirdars collected rout either in cash or in services. All the benefits from the assigned lands went to the holder of the jagir or to the muafis and none to the State. The rights of 396 jagirdars and 2,347 mukarriders were abolished as a consequence of this enactment of the J.K. Big Landed Estates Abolition Act, 1950. This was further amended in 1955, 1960, 1965 and 1970. To remove the flaws and gaps, the J&K Agrarian Reforms Act, 1976 was promulgated. It reduced the ceiling to a scale of 5.06 hectares from 9.2 hectares. All types of lands were converted into standard acres as per the quality of land. In both the Acts, orchards which constitute an important part of the agrarian economy of Kashmir Valley and forest lands have been exempted from ceilings.

To rationalise the distribution of land declared surplus, the Agrarian Reforms Act, 1976 gave the first priority to tillers having less than 1 (one) hectares followed by ex-owners having less than 1 (one) hectare, refugees having less than 1 (one) hectare of land and landless agricultural labourers taken in order. As per J&K Constitution, these landlords were not to be given compensation as their properties were acquired in the public interest. From tillers, only a nominal price of land was realised. An estimated 4,50,000 acres of land was distributed to the actual tillers within a short period spread over a couple of years. The success can be very well appreciated from the fact that out of 9,50,000 acres of land distributed throughout the country till 1970 about half (4,50,000) was distributed in J&K alone. 5,33,222 persons have been declared prospective owners and absolute ownership has been conferred on 1,62,041 persons as per L.B.S. Academy report.[1]

The ceiling limit as usual has been circumvented in some cases by transferring land within the family. Due to non-classification, naturally landlords exercised their option to retain the last irrigated land to the tune of 22.5 acres. The resumption of land was only for personal cultivation which the ex-owners could not prove yet the progress achieved under the Agrarian Reforms Act, 1976 is not satisfactory. Due to poor maintenance and lack of updatation of land records, the progress has been further slackened. Perhaps the administration got preoccupied with the militancy sponsored by Pakistan. However, there is a lot of unfinished work yet to be done in the field of land reforms in J&K which is very obvious from the figures as per Government of India's report that consideration has taken place in respect of 1.32 lakh acres of land upto September 2006.

It is anticipated that total of 6,60,000 acres of land would pass on to the tillers or tenants. The landlords could still retain over 2,00,000 within the ceiling limit.

Tenancy Reforms

As per Government of India's report,[2] total 6,10,000 tenants have been conferred ownership upto September 2006. Another area of land reforms in which State's record is indeed creditable is tenancy reforms. Incidence of tenancy, both in terms of number of households leasing-in/leasing-out land and land leased in/leased-out as percentage of area owned, has sharply declined in the State between 1971 and 1981. In 1971, 13.15 per cent of the house holds (23.72% all India) in rural Jammu & Kashmir leased-in land. The leased-in area was equal to 8.03 per cent against 10.69 per cent at the all India level of the area owned. The correspondence percentages for 1981 are 5.40 (compared to 18.53 at the all India level) and 2.74 (compared to 7.46 at all India level). Percentage of households leasing-out land decreased from 3.73 in 1971 to 1.54 in 1981. Area leased-out as a percentage of owned area decreased from 3.21 in 1971 to 0.97 in 1981. Matching percentages for the country as a whole area 9.87 and 5.53 for households and 5.77 and 4.29 for leased-out area in 1971 and 1981 respectively. The leased market has thus, moved in favour of marginal and small holdings. The percentage of area leased-in for share produce in 1971 was 86.85 compared to 47.87 at the all India level, the second highest after West Bengal.

The achievement in the area of tenancy reform can be attributed to the various Acts enacted in the State from time to time. The Jammu & Kashmir Agrarian Reforms Act, 1976 made comprehensive provisions that, with a few exceptions which are in general public interest, ownership follows personal cultivation. The Act prohibits the creation of new tenancy and extinguishes existing tenancy except in certain cases. Decrease in the incidence of tenancy has had a positive impact on equitable land distribution.[3]

Concluding Remarks

The State has demonstrated that inequality can be reduced

considerably through serious implementation of land reform measures in the field. It can be safely concluded that there is a basically an egalitarian society in Jammu & Kashmir which every religion including Islam professes. The cultivation is a matter of pride in Jammu & Kashmir. The State stands at the top of the table in the country in the field of implementation of land reforms. However, one gets a setback while rating the State as number one when one finds that Jammu & Kashmir is also the first ranker in violence specially terrorist's violence. An egalitarian society like that of Jammu & Kashmir can allow neither terrorism nor communalism to grow. This calls for deeper research and working out solution in the area. There is lot of grant earmarked for development of the State which is not being fully utilized. It is the appropriate time that Jammu & Kashmir's marginal and small farmers rise in revolt against the militancy as because they are the worst sufferers and they are the only ones who can fight against the militants and defeat their nefarious designs to divide the country.

REFERENCES

1. L.B.S. National Academy of Administration Mussoorie: *Land Reforms in India: An Empirical Study*. 1989-90, p. III.
2. Government of India, Ministry of Rural Development: *Annual Report, 2006-07*, Annexure XLIX, p. 258.
3. Bhatt, M.S. (2000) Land Distribution in Rural Jammu & Kashmir: An Inter-temporal Analysis, *Land Reforms in India*, p. 166, Vol. 5 ed by B.K. Sinha & Pushpendra, published by Sage Publications.

22

Land Reform Scenario in Himachal Pradesh

Himachal Pradesh is a hilly State of India. It has 55,673 sq. km. geographical area and has 60.78 lakh population as per 2001 census. It has 24.72 per cent Scheduled Caste population whereas population of Scheduled Tribe is only 4.02 per cent.

Over 93 per cent of the population in Himachal Pradesh depends directly upon agriculture which provides direct employment to 71 per cent of its people. New industrial hubs have grown in the foot hills of the beautiful State but that is only solving a tip of the problem iceberg in otherwise very peaceful state.

Area of operational holding is about 9.79 lakh hectare owned by 9.14 lakh farmers. The marginal and small farmers possess 86.4 per cent of the total land holdings. The cultivated area in the State is only 10.4 per cent. About 80 per cent of the area is rain-fed and farmers depend on Indira, the God of rains.[1] Fruit cultivation has, however, provided safety net to the farmers. Over Rs. 2200 crore are fetched annually from fruit crops.[2] It has helped to place Himachal Pradesh in high per capita income group state in India.

The agrarian reforms undertaken in the state by the government has also helped a great deal in the advancement in agriculture. In 1954, a revolutionary land reforms legislation, the Himachal Pradesh (H.P.) Abolition of Big Landed Estates and Land Reforms Act was enacted. This Act took away land beyond a certain limit from big landlords and erstwhile rulers and transferred these to tenants on payment of compensation amounting to 24 times of the land revenue paid on the land. In 1972, the H.P. Ceiling on Land Holding Act was passed which had the land ceiling fixed on various lands and tenants who could not be evicted. It also directed that every agricultural family must be given at least five bighas of land. As a result of these measures, 2500 big landed estates were abolished and an area of about one lakh acres was declared surplus and distributed to the landless. In 1974, H.P. Village Common Land Vestment and Utilisation Act was passed to enable the Government, to give shamlat lands to the landless. Under these agrarian reforms, out of about 5 lakh agricultural families, about 4.5 lakh families have become landowners.

The main sources of irrigation are Kuhls (small water channels) fed from perennial or seasonal springs. Well irrigation is possible in some areas near the plains. Lift irrigation is another source of irrigation. Efforts have been made to improve irrigation facilities since the beginning of the five year plans and about 1.60 lakh hectares of lands have been provided with it so far.

Availability of cheap credit, organization of marketing facilities and provision of agricultural inputs are very important for the development of agriculture. Besides govermental agencies, co-operative societies are the only agencies which performs some of these functions. Co-operative societies numbering around 3841, cover about 93 per cent of rural population. Some agricultural societies provide short and medium term credit facilities to their members. Other functions of the co-operatives, is the mobilization of deposits and the marketing of agricultural and horticultural produce. They also pay a vital role in the public distribution system and are running a lot of fair price shops in the state.

Position of Excess Ceiling Land

The progress on implementation of Land Ceiling Laws upto December 2007[3] as per Government of India's report is given below:

1.	Area declared surplus	3,16,556 acres
2.	Area taken possession	3,04,895 acres
3.	Area distributed to individual beneficiaries	6167 acres
4.	Total number of beneficiaries	6259
5.	Number of Scheduled Caste beneficiaries on 2727 acres of land	3912
6.	Number of Scheduled Tribe beneficiaries on 245 acres of land	329
7.	Other beneficiaries on 3195 acres of land	2018
8.	Area involved in 5 cases	8072 acres

By no logic whatsoever, it can be justified why only 6167 acres of land has been distributed out of 3 lakh acres (approx) ceiling surplus land taken possession of. This shows the most dismal performance on the land reform front in the State. It is also not clear why out of 5 court cases, no case could be disposed of for a long time. It seems that there was no requisite political will or administrative will on the part of successive governments in Himachal Pradesh. Central Government should intervene to take the state out of this morass.

Himachal Pradesh has performed well by distributing 17,000 acres of government wasteland by December 2005.[4] But the ceiling surplus land is a better quality land and is available for cultivation just after its allocation whereas the wasteland has to be developed first. The study of a village by IAS probationers of the L.B.S. National Academy of Administration during late nineteen eighties reveals that lot is yet to be done on account of implementation of ceiling legislation in Himachal Pradesh.

In the district of Simla, the village of Karasa in Tehsil Rohroo was selected for study. In this village only one case of landowner having land holding in excess of ceiling limit was identified on the cut-off date. He owned 16 hectare of land in all and 5 hectare of such land was located in the village under study. He had filed returns and the case is still pending in the Civil Court. This shows that even 17 years after the enactment of Himachal Pradesh Land Ceiling Act, no land has been declared surplus so far in this village. The easiest and popular method of evading ceiling is what is commonly known as *Gharelu Taksim* or *Jhangi* or private partition. Most of the big landholders came to know about the ceiling law much before they were brought into force and they all divided their land by splitting in into as many families as the number of individuals in the house. They got the land partitioned under Section 123 of the Himachal Pradesh Land Revenue Act and because of this, hardly anyone came under the purview of the Ceiling Act. The big holdings now are mostly with the few apple growers and they are so powerful that this hardly affects them. The total land in fact taken over under ceiling lands remains very less and is less than a hundred acres for the whole of Shimla District.

The ceiling laws have not been all that effective too. The various Acts were silent about orchards. Thus, landowners concealed lot of ceiling surplus land under orchard until 1974 when orchards were brought under the definition of the land.[5]

In few cases, the ceiling law was evaded by ceiling tenancy in favour of the family members. Even the mutations got sanctioned in connivance with the revenue officials.

There is a practice of collection of Chula Tax in the village by the Numbardar of the village. It is evidence of whether the families are living jointly or separately. In case of part-time of joint family, each family will pay *chula* tax separately. Had this tax system been taken into account, evasion of ceiling could have been easily plugged.

Tenancy Reforms

In Himachal Pradesh, only 3.20 per cent operated area under cultivation is under sharecropping as in 1981-82.[6] It has come down from 10.20 per cent in 1971-72. It means that the informal tenancy has gone underground. Even then 4.01 lakh tenants have been conferred ownership rights or have been recorded as tenants.[7]

Balancing Between Land Reforms and Industrial Development

Under Section 118 of the Himachal Pradesh Tenancy and Land Reforms Act, 1972, the transfer of land to non-agriculturist has been banned.

Agriculturist has been defined as a person who cultivates land personally in an estate situated in Himachal Pradesh.

However, creation of a tenancy shall be valid in favour of a person who is not an agriculturist. It is also permissible for any public purpose under the Land Acquisition Act, 1894. The industrial estates in H.P. have been developed under this provision.

However, a strict provision has been inserted so that the industrialists or service providers who intend to set up their units, must use these lands within a period of two years or further such period, not exceeding one year, as may be granted by the State Government from the date of registration. If he fails to do so, the land so purchased by him shall vest in the State Government free of all encumbrances under the Himachal Pradesh Ceiling on Land Holdings (Amendment) Act, 1999[8]. The Government can assess the real requirement of all industrial units including hydel project and tea garden and can vest excess land which is not being used for the declared purpose.

Conclusion

Himachal Pradesh is dominated by Rajas, Maharajas, Landlords, Zaminders etc. Therefore, ceiling laws have not been effectively implemented. If the State Government can distribute the ceiling surplus land only, it will be a great milestone in the field of land reform not only for H.P. but also for the country because by doing so, about 3 lakh acres of land will be distributed benefiting about 3 lakh landless persons or marginal farmers who have great hunger for land. No other state can accomplish this feat, as so much ceiling surplus land is not available anywhere else. I am sure that public conscious administration will do this job for the well deserving poor people.

The industrial units, hydel projects and tea gardens have also been clearly warned that the unutilized land for the declared purpose will vest to the State. This indicates that the industrial units or employment generating units should not be treated like son-in-laws. They should also be under the discipline of land reform principles.

REFERENCES

1. Government of India, Ministry of Information & Broadcasting, Publication Division: India 2008, Soochna Bhawan, CGO Complex, Lodhi Road, New Delhi-110003, p. 956.
2. *Ibid*, 957.
3. Government of India, Department of Land Resources: *Quarterly Progress Report* (cumulative) on Implementation of Land Ceiling Laws for the quarter ending December, 2007.
4. Government of India Ministry of Rural Development: *Annual Report, 2006-07*, Annexure-XL VIII, p. 257.
5. L.B.S. National Academy of Administration, Mussoorie: *Land Reforms in India, An Empirical Study, 1989-90*. Volume I, p. 75.
6. *Ibid* 5, p. 7.
7. *Ibid* 4, Annexure XLIX, p. 258.
8. Government of H.P. Gazette, Extraordinary: Shimla, 11th April, 2000, Act No. 7 of 2000.

23

Land Reforms in Goa

The erstwhile U.T. of Goa was conferred full Statehood on 30th May, 1987. It was liberated from the Portuguese domination on 19th December, 1961.

It is a small state having an area of 3,702 sq. km. and population of 13,47,668 as per 2001 Census. It has most of the Christian population and the old customary Portuguese laws still hold sway even in case of agrarian relations. The spurt in tourism has upgraded Goa as the richest State in India where per capita income is the highest.

Rice is the main food crop. Pulses, ragi and other food crops are also grown. Main cash crops are coconut, cashew nut, arecanut, sugar cane and fruits like pineapple, mango and banana. It has good irrigation facilities. As much as 43,000 hectares of land is irrigated but the people do not pay so much attention to agriculture as they get easy money serving the foreign tourists. This has changed the whole socio-cultural ethos of Goa, yet that is there. It is hoped that the Goanese turns to cultivation with the same vigour and interest as tourism. Goa is rich in forest cover of more than 1,424 sq. km.

Thus on the whole, there are adequate land resources available to the local populace.

Under the Goa Agricultural Tenancy Act, only 1/6 of gross produce is recovered as rent from cultivating tenants who have all the rights in the land. Further, through the Fifth Amendment passed by the Assembly in 1976, a provision for resumption of land by the landlord has been omitted.

A special provision also exists for granting necessary relief against threatened wrongful dispossession and also to provide for action against eviction. Similarly, a provision has also been made against wrongful dispossession of any land or dwelling house. In the matter of surrender of land by tenants, the Mamlatdar who is the local Revenue Officer has to be satisfied with the genuineness of the request and that surrender is not under duress.

A progressive piece of legislation relates to the protection of homesteads on agricultural land to the persons known as "Mundcars". This legislation has given protection from eviction to large number of rural and semi-urban people from dwelling houses.

There are directives issued by Revenue Department No. 12, dated 19th June, 1975 that every Gram Sabha and B.D.O. will enforce cultivation of lands by the farmers in each community consistent with the spirit of the Agricultural Tenancy Act, 1964, read with rule 15A of the Agricultural Tenancy Rules, 1965. If the landlords does not comply with the mandatory provisions, their lands may be vested to the Government and may be allotted to the local youth willing to take up agriculture specially modern agro-horticulture. The absentee landlords should thus be given rough treatment by the State which they deserve under Section 36 of the Goa Tenancy Act, 1964. Thus, about 20,000 hectares good and fertile land is being deliberately kept uncultivated, cannot be left fallow. It should be cultivated at all costs in the overall interest of the community to ensure high productivity and to ensure the food security in the State. This is also the ultimate object of the land reform measures. In Goa, the land belonged to the village communes and there was no system of private land holding.

The progress of implementation of land reform measures in Goa is distribution of 5,000 acres of waste land by March 1992[1] and nothing else has been done as per Government of India's report. It shows that the political elite are not doing their due and are keeping people diverted on non-issues. I hope that good sense prevails among the popularly elected representatives before they are disowned or boycotted by the people of Goa.

Moreover, Goa has done well in the field of updation and maintenance of land records of the land and tenants. This is the first State which has completed land records computerization. The Dharni Project is an integrated system in which mutation has been automated and updated copies of RORs are being issued to landowners along with locational details. Though legal sanctity has been accorded to computerized copies, issue of manual records has not been stopped because the State is providing computers to the village officers in a phased manner.[2]

REFERENCES

1. Government of India, Ministry of Rural Development: *Distribution of Government Waste Land*, Annexure-XLVIII, p. 257.
3. *Ibid.*, p. 142.

24

Land Reforms in North Eastern States

The group of North Eastern States consists of Assam, Arunachal Pradesh, Manipur, Meghalaya, Mizoram, Nagaland, Tripura and now the new entrant State of Sikkim.

The population and total area profile of these States is as follows as per 2001 Census:

Sl. No.	*Name of State*	*Total Population [in lakhs]*	*S.C.*	*S.T.*	*Total Area Sq.Km.*
1.	Assam	266.656	18.26	33.09	78,438
2.	Arunachal Pradesh	10.98	.06	7.05	83,743
3.	Manipur	21.67	.60	7.41	22,327
4.	Meghalaya	23.19	.14	19.93	22,429
5.	Mizoram	8.89	0	8.39	21,081
6.	Nagaland	19.90	0	17.74	16,579
7.	Tripura	31.99	5.56	9.93	10491.7
8.	Sikkim	5.41	.27	1.11	7,096

Since these states have some common features of land like concentration of hilly regions and concentration of tribal population, we shall take them together from land reforms point of view so that repetition can be avoided.

1. Assam

Assam is the leader of the North-Eastern Region. Immediately after independence, Assam has initiated several steps for protection of tribal lands as well as for land reforms. In 1951, the Assam State Acquisition of Zamindaris Act was passed by which all intermediaries in the land system were abolished in the permanently settled districts of Goalpara, Dhubri, Kokrajhar and Karimganj. As a result of this Legislation, 3628 Zamindari Estates were abolished and the State Government acquired 6.76 lakh hectares of land.

For ensuring equitable distribution of land, Land Ceiling Acts were enacted for rural areas in 1956 and for urban areas in 1976. The ceiling in rural areas has been fixed at 6.68 hectares per family while in urban areas the ceiling is 2000 sq. metres per family. Implementation of the Ceiling Acts have been completed both in rural areas as well as in urban areas. In rural areas alone 2.34 lakh hectares have been acquired. These ceiling surplus lands have been distributed amongst rural landless farmers.

As a part of the land reform measures, the Assam (Temporarily settled areas) Tenancy Act, was passed in 1971 by which the rights and obligations of occupancy and non-occupancy tenants were recognized.

These measures have benefited the poorer sections of the community and especially the small, marginal and landless agriculturists. As a further step towards assisting the similar landholders, in 1979 the State Government have exempted landholders owning less than 10 bighas from land revenue.

Soon after independence special provisions were incorporated in the land laws for protecting lands belonging to tribals by constituting protected belts and blocks. Legal provisions have been made prohibiting transfer of protected lands to non-tribals and even any registered document evidencing such transactions has been made void. In March 1990 Government has further strengthened the legal provisions by providing for stringent punishment by way of imprisonment and fines for violation of the legal provisions in this regard. The administrative machinery has been strengthened by providing whole time Additional Deputy Commissioners and Circle Officers for this purpose.

For ensuring more effective implementation of the land reform measures, as also the provisions relating to protection of tribal lands, requisite infrastructure facilities have been created.

Land Ceiling Situation

In 1958, the ceiling was fixed at 150 bighas per person/family for all kinds of land (except lands utilized for cultivation of tea and ancillary purposes) irrespective of size of family, nature of soil and availability of irrigation. The ceiling was brought down to 75 bighas and further to 50 bighas by two separate amendments of the Act in 1970 and 1972 respectively. A further amendment of the Act in 1975 aimed at preventing owners from circumventing the ceiling provisions by showing a sizeable part of excess land as land under orchards.

The zamindari system was finally abolished in 1955. The Act enabled the government to acquire all the interests associated with these estates like rights to minerals, forests, fisheries, redistribution of rent, etc. It also provided the tenants in these estates to continue to hold land on the same conditions as before.

As per the study of few villages by the IAS probationers of L.B.S. National Academy in Assam from 1988-1991, it was found that the extent of land allotted to beneficiaries in the studied villages was only 70.96 per cent of the total land declared surplus. All the lands allotted were unirrigated and uncultivable lands because these were surrendered by ex-Zamindars. Even the average extent of land allotted was only 0.40 hectare per beneficiary. The Scheduled Castes and Scheduled Tribes were hardly included among the allottees of surplus land. They constituted 0.65 per cent and 0.98 per cent of the beneficiaries whereas 'Other Castes' constituted bulk of the beneficiaries (98.33%). This is a great setback to the implementation of land reforms in Assam. In few cases allottees have left the place but the land records have neither been corrected nor their lands have been distributed to other equally deserving landless persons.

"The Assam State Acquisition of Lands belonging to Religious or Charitable Institutions of Public Nature Act, 1959" had brought about a massive change in the land distribution pattern in Assam. It controlled the powerful feudal lords 'Sutradhikars' of upper Assam and Majuli of Jorhat. More important was the fact that implementation of this Act was done with all seriousness and today almost all satras in Assam have been stripped of the land and are on an annuity. The tenants who already existed on the satras lands, have been automatically made owners.[1]

The following pattern of distribution of land in Assam satisfies the assumption/statement (Table 21.1):

Table 24.1[2]: Number and Area of Operational Holdings in Assam

Size Class (hectares)	*No. of operational holdings according to size*	*Percentage to total*	*Area of operational holdings according to size (in hectares)*	*Percentage to total hectares*
Below 0.5	651,992	33.3	109,486	6.4
0.5-1.0	468,413	23.9	339,812	11.5
1.0-2.0	466,691	23.6	661,528	22.9
2.0-3.0	189,089	9.6	459,399	15.8
3.0-4.0	86,691	4.3	297,809	10.2
4.0-5.0	43,540	2.2	93,108	6.3
5.0-10.0	50,384	2.5	327,236	11.3
10.0-20.0	5,962	0.5	76,195	2.5
20.0-30.0	593	0.03	14,051	0.6
30.0-40.0	181	0.01	6,227	0.3
40.0-50.0	88	0.005	3,897	0.2
50.0 and above	752	0.04	333,825	11.0
Total	1,964,376	100.00	2,882,573	100.0

Source: (i) Columns 2 and 4 are taken from all India Report on Agricultural Census, 1970-71, Ministry of Agriculture and Irrigation, Government, of India, New Delhi.

(ii) Columns 3 and 5 are calculated by the author.

As per Report of Government of India, Department of Land Resources, Ministry of Rural Development, the implementation of land ceiling laws upto December 2007, is as below:[3]

1.	Area declared surplus	6,13,405 acres
2.	Area taken possession	5,75,337 acres
3.	Area distributed	5,45,875 acres
4.	Total number of beneficiaries	4,45,862
5.	SC beneficiaries	43,723
6.	Area allotted to SCs	86,069
7.	ST beneficiaries	42,365
8.	Area settled with STs	58,986
9.	Other beneficiaries	3,59,774
10.	Area for other beneficiaries	4,00,820
11.	Area declared surplus but not yet distributed	1,07,529
12.	Area involved in litigation	38,461
13.	Out of area, area involved in revenue courts	34,459

Thus, there is clear discrimination against SC & ST beneficiaries in land distribution. It may be one of the causes of terrorist violence in the State. There is lot of surplus government land available for distribution. That should be exclusively distributed among SC and more among ST beneficiaries-to undo injustice done to them in land distribution. Not much has been done to restore the tribal lands to the tribals. Out of 4211 acres of land, 1992 cases involving 4192 acres of land are still pending upto September, 2006.

Apart from surplus ceiling land, the following lands are available for distribution in Assam:

Waste land: 5.89 lakh acres[4]

The pace of distribution of wasteland among the landless is very poor. From April 2007 to February 2008, only 284 hectare could be distributed. There are number of Government of India schemes for reclamation of wasteland. Even 100-days employment generation scheme (NAREGA) can be used for the purpose apart from so many types of water harvesting schemes.

I am sure that forward-looking administration of Assam will come up to the challenge and do the needful.

Position of Tenants or Sharecroppers

The Assamese peasantry rose in revolt against the Britishers directly against the 'paik and khel' systems introduced by the Ahoms in the 19th Century.

The lot of the *Adhiars* or sharecroppers did not improve considerably even now though the Tenancy Act of 1971 recognizes *Adhiars* as tenants. The good feature is that only 4 per cent of land in Assam is under tenancy.

The main features of the Tenancy Act of 1971 are as follows:

(1) Sharecroppers have come within the definition of 'tenant' and hence all protections under the Tenancy Act will be available to them.
(2) There will be only two classes of tenants, namely occupancy and non-occupancy tenants as against earlier 5 classes of tenants.

(3) Right of occupancy will accrue on 3 years occupation as against 12 years of earlier law.

(4) Rights to acquire the ownership and intermediary rights and to confer the same to the cultivating tenants both occupancy and non-occupancy tenants including former under-raiyats, have been granted.

(5) An enabling right has been given to both occupancy and non-occupancy tenants to acquire the ownership rights of their landlords by filing application and depositing compensation which is 50 times the land revenue payable for such land.

(6) While occupancy tenants are fully protected against ejectment, the non-occupancy tenant can be ejected on certain specified grounds only.

(7) A limited right to mortgage has been given to non-occupancy tenants while occupancy tenants have heritable and transferable rights.

(8) One-fifth of the produce of one principal crop has been prescribed as uppermost limit for fair rent in respect of crop rent whereas cash rent should not exceed three times of the land revenue. There is a provision for payment of money rent in case of failure of crop which is double the amount of land revenue.

Under the existing tenancy law, the sharecroppers working with the same landowner continuously for three years are entitled to be conferred with the status of 'Occupancy tenant'. Unfortunately, the empirical reality does not accord with the legality. The data collected by the probationers demonstrate unmistakably that the aforesaid mandate of law is not being implemented properly and effectively. It has been rendered a mere paper tiger. Hence, it is absolutely necessary that adequate steps be taken through appropriate crash programme for implementation of the relevant legal provision so as to ensure realization of the mission of law.

Although the Tenancy Reforms Act, 1971, provides that one-fifth of the produce of the principal crop should be paid to the landlord by the tenant as crop rent, in actual practice the sharecroppers are being compelled to pay as much as 50 per cent of the gross produce. This is causing immense hardship to the sharecroppers. It is, therefore, very necessary that rigorous steps be taken for implementation of the legal provisions so as to actualize the benefit sanctioned by law in favour of the tenants.

The ownership rights should be conferred on erstwhile occupancy tenant on the payment of compensation amount of not more than 25 times the annual revenue. Many of the occupancy tenants are continuing in the same status for a number of years as they are unable to pay the required compensation amount equal to 50 times the full rate of annual land revenue. The law demanding such higher compensation should be amended accordingly.

The average area of land leased-in by tenants is very low and is also devoid of irrigation potential. Steps should be taken to generate irrigation potentiality and link them with financial institutions and rural development schemes.

In Assam upto September 2006, as per Government of India's Report 29.08 lakh tenants have been conferred ownership involving 31.75 lakh acres of land. Though there may be some lacuna here and there as land reform is a vast field, the performance of Government of Assam can be hailed as excellent and satisfactory on this front. However, in second phase of tenancy reform, there is scope of large operation type campaign so that the remaining sharecroppers can at least be recorded even without giving ownership right.

Conclusion

Assam has really shown the leadership in the field of land reform in the North Eastern Part of the country. It proves that it is not difficult to implement components of land reforms in this region as people advocate. As there is relatively less consciousness, the assignees of vested land and sharecroppers may be advised to indulge less in drinking and more in cultivation through socio-religious reforms and awareness programmes. Secondly, the revenue administration of this region has to be thoroughly geared up so that the remaining returns of vested lands and cases for restoration of tribal lands are attended on priority. The tribal population of the region deserves its due share in the prosperity of the nation. For this, extensive training of revenue officials outside the State will be required. West Bengal can be one of the favoured destination. Thirdly, technological innovations in agriculture in the region should be implemented in a big way so that man-folk is more attracted towards cultivation and justice is done with the female folk. Their names should be invariably recorded in government leases or pattas as in other states so that their labour in the field is well recognized and honoured.

2. Tripura

Leader in Land Reforms in the Region

Tripura welcomed cultivating immigrants from the Maharajas times as there was plentiful supply of virgin land in the valleys. These immigrants resulted in two and half times increase in population during the period from 1951 to 1971. As a result, it caused heavy pressure of population on land. Over the years, the tribals have been forced to move into the reserve forest areas where unfortunately no land can be allotted to them. In 1973, out of the total population of about 16.5 lakhs, as many as 2.59 lakh people, including Scheduled Castes and Scheduled Tribes were landless.

The Tripura Land Revenue and Land Reforms Act, 1960 (hereinafter referred to as TLR Act) was a revolutionary Act which abolished intermediaries which also conferred security of tenures on under raiyats and sharecroppers.

Ceiling on Land-holding

The TLR Act, 1960 fixed ceiling on land holdings at 10 standard hectares for a family of 5 members. For each additional member above five, the ceiling could be raised by 2 standard acres subject to a maximum 2 standard hectares. Subsequently, the Act was amended and the TLR (Second Amendment) Act, 1974 lowered the ceiling limit to 7.2 standard hectares with retrospective effect from January 24, 1971. Under the principal Act, a family of a person included all children and grandchildren but under the TLR Act (Fourth Amendment), 1976 a family does not include married and unmarried adult sons who hold any land.

The following are exemptions:

(a) land held for cultivation of tea, coffee or rubber;
(b) land held by a cooperative society.[5]

The fixation of ceiling at a very high level and the relaxation of ceiling limit for orchards, sugarcane farms etc. in original Act, and inordinate delay in the implementation of legislative measures rendered ceiling legislation ineffective.

The TLR Act is one of the unique in the country which provides to prevent fragmentation of holdings less than 0.80 standard hectare.

The courts have allowed landlords to defeat in large measure the spirit of the Act. Delays in assignment of land after declaration of it as surplus, have been inordinate. A major source of delay is the preparation of subdivision records by the survey staff.

Most of the allottees are still below poverty line. However, the allotment of house sites has given them confidence in rural society. Many of these allottees have been given credit and development assistance.

The position of implementation of land ceiling upto December 2007 is as below, as per Government of India's report[6]:

1.	Area declared surplus	1995 acres
2.	Area distributed	1598 acres
3.	Total number of beneficiaries	1424
4.	SC beneficiaries	256
5.	ST beneficiaries on 448 acres of land	359
6.	Surplus land not yet distributed	397 acres
7.	Area involved in litigation	59 acres

It shows that the revenue administration is not doing its normal job of distribution of land.

However, Tripura shows a satisfactory state of affairs as regards distribution of government wasteland. So far 1.32 lakh acres has been distributed which deserves acclamation on all counts.

As per the 1985-86 figures, in Tripura total number of operational holdings are 3.2 lakhs. The average size of operational holdings is 1.02 hectares when 7.2 hectares is the ceiling limit. One can conclude that majority of the cases would be outside the ceiling limit except few large holdings from 40 hectares to 50 hectares which should be detected and should be sternly dealt with.

Restoration of Tribal Land

The TLR Act provides for restoration of land and sale of land by tribals only with the approval of State Government. Government have achieved good results.

Upto September 2006, the position is as follows: (GOI's Report)[7]

1.	Cases disposed of	29,068
2.	Area	25,377
3.	Cases rejected	20,041
4.	Area involved	18,123
5.	Cases decided in favour of tribals	9027
6.	Area involved	7255
7.	Cases pending in Courts	1067
8.	Area locked in cases	2355

Thus, there is lackadaisical response to the restoration of alienated tribal land. This is one of the causes of tribal unrest in Tripura. The Government should gear up the machinery for restoration of tribal land. Administrative Officers like Welfare Officers of the Tribal Welfare Department should be invested with the power of restoration of tribal land. After an *in-depth study, Tripura* Government has brought Sixth Amendment of Tripura Land Revenue and Land Reforms Act where the definition of transfers has been made very broad to cover all contingencies. Civil Court jurisdiction has been barred and for alienation of land, stiff monetary penalties as well as imprisonment have been imposed.

Tenancy Reforms

The TLR Act aimed at protection of all types of under-*raiyats including* '*bargadars*' against rack-renting and eviction.

In the cases of 'Bargadar', rent payable by him has been fixed at one-fourth of the produce where the raiyat (landlord) supplies plough cattle and one-fifth of the produce or its value if plough cattle is not supplied by the raiyat.

The 'permissible limit' for resumption of land by a raiyat from under-raiyat for personal cultivation has been fixed at the ceiling limit of 7.20 standard hectares. Thus provision seems to be a photo copy of the relevant provision of the WBLR Act, 1955. There was large scale eviction of bargadars or concealment of share tenancy after enactment of the TLR Act, 1960.

One study showed 20 per cent of the cultivation by bargadar. In 1974, the TLR Act was amended to record bargadars in the r-o-rs but the effort failed to achieve much success. This was because of two reasons, namely:

(a) eviction and leasing out of land under informal agreement; and
(b) unwillingness on the part of the bargadars to incur displeasure of the land-owners.

As per report, only 4.5 per cent area is cultivated through bargadars. As per Government of India's report, 14,000 bargadars have been recorded in Tripura upto September 2006.[8]

As per survey by IAS probationers, things were pretty bad until 1978-79 when the Government launched a special programme 'operation barga' on the pattern of West Bengal for recording of bargadars. Even legal aid was provided to bargadars to defend their cases in courts.

The implementation of laws relating to tenancy due to lack of awareness on the part of bargadars and lack of organizational strength, has been very ineffective. Although maximum rate of rent has been fixed between 20 per cent to 25 per cent of produce, the actual rate continues to be about 50 per cent of produce.

Conclusion

(i) Speedy preparation of 'barga khatian'.
(ii) Checking of benami land transfers from poor tribals to rich tribals or non-tribals.
(iii) Rehabilitation of non-tribal cultivation affected by restoration of alienated tribal land.
(iv) Acquisition of land in excess of the *bona fide* requirements of tea estates and its distribution among landless families.
(v) Extension of irrigation facilities and financial assistance for timely supply of credit and inputs to the small and marginal farmers.

3. Agrarian Relations in Arunachal Pradesh

About 61.9 per cent of the total geographical area of Arunachal Pradesh is covered by forests. Just over 4 per cent of the area is suitable for agriculture operations. More than 70 per cent of the available land is subjected to shifting cultivation. Permanent or settled type of agriculture has thus far been extended to only about 30 per cent of the available land.

The age old tribal economic system based on slash and burn (Jhum or shifting) cultivation survived intact well so far. The Chinese invasion of 1962 turned the region, then known as NEFA, into a sensitive security zone.

The community ownership is the basis of the tribal system. Therefore, there is not much scope for redistribution of land, i.e. land reform. The individual raiyat does not have absolute ownership right over the land cultivated by him. He has the right to hold land as long as he makes effective use of it. As soon as he stops operation, his right over the land ceases.

The Gaonbura or Chief of the village usually allots a plot of land to each family for cultivation purposes. After it has been abandoned, it becomes the common property of the village.

If a new selter, or any household of a village turns some of the communal Jhum land into irrigated terraces usually known as Panikhati, the man who has transformed the land in this way by his own efforts, can claim these rice terraces as his individual property. The owner has the right to transfer the land in anyway as he desires. The instances of individual ownership may be traced in Jorum land and Kamla valley.

An Akas tribal can also lay claim to a piece of land by the mere fact of having wrested it from the forest. Among the Khamtis, the whole community tills the land on cooperate basis.

The Monpas have complicated system of land rights which differs fundamentally from that of the most of other population of the State. Cultivable common land can be tilled by the members on payment of a modest tax collected by in-charge of the village *in-charge* or group of villages. There is no land revenue payable to the Government. The tax is often used for social and ritual purposes.

Though there is no system of giving out land or lease yet the people are now engaging in business. Therefore, absentee landlordism is coming into vogue gradually. Similarly, the disputes over land are now coming on surface.

Transfer of Land to Non-tribals

A non-tribal married to a tribal woman or a tribal wife married to a non-tribal can apply for allotment or purchase of land in his or her name. Similarly, a non-tribal can purchase land in the name of an adopted tribal son or even tribal servant.

Preparation of Land Records

No cadastral survey of the region has been done except the recognition of rights by the village councils.

Suggestions

(1) The rights of the person cultivating even by way of Jhum or shifting cultivation should be recorded in a field book—Khatian or Patta under the village council. That will provide them incentive to improve the land.

(2) The land records should be created so that they may get financial incentive assistance for cultivation from banks or cooperatives like in other States. The Scheduled Areas and Scheduled Tribes Commission of 1960-61 also suggested for completion of records of rights for the tribals.

(3) Thus, we should try to imbibe factors of land reforms with the social fabric of Arunachal Pradesh slowly as the basic object of land reform has already been enshrined in the present community system of land in this beautiful region of the country.

4. Lacuna in Land Reforms in Manipur

Taking a serious note of the possible danger of increasing concentration of wealth, status and power, an attempt was made by the Government of Manipur to introduce the Manipur Land Reforms and Land Revenue Act, 1960. The said Act got implemented after a lapse of 15 years.

About 98.70 per cent of the holdings in Manipur are below 4 hectares and the holdings constitute 94.5 per cent of the total agricultural land. However, more than 40 per cent of the farming population are the tenants in one form or the other. As such the existing rural economy appears to be characterized by the agrarian relations of a submissive type rather than the exploitative type with less impulse of competitive interaction and enterprising exposure. Hence the tenancy reform appears more imperative and demands immediate attention.

The MLR and LR Act has provisions for the transfer of ownership of land to tenants by payment of nominal compensation to the land owners. The provision has not been implemented but will be implemented in a phased manner so that the age-old socio-economic condition of the society is least affected and undue hardship is not caused to the land owners who depend solely on the produce of their lands for their livelihood. Modalities are being worked out in this regard.

The MLR and LR Act has adequate provisions to safeguard tenancy rights. There names are recorded in the Tenants Khatian which is a record of rights. They are not subjected to arbitrary eviction as their right is heritable. Maximum rent is laid down in the Act between one-fifth and one-fourth of the gross produce.

The Revenue Tribunal is dealing with cases under the MLR and LR Act in place of conventional judicial courts. Disputes are very few and the Tribunal can effectively handle the cases.

There are adequate provisions in the MLR and LR Act to prevent alienation of land from a tribal to non-tribal. Though the Act has not been extended to the hill areas, it is followed in spirit. Such tenant is not allowed without permission of the Deputy Commissioner and the consent of the Autonomous District Council. No fraudulent transaction in this regard has been reported so far. Regarding the need for protection of tribal lands from alienation, it may be pointed out that 90 per cent of the total area of 22,327 sq. km., in the State is occupied by 28 different tribes spreading under 5 hill districts. Unlike most other States of India, the threat or hunger of alienation of tribal lands arises mostly due to exploitation of the Chief/Headman and well to do tribal families from non-tribals from outside. These problems arise because of defective land holding system. In the tribal areas of Manipur, 3 different land holding systems operate:

(i) Lands owned by Chiefs/Headmen.
(ii) Lands owned by village community.
(iii) Lands owned by the individual.

In most of the non-Naga villages, the land belong to the Chief who has got absolute right over the land. As a result, the villagers are practically tenants of the village Chief. Even in many Naga villages, substantial area of village land is owned by the Headman. Of late, new well-to-do tribal families have started purchasing large tracts of land from the Chief/Headman. These two factors have led to exploitation of the poor tribal families. There is, therefore, need for restricting ownership of large area by Chief to Headman and influential persons. The danger of alienation of tribal lands to non-tribals is presently marginal.

Fixation of Ceilings

The ceiling on land holdings in Manipur is 5 'Paris' (or 12.5 acres) for a family of five or less. It has been increased at the rate of one "pari" per head up to 10 'paris' (or 25 acres) for a family of ten or more.

The surplus land since 1946 in Manipur has been decreased as 732.86 acres. Out of this, only 36.74 acres was distributed by 15th January, 1983.

As per latest report of Government of India, Department of Land Resources, Ministry of Rural Development, the land vested to the Government and distributed among the eligible persons is given below upto December 2007.[9]

1.	Area declared surplus	1830 acres
2.	Area taken possession	1685 acres
3.	Area distributed	1682 acres
4.	Total number of beneficiaries	1258
5.	S.C. beneficiaries	82 on area 12 acres
6.	S.T. beneficiaries	70 on area 97 acres
7.	Other beneficiaries	1106 on area 1457 acres
8.	Area yet to be distributed	45 acres

It means that the distribution of land is asymmetric. The tribals have not been given one-third share in government surplus land. This may be one of the causes of separatist or terrorist movement being waged in Manipur. The non-tribals are being favoured at the cost of simple and deserving local tribals.

About 150 cases of land involved in court cases before taking over possession, should also be made available for distribution among the landless tribals and the dalits.

On the whole Manipur has democratic character of land. The table, below indicates that small-sized holdings have the predominant characteristic of the State land system in respect of both the hills as well as the valley.

Table 24.2[10]: Estimated Households and Area Operated (in per cent) by size of Operational Holdings: Manipur Valley and Hills

Size class of Household	*Percentage of Households in*		*Percentage of Area Operated in*	
Operational Holdings (Acres)	*Valley*	*Hills*	*Valley*	*Hills*
Operating no land	9.77	7.44	0.00	0.00
0.01-0.49	10.16	5.37	1.12	0.34
0.50-0.99	8.27	6.48	2.41	1.78
1.00-1.24	0.81	4.95	0.40	1.99
1.25-2.49	31.91	27.18	24.73	20.09
2.50-4.99	28.51	35.02	41.24	44.48
5.00-7.49	7.94	11.20	19.91	23.60
7.50-9.99	2.15	1.65	7.43	5.00
10.00-12.49	0.28	0.71	1.42	2.72
12.50-14.99	0.10	—	0.61	—
15.00-19.99	0.10	—	0.73	—
20.00 and above	0.00	—	0.00	—
All Classes	100.00	100.00	100.00	100.00

Source: Economic Review, 1981-82, Government of Manipur, Imphal.

In Manipur, the floor or minimum limit of land holding has been fixed at one 'pari' or 2.5 acres. A good work has been done in Manipur as 32,000 acres of government waste lands have been distributed among the beneficiaries. Reclamation of waste land is generally done through cooperative farming societies. More than 195 of such societies are functioning in the State.

Tenancy Reforms

These include regulation of rent, security of tenure, peasant proprietorship etc. The chief features are as follows:

(a) No defaulting tenants can not be evicted except for personal cultivation by the land-owner,

(b) There should be provisions for helping tenants to become owners.

(c) The minimum rent to be paid by the tenants should be fixed between one-fourth to one-fifth of the gross produce.

Measures Suggested

(1) Like other N.E. States, Manipur should also ensure updation of land records and distribution of records of rights to every land-owner or tenant.
(2) Injustice perpetrated on tribals in land distribution should be made good by making more lands available to them either from the ceiling surplus land or from Government waste land or by way of purchase by the Government from the open market on the pattern of one scheme prevalent in some states like West Bengal, Karnataka etc.
(3) The terrorist or extremist elements should allow politicians—statesmen to come and take rein of the State administration so that they can pay attention to the basic land reforms rather than engaging in fire-fighting job.
(4) Schemes for financing assigness of government surplus land or sharecroppers should be implemented so that Manipur can continue to lead N.E. States in agriculture production.
(5) The tenants or sharecroppers should be recorded in land records so as to ensure them security of tenure.

If the foregoing tenure measures are implemented, violent agitation in Manipur will come down considerably.

5. Meghalaya

The land tenure system is very different in Meghalaya and Government do not disturb drastically the community ownership of land but always involve the community in this matter. Government have strong legislation to ensure that alienation of tribal land does not take place. Proposals for acquisition of land even for public purposes are subject to detailed scrutiny by people's representatives and involve the community.

However, there is not much problem as more than 75 per cent are tribals and there are sufficient land resources available. However, there is a cause of worry as non-tribals are slowly getting entrance into Meghalaya and are disturbing their cultural and social unity. Thus, there are genuine concerns for land records as follows:

(i) Land records would be prepared and should be distributed so that non-tribals may not win land except in urban areas like Shillong etc.
(ii) The land transferred to the non-tribals unauthorizedly should be restored back to the tribals.
(iii) The excess land with big tribal landowners be determined and distributed among the landless or deserving tribals on the advice of village councils or panchayats.

Basically, there is equity in Meghalaya social structure. During the year 1976-77, 34.6% were found marginal farmers whereas 30.1 were small farmers and 26.6 per cent were found semi-marginal farmers. The large farmers were only 0.6 per cent. In such a well constituted or well grooved rural society, there is bound to be peace and tranquility. The problem arises when the rural folk looks at the urban areas and try to enjoy life which is not possible through agricultural production specially in not so suitable terrain. In such cases, only alternative is to spread social and religious reforms in rural areas and arrange heavy dose of bank loans and government subsidies through agricultural inputs like seeds, fertilizers, insecticides and plough and cattle.

6. Status of Land Reforms in Mizoram

In Mizoram, prior to the advent of the British each village was having Chief who had an absolute rights over the land within his jurisdiction. The institution of Chieftainship was utilized by the British solely for the purpose of maintaining law and order in the region. Following the abolition of Chieftainship, a District Council was set up in 1952 under the Sixth Schedule of the Constitution of India. The land administration then passed into the hands of the District Council.

Thus, the revenue administration from the year 1955 remained under the Mizo District Council till Mizoram was carved out from Assam and raised to the status of a Union Territory on 21st January, 1972. Mizoram was granted statehood on 20th February, 1987 under the State of Mizoram Act, 1986. During the period the land administration remained under the control of Mizo District Council a number of Regulations and rules had been framed and Acts were passed by the then Mizo District Council for the administration of land in Mizoram. These legislations still form the basis of revenue administration in Mizoram till today.

Lands in general thus belong to the Government and allotment is made to individuals either for agricultural or non-agricultural purposes. Initial allotment is made for a specific period and a specified purpose. If it is found that the land is fully utilized for the purpose for which it was allotted, permanent settlement is allowed and land settlement certificate is issued. It is, therefore, evident that whatever settlements have been carried out, they are based on individual land-holdings in isolated pockets.

Abolition of Intermediary Tenure

The intermediary tenure system was abolished by the Assam Lushai Hills District (Acquisition of Chief's Right), 1954. Now, no problem has been faced in Mizoram with regard to intermediary tenure as transaction of land is between Government and individuals. No tenancy problems have been faced in Mizoram until recently. As such, there have been no enactments of tenancy laws in Mizoram till today. However, there is possibility of tenancy problem being cropped up in Mizoram particularly in the border areas where there are agricultural potentials.

Besides the Government is deeply concerned with the productive, development and a democratic social orders.

The Tenancy Acts enacted in the mid-fifties affected the largest number of people in the State and brought about the transfer of ownership of a very large area of agricultural land from owners to their tenants.

As a result of the implementation of the Tenancy Acts, by the end of September 1970, ownership of leased land was partly or fully transferred to the tenants in about 8.75 lakh tenancy cases, out of a total of about 26 lakh recorded tenancy cases in the State. The total area of land of which the ownership was transferred to the tenants was around 10.4 lakh hectares.

The Mizoram Agricultural Lands (Ceiling on Holdings) Act, 1961 came into force on 26th January, 1962. An area measuring 1,24,493 ha was declared surplus under the provisions of the said Act.

The ceilings were lowered in 1975, as a consequence of which an area of 1,60,962 ha. was declared as surplus. Out of the total area of 2,85,455 hectares declared as surplus under these enactments, 2,51,522 ha. have already been distributed.

Lands measuring 18,422 ha. had to be excluded from distribution because this was either uncultivable or was needed for a public purpose or was involved in exemption claims. An area of 6204 hectares is involved in litigation.

The proportion of Scheduled Castes and Scheduled Tribes allottees in Mizoram has been as high as 53 per cent. The ceiling which was initially imposed on agricultural holdings in 1962 was substantially lowered within a short span of just about 13 years.

A good work has been done in Mizoram by distribution of about 74,000 areas of Government waste land by September 2006. Such a tempo of land reforms requires to be maintained and should be encouraged.

7. Scenario of Land Reform in Nagaland

Nagaland is the eastern most state of India. The density of population as per 1981 census was 47 per sq. km. The State is hilly with deep gorges and steep terrains with a few valleys on the border of Assam. The topography being severe, land available for cultivation forms small proportion of the geographical area.

As heavy majority of population is tribal and matters relating to land are guided by the customary laws which means ownership of the community on land. The concept of ownership, therefore, varies from tribe to tribe. The Jhumland Act of 1970 governs following types of ownership.

Most part of Nagaland comes under shifting cultivation. Therefore, under the broad regulation of Jhumland Act of 1970, the following types of ownership are found.

(1) "Except in the Sema and Konyak areas, the land is owned by the Village Community as a whole or by a clan within the village or by an individual. There is no record for conferring such ownership rights but it is usually determined by tradition and customary laws. The village Councils are the authority for directing community actions on land and interpretation

of customary laws in regard to ownership of use of land by individual". This is the general rule prevailing in the State.

(2) However, individual ownership has been established or getting established where terrace cultivation is practised or has been introduced. Terrace is mainly practised among the Angamis and Chakhesangs and among the individual, right on terrace land is found. The right is permanent, heritable and transferable. There are few cases among them where the land is held jointly by the clan. In such cases, the village elders decide by whom the land should be cultivated, and generally it goes to the eldest or poorest of the clan. Such clan lands cannot be sold or transferred by any individual. Among the Angamis and Chakhesangs, the land goes from the father to the sons, but not to the daughters, and it is the father who will distribute his landed and other properties according to his sweet will amongst his sons; but usually the lion's share goes to the eldest son in expectation that he would look after others. Daughters are not entitled to any landed property, but in rare cases the father by a special gift may give her some land. If the father dies without a male heir the property goes to his nearest kin.

(3) Among the Ago tribe the ownership of land is based on two systems. First, the cultivable land is held by the village community or the clan or even the individuals and secondly, the forest land is held by the entire village collectively. In case of cultivable land the village or clan elders distribute it among the individuals for cultivation for a particular period of Jhum cycle. In case of individual holding, it goes directly from father to sons. But forest land is controlled by the village Council and the people are allowed to use it as and when needed. So far individual land is concerned, it goes directly from father to sons and not to daughters. Females are not allowed to inherit landed properties. If a man dies without a male heir, the land goes to his nearest kin, but however, if he is extremely desirous to give a part of his land to his daughter he can do so with the consent of the village Council who will arbitrate in the matter. Aoo as well as others are very democratic and considerate people and so a landless person is also allotted land for cultivation for a particular period.

(4) Among the Sema villages, all the land is held by the Chief of the village and he allows others to cultivate it, but his cultivators do not own the land, and all these landless peoples are called Mughemi or dependants of the Chief. But in practice the cultivators own it by inheritance.

(5) Among the Konyaks there is the system of Ang or Kingship. The Ang is the owner of all the lands of the village and he distributes it among his subjects to cultivate and possess. Though technically the Ang is the owner of the lands, in practice the cultivators own it by inheritance.

(6) The system of recorded individual holdings is found in Dimapur Mouza (259 sq. km.) which is a plain place in the south-west of the State and adjoins the plains of Assam. Here the Assam Land and Land Revenue regulations apply.[11]

The prevailing form of cultivation in Nagaland is Jhuming and at the same time a small percentage of the land is under terrace. In both the forms the main crop is rice. Table 24.3 shows the land use pattern in Nagaland.

Table 24.3: Land use pattern in Nagaland

	Particulars	Area in sq. km.	Percentage of Total Geographical Areas
1.	Land set apart for cultivation	6,905	41.9
2.	Reserved Forests	329	2.0
3.	Protected Forests	518	3.1
4.	Civil use	388	2.4
5.	Remaining areas including village, forest, wasteland, etc.	8,345	50.6

From Table 24.3 it is seen that the land set apart for cultivation is 41.90 per cent of the total geographical area of the State.

Since everybody cultivates his own land and there is practically nobody without land. There is no landless person in the State. On the other hand, during the peak agricultural operation, same families borrow labour from other families and repay the labour by working in their fields. Thus, no external credit facilities are needed. But there is a need to introduce credit facilities or if not heavy subsidies for cultivation by the government so that agricultural production may improve and land will itself have better meaning for them rather than going for an industrial society which will take many decades.

Thus, no fresh land reforms are required. But there is an urgent need for cadastral survey and preparation of land records and giving over to the village councils or to the individual farmers or owners so that permanent peace may prevail and they may not be misguided by the militant outfit, for violence on one alibi or pretext of discrimination against them by State or the Central Government.

8. Status of Land Reforms in Sikkim

Sikkim is bountiful with nature situated in the lap of the Himalayas. The altitude varies from 800ft, above sea level to above 28,000ft, at Kanchenjunga—the second highest peak in the world. The area between 7000ft and 14,000ft is almost unhabited except some seasonal grazers like the Bhutias and Sherpas as or Gurungs visit the area which is generally covered with glaciers. The state is surrounded by China-Tibet, Nepal, Bhutan and West Bengal on the North, West, East and South respectively.

The oldest form of land measurement in Sikkim was Dhoors or paces of lands. Taxes from the tenants were collected from the earliest period by the Zamindars. But they could not sell the land.

The raiyats had to render free services to their landlords, mondals (headman). The landlords meaning the kazis and 'thikader' had magisterial power in civil and criminal matters and could easily dispossess a raiyat if he did not satisfy him.

According to Government Notification No. 2627/2727 dated 06-07-1948, the private estates and monasteries' lands were abolished.

As per notification in 1950, the raiyats were classified into two broad categories—

1. Primary Holders—They are known as bestowals also. It means a person who has right to possess, use, sell, mortgage and inherit the land.

2. Secondary Holders—It refers to Kutiadars and Adhiadars. A kutiader means a sharecropper who will be giving half of the produce to the primary holder.

Land Ceiling

In 1974, a land ceiling was imposed *vide* Notification No. 8545/G that the bastiwallas could not hold land more than 20 acres, mondals not more than 30 acres and Kazis, Thikaders etc. not above 100 acres. The last category could hold upto 200 acres with government's approval. However, there was no limitation imposed on their holding of Cardamom fields, orange garden, homestead, fodder and fuel forests etc.

The revision of agrarian laws for effective implementation of land reforms has been an important objective of the Government. Sikkim Government already has a land reforms law which aims at effectively implementing these policies so as to eliminate poverty and bring about a more equitable distribution of land amongst the people. The State had enacted the Sikkim Agriculture Land Ceiling and Reforms Act in 1977 which provides for the implementation of the above objectives. The cadastral survey in the State has also already been completed a decade ago by the government and most of the aspects relating to land reforms have been covered under the Act and its provisions. The surplus lands have already been identified and the government is now attempting to achieve the allotment of such surplus lands to the beneficiaries.

The State legislature has already passed a legislation, namely the Sikkim Transfer of Land (Regulation) Bill, 1989 which will be implemented after the assent of the President. This Bill aims at supplementing the old laws which protect the interest of the tribals of Sikkimese origin of the State. The old Sikkim laws of the State like the Revenue Order No. 1 of 1917 and the Proclamation of 1956 on the subject have the protection under Article 371(F) of the Constitution. The Sikkim Agricultural Land Ceiling and Reforms Act, 1977 provides for restriction on alienation of lands by the tribals.

Therefore, the State has already taken ample measures for safeguarding and protecting the lands of the tribals with proper legislations.

The Government is also proposing to compile, maintain and update the land records and monitor and computerizes these with a scheme of computerization of the land revenue administration. This by itself will go a long way of providing remedial benefits to the rural masses.

Tenancy Reforms

It was only after the Sikkim Cultivators' (Protection) Act, 1975 was enacted that these people were legally provided with protection of tenancy. But since the Government did not maintain any tenurial records, the above provisions did hardly had any effect. The State Government also enacted a law being the Sikkim Cultivators Protection Act, 1985 for the protection of the rights of cultivators. There are hardly incidents of atrocities against tenants in any major measure as law is implemented with sincerity and in spirit. There are effective provisions under this Act to ensure that there is no arbitrary termination of cultivation, as well as providing for restoration of possession of the cultivation. It is found that the sharecroppers are more interested in cultivating irrigated land than non-irrigated ones.

Secondly, the lower altitude villages in general have a higher percentage of sharecroppers as the production is higher in such lands.

Conclusion

A large number of the landowning people are otherwise very poor and have little or no difference with the sharecroppers or agricultural labourers. There is lot of hiatus between the most affluent landowners and the poorest of the poor. The peasants' lot has improved little over the past, few decades after the 'No Rent Movement' of 1949 and the 1973 Movement, which were political. However, economic differences and creating caste and ethnic conflicts between the Lepchas or Bhutias and the Nepalese on the other hand can be done away with if the land reforms are implemented with requisite 'political-will' in spite of temporary set backs. Then, the 'Sunrise' State will scatter rays the way to other small states and UTs also.

Summary

The six North Eastern States are called as six golden sisters, which are great nature reservoirs of the country. The Supreme Court has rightly prevented deforestation of forests in the area so that the natural beauty can be maintained. As a result, the tourism is increasing day by day. So is the case with its twin diamond brother States, viz., Tripura and Sikkim. There is basic stability in the agriculture society of the region, which is very evident from the following Table 24.4.

Table 24.4[13]**:** Distribution of Holdings and Area by Size Class, 1970-71 and 1976-77

(*In percentage*)

State/UT		*Marginal (below 1 hec) 1970-71 to 1976-77*		*Small (1 to 2 hec) 1970-71 to 1976-77*		*Semi-medium (2 to 4 hec) 1970-71 to 1976-77*		*Medium (4 to 10 hec) 1970-71 to 1976-77*		*Large (10 hec & above) 1970-71 to 1976-77*	
Assam	H	57.0	59.6	23.8	22.6	14.0	13.1	4.8	4.3	0.4	0.3
	A	17.7	19.3	23.0	23.3	26.3	26.3	18.1	17.2	15.1	14.0
Arunachal	H	7.7	9.7	12.0	18.3	25.9	27.4	36.4	27.3	18.1	17.3
	A	0.7	1.0	2.8	4.4	11.6	12.8	35.0	28.3	49.9	53.6
Manipur	H	40.9	49.5	42.9	34.8	15.0	14.2	1.2	1.5	0.03	0.03
	A	18.9	24.0	44.0	38.6	31.6	30.9	5.1	6.3	0.4	0.3
Meghalaya	H	36.8	34.6	34.6	30.1	24.1	26.6	4.3	8.1	0.2	0.6
	A	14.9	10.7	31.1	22.7	38.9	38.7	3.9	23.4	1.3	4.5
Mizoram	H	0	33.7	0	39.6	0	23.0	0	3.4	0	0.2
	A	0	15.1	0	33.6	0	374	0	11.6	0	2.3
Nagaland	H	9.4	9.5	17.6	14.0	27.8	19.4	31.6	32.6	13.6	24.5
	A	1.1	0.8	4.0	2.9	13.7	7.7	34.8	29 1	46.3	59.6
Tripura	H	69.5	58.8	18.8	24.4	8.9	13.3	26	3.3	0.3	0.2
	A	27.6	22.9	26.0	29.5	23.6	30.3	14.0	15.0	8.7	2.3
All India	H	50.6	54.6	19.1	18.0	15.2	14.3	11.3	10.1	3.9	3.0
	A	9.0	10.7	11.9	12.8	18.6	19.8	29.8	30.4	30.9	26.3

Note: 'H' and 'A' stands for 'Holding' and 'Area' respectively.

But Governments cannot sit contended on the plank of land reform alone. The expectations of better consumption life have increased considerably in the area alongwith other parts of the country. Secondly, the educated youth does not want to go for cultivation personally and exclusively. To avoid conflagration of violence, the State Governments and Central Government should have huge investment in agriculture in the region to make agriculture or cultivation remunerative in the region if not at par with other avocations by means of technological innovations like green revolution, white revolution and also through plantation of new cash crops like rubber, tea, etc. in the hilly and hostile terrains of the region. The updation of land records is also one of the major area of priority for the region.

I am sure that the peaceful people of the region will shun violence soon and will join the train of high production and high consumption with other parts of future prosperous India.

REFERENCES

1. L.B.S. National Academy of Administration Mussoorie: Land *Reforms in India, An Empirical Study, 1989-90*, pp. 98-99.
2. Goswami, Atul: *Land Reforms and Peasant Movement*, Omsons Publications, Jasomanta Road, Pan Bazar Guwahati, p. 195, 1986, p. 232.
3. Government of India, Department of Land Resources: *Quarterly Progress Report* (cumulative) on Implementation of Land Ceiling Laws for the quarter ending December, 2007.
4. Government of India, Ministry of Rural Development: *Annual Report, 2006-07*, Annexure-XLVIII, p. 257.
5. *Ibid.* Annexure—XLIX, p. 258.
6. *Ibid.* 3.
7. *Ibid.* 4. Annexure—LI p. 260.
8. *Ibid.* 4, Annexure—X LIX p. 258.
9. *Ibid.* 3.
10. *Ibid.* 2, p. 172.
11. *Ibid.* 2, pp. 185-187.
12. *Ibid.* 2, p. 187.
13. *Ibid.* 2, p. 20.

25

Land Reforms in Union Territories

The 7 (seven) Union Territories are Andaman & Nicobar Islands, Chandigarh, Dadra & Nagar Haveli, Daman & Diu, Lakshadweep, NCT of Delhi and Pondicherry. The land reform is not very important factor in UTs because UTs have small area and small population. Secondly, all UTs except Andaman & Nicobar Islands, Lakshadweep and Dadra and Nagar Haveli are urbanized. There is hardly any scope of land reform. If there are few farmers, they also want to become businessmen or industrialists. However, to ensure sustainable development of UTs, basic farming land should be preserved and highly subsidized to save those UTs from unforeseen market exploitation or even starvation of large population like in Delhi. Let us examine the state of affairs of land reform UT-wise.

1. Andaman & Nicobar Islands

A & N Islands are famous for its blue sea water, dense forests and its primitive tribals.

They have 3,56,152 population as per 2001 Census.

These have 29,000 tribals who constitute 8.27 per cent of its population. They have an area of 8,249 sq. km.

There are 38 inhabited Islands, including 25 in the Andaman district and 13 in the Nicobar district.

There are tribes, namely Andamanese, Ongo, Jarwa, Sentinalese, Nicobarese & Shampens. Jarwas are still hostile and have naked bodies and live on forests by hunting and fishing. Constant attempt is being made to bring them into the mainstream but the efforts are not so successful. About 8068.71 hectares of land under agriculture and plantation out of total 51,694.35 hectare was damaged in December 2004 Tsunami/Earthquake. Coconut and areconut are main cash crops of the Islands. Recorded forest is 7,171 sq. km. which is 87 per cent of the land area.

There is a need to balance the great natural resource of the country and also to provide adequate living of the people of Islands so that they may not be deprived of in their own land.

In this Union Territory, Land Revenue and Land Reforms Regulation, 1966, is operative on revenue land. 86 per cent of the areas in this Union Territory is comprised protected/reserved forests to which Land Revenue Regulation, 1966 does not apply. Almost the entire Nicobar district excluding 7 revenue villages in Great Nicobar has been declared as tribal area where also the revenue regulations are not applicable.

No intermediary tenure exists in the territory. However, sub-letting of land by a tenant is allowed under the specific conditions. Regarding tenancy system, the ownership of the land is absolutely vested with the Government and land is allotted to the individuals under these Rules. The Government is the owner of the land of these islands and land allotted to the individuals by the Government can also be resumed. The licensees are conferred Occupancy Right who cultivate the land continuously for a period of two years. There is no bar in transfer of the interest of an occupancy tenant and grantees which is allowed with the permission of competent authority to non-agriculturist. No land ceiling has been prescribed in this territory. However, 10 acres of paddy/ hilly land was allotted to such settlers in colonization schemes. 5 acres of paddy land and 1 bigha of Homestead land was allotted to such settler settled under Rehabilitation Scheme and 10 acres of agricultural land and 1 acre of Homestead land was allotted to each settler settled under the scheme regarding settlement of ex-servicemen.

Homestead Rights

The Administration is allotting land to landless poor persons free of cost and to the non-poor on payment of premium at prescribed rates. The Administration is also providing credit facilities for construction of houses to the extent of Rs. 23,500 for LIG and Rs. 40,000 for MIG housing schemes. It has also taken up the work of updating and modernization of land records for 197 revenue villages of Andaman district, 7 villages in Nicobar district and the Port Blair township.

The administration had also decided to issue Patta-Pass books to all the tenants after the records are updated.

Regarding, consolidation of land holdings, the position in these islands is that the land of the individual agricultural holdings is located in compact areas which is manageable conveniently and therefore, there is no need for consolidation.

There is peoples' involvement at the time of allotment of land to individuals at Panchayat level and also at the higher pradesh council level. They are also fully alive to their requirements and rights.

Protection of Aboriginal Tribal Land

In Andaman & Nocobar Islasnds, (Protection of Aboriginal Tribes) Regulation, 1956 takes care of provision of alienation of tribal land which provides that no member of an aboriginal tribal except with the previous sanction of the Administrator can transfer by way of sale, exchange, mortgage, lease or otherwise any land to any person other than a member of an aboriginal tribe and no such land can be attached or sold in execution of any decree or order of the Government. Such transfer, attachment or sales of any land are illegal in this territory and therefore, the interests of the tribals are safeguarded by the provisions of Regulation of 1956.

The challenge before the administration is to put the aboriginal sons of the soil into actual possession and ownership of land and to ensure that they use these lands properly through cultivation. Crop is their choice. India is not a country who will leave their aboriginal people in forest museums unlike the most developed countries of the world, viz., USA and Australia.

Thus, there is no problem as local tribals are concerned. The influx of the outsiders is to be checked. If it cannot be checked, then usual regulation of ceiling and recording of sharecroppers should be brought in place. There is no point in sitting in ivory tower saying that government regulation to settle land can manage the land. It has never been successful specially in democracy. It is better to give a fresh look, prepare updated land records and have regular statutes to regulate agrarian relations in the Islands.

2. Chandigarh

Chandigarh UT is called the 'Beautiful City'. It is the best laid down city in India and functions as buffer between the two States of Punjab and Haryana.

It has 9,00,635 population and covers an area of 114 sq. km. only.

There are negligible cultivable lands on the foothills of Shivalik hills. The village Rampur Kalan has the Sewage Treatment Plant for the city. That can be one centre used for selected vegetable cultivation also along with some small villages. These villages will soon be converted into hinterland of the urban areas. Therefore, there is not much need for land reform in UT of Chandigarh.

3. Dadra and Nagar Haveli

Thus UT has 2,20,490 population as per 2001 Census. Out of this population 62.24 per cent are tribals. It has total area of 491 sq. km. Silvassa is its capital. It has 21,115 hectares under cultivation.

Forests covers 40 per cent of the total geographical area. Major crop is paddy. These tribals will be soon converted into urban population. Perhaps, land reform cannot catch hold of them in view of fast urbanization.

In D and N Haveli, 7267 acres of land was found surplus under Dadra & Nagar Haveli Land Reforms Act, which has been distributed among 3749 beneficiaries upto December 2007[1] as per Government of India's report. Similarly, 7000 tenants or sharecroppers have been conferred ownership or their right of cultivation protected on 21,000 acres of land.[2] Unfortunately 850 acres of area is still locked in court cases at the High Court in 11 cases which require to be disposed of soon so that landless persons or eligible beneficiaries can be benefited by distribution of government vested land.

I am sure that UT administration will come up to the expectation and will do the needful early.

4. Daman and Diu

Daman & Diu has 1,58,204 population. Its geographical area is 11,259 Km.

Daman & Diu was a colony held by the Portuguese upto 1961. The Portuguese land laws were prevalent. But these are slowly going in oblivion. Total irrigated area is 393.393 hectares and un-irrigated area is 3304.73 hectares as per Agricultural Census 2000-01. The net area under cultivation was 3375.65 hectares.

The area is full of industries. There are 2930 small scale and medium scale industries. The industry hub is gradually taking over agricultural land. And land reform has gone hiding in the small UT where cultivators are not organized at all.

5. Lakshadweep

The UT has 60,650 population as per 2001 Census and has an area of 32.99 km. It is in down south. It has agrarian islands. Fish resource is enough for islands. Lakshadweep stands first in coconut production in the country. There are no agrarian problems and there is no demand for land. However, land records should be updated in the UT to start with the land reform work in the UT.

6. NCT, Delhi

NCT, Delhi, has a population of 138 lakh people as per 2001 population. It has 148,339 km. area. There is no Scheduled Tribe population but Scheduled Caste population is staggering 16.92 per cent which itself calls for land reform measures.

There are few villages in NCT, Delhi. But those are villages in names. Their activities fully bear urban life style. The emphasis is now shifted from food crops to vegetables and fruit crops, dairy and poultry farming, floriculture etc., as these are more remunerative than food crops in the territory.

There are the required statutes on land reforms like the Delhi Land Reforms Act, 1954, the Delhi Land Holdings (Ceiling) Act, 1960. The Delhi Land Reforms Act, 1954 is on the pattern of U.P. Zamindari Abolition and Land Reforms Act, 1950. It *inter alia* provided for termination of intermediaries rights, classification of raiyats into Bhumidhar, Asamis and Sirdar tenants, role of Gaon Sabha and Gaon Panchayats in land reforms works, cooperative farms from Sections 163 to 180 etc. The Delhi Land Holdings (Ceiling) Act has been amended in 1976 to accommodate urbanization and to plug loopholes. Even then the builders and real estate owners are likely beneficiaries of all government laws. Under the benami names of the land reform beneficiaries, the builders are there. On the other hand, under the garb of agriculture, large farmhouses have come in existence. There is agriculture on those farms but the sharecroppers are not recorded because they are paid high daily wages. Thus, there is no possibility of tenancy reforms in NCT, Delhi. If Government of NCT, Delhi, can preserve adequate agricultural land for cultivation for unforeseen situation like war, blockage, floods, etc., that will in itself be considered an achievement. It is more essential because the country's capital is situated within NCT of Delhi. The efficiency is there in revenue administration. About 99 per cent entry work has been completed and computerized copies of R-o-Rs are being issued to land owners in West District of NCT, Delhi. But corruption is plaguing the efforts of implementation of land reforms in NCT, Delhi.

The position of implementation of land ceiling laws upto December 2007 as per Government of India's report is as below:[3]

(1) Area declared surplus	1132 acres
(2) Area taken possession	394 acres
(3) Area distributed	394 acres
(4) No. of beneficiaries	654
(5) No. of S.C. beneficiaries on 277 acres	495
(6) Other beneficiaries on 117 acres	159
(7) Area involved in litigation in 13 no. of cases	183 acres

6000 acres of wasteland has also been distributed in NCT, Delhi.

Thus, there is a huge gap between cultivable land area declared surplus and taken over possession.

About 500 acres is being pocketted by the benamidars, land mafia or builders in connivenance with the land revenue machinery. This calls for thorough enquiry and necessary corrective actions. Poorest of the poor can be settled on these lands on the pattern of the cooperative farming under the full management by the Government as in Pune Farm in Maharashtra. This will also ensure basic food security for the NCT, Delhi. Similar Cooperative Farming can be experimented in cases of other lands allotted to the beneficiaries provided land is available in one or two blocks.

Thus, implementation of land reform in Delhi calls for introspection and some innovative steps keeping with the great tradition of the country's capital.

7. Pondicherry

UT of Pondicherry has 479 sq. km. area surrounded by sea and has a population of 9,74,345 as per 2001 Census. There is no tribal population but like NCT, Delhi, there are 16.19 per cent Scheduled Caste population.

The UT is famous for Aurobindo Ashram. Nearly 24.37 per cent of the population of the Union Territory is engaged in agriculture and allied pursuits. 86 per cent of the cultivated area is irrigated. Paddy is the predominant crop (65%) followed by pulses and cash crops.

It was once the capital of French India. Therefore, many laws relating to land continue as customary land laws. Yet popular governments are trying their best to implement land reforms because Pondicherry is the land of justice and love for the poor. Direct entry work has been completed and updation of land records R-o-Rs. are being distributed to the land owners.

The position of land system in the Union Territory of Pondicherry, by virtue of its colonization is totally different from the system in the rest of the nation. The French Administration has determined the mode of possession of land and levy of royalties. This has found its expression in the Ordinance dated 07-08-1828, by virtue of which the tillers of the land were allowed to enjoy as owners. As a result of this progressive legislation early in the 19th Century, there was no possibility of intermediary tenure in this Union Territory. Even in the cases where there were customary intermediaries, they were abolished particularly in Mahe region, a pocket in the Kerala coast.

Administration has brought in legislation on fixity of tenure like Pondicherry Cultivating Tenants Protection Act, 1970 in all the regions except Mahe region for which a comprehensive Land Reforms legislation was brought into force on the model of Kerala Land Reforms Act, which include *inter alia* fixity of tenure, ceiling on holdings, fair rent, assignment of ownership rights and vesting of landlord rights with Government.

The National policy of fixing the Fair Rent in the range of 60:40 has been adopted in all the legislations regulating the payment of fair rent to the landowners. The Administration has also enacted legislation for protecting the insecure and oral tenants from being evicted of their lease hold lands. Legislations for protecting the interest of cultivating tenants in original forms till 1982 provided for resumption of leased lands by landlords under certain conditions. This right of resumption for personal cultivation was withdrawn totally. Only those from the Armed Forces on their retirement/

discharged were entitled to resume tenancies. It can therefore be said that, once a tenant's land, it will for ever be the same. More than a decade before a legislation for conferment of ownership in respect of homesteads was enacted and as many as 3,816 agricultural labourers have been conferred with homestead rights. Besides, a scheme for providing free house sites to landless labourers in rural areas is also under implementation. So far 21,622 houseless persons have been provided with free house sites. Adequate subsidy is given to every beneficiary for construction of hutments. According to the agricultural census conducted in 1980-81, there were 33,783 operational holdings in the Union Territory spread over an area of 34,973 hectares. Of these holdings, 23,569 hectares were wholly owned and self-operated, while the remaining were either wholly owned or partly leased.

Pursuant to the National guidelines on ceiling on holdings, the Pondicherry Government enacted three different ceiling laws on land holdings, depending upon the pattern of such laws prevalent in the States adjoining the three linguistic regions of this Union Territory. None was found to be in possession of surplus land in Mahe and Yanam. In Pondicherry and Karaikal regions, out of an extent of 3,080 acres, estimated as surplus, based on revenue records, so far an extent of 2,296 acres have been declared surplus and actually 1,015 acres have been distributed to 1,351 beneficiaries, which include also 795 Scheduled Caste members. The remaining area, viz. 1,281 acres have also been declared as surplus, but could not be taken up for distribution, due to litigation on behalf of landowners. The Union Territory Administration is making all concerted efforts to complete the process of distribution of surplus lands to the landless, after surmounting the delay caused by litigation. No problems of tribal lands are faced in the Union Territory, in the absence of tribal areas.

The ex-French system of cadastral records was replaced by resurveying and resettling the land on Tamil Nadu pattern and records are more or less updated with the implementation of scheme of updating of land records in the VII Plan.

In pursuance of the deliberation of the Revenue Ministers Conference held earlier, the Administration has also forwarded schemes to the extent of Rs. 6.85 crores for assistance from the Finance Commission for strengthening and modernizing the Revenue Department which implements these socialistic legislations.

The progress of land reform measures in U.T. is as below as per Government of India's report upto December, 2007:[4]

(1)	Returns of surplus land filed	311
(2)	Pending returns	47
(3)	Area declared surplus	2326 acres
(4)	Area taken possession	1286 acres
(5)	Area distributed to the beneficiaries	1070
(6)	Number of beneficiaries	1464
(7)	S.C. beneficiaries on 640 acres of land	858
(8)	Other beneficiaries on 430 acres	606
(9)	Surplus land not yet distributed	1255 acres
(10)	Area involved in litigation	929 acres
(11)	Area involved in High Court cases	776 acres

Thus, there is lot of work to be done by the revenue department to dispose of 47 returns and also to distribute pending ceiling surplus 1255 acres of land. It is not understood why so much land was not taken possession of. It is the responsibility of revenue machinery to see disposal of cases at the High Court involving 776 acres of land.

There is one very good feature that 3000 sharecroppers have been recorded on 700 acres of land and 5-hectare wasteland has been distributed from April 2008 to February 2007.[5] It is hoped that the pace of land reform will go in a similar in vein.

REFERENCES

1. Government of India, Department of Land Resources, *Quarterly Progress Report* (cumulative) on Implementation of Land Ceiling Laws for the quarter ending December, 2007.
2. Government of India, Ministry of Rural Development, Annual Report, 2006-07, Annexure XLIX, p. 258.
3. *Ibid* 1.
4. *Ibid* 1.
5. *Ibid* 2.

26

A Scheme to Purchase and Distribute Land by the State

Increase of productivity is the ultimate aim of the land reforms. It was debated by some economists that the minimum farm size should always be there to ensure due productivity of land. The minimum size was estimated upto 2 ha (5-6 acres approx). On this premise green revolution was launched. But the green revolution turned red in the bastion state of green revolution, i.e. Punjab. There was terrorist violence and large scale migration to foreign countries from Punjab. One of the reasons of terrorist violence in nineties was uneven distribution of land and wealth in Punjab.

According to Professor S. Swaminathan, only 10 million ha[1] land is sufficient for production of 100 million tons of foodgrains in the country but the country will never be able to invest even in fertilizers at par with advanced countries. What will 70 per cent masses do in villages who are dependent on agriculture and know only how to cultivate land?

The Indian economy has not yet reached the stage to provide them employment. At present there is lot of disguised unemployment. Only the rural folk is employed to about 30 per cent of their capacity. Therefore, the economic liberalization should not create more unemployment and disguised unemployment in rural areas which will ultimately result into violence destroying all the palaces, malls, structures and buildings erected by the fast running Indian economy. At present, upsurge of the Naxalism is one of the offshoots of inequitable growth in rural India. Similarly, the animal resource is available in plenty in rural India which cannot be otherwise employed by the modern economy. What will bullocks do if there is no work available in rural India for them?

The recent study by the Food and Agricultural Organization of the United Nations has found that small land holdings given by Government is creating confidence in rural masses.

"In the later phases of the land reform, the administrators began allocating the vested land in smaller parcels. Given the fact that large numbers of landless are owning even a very small parcel of land, this implementation of policy made good sense.

Most interviewees who commented on the relative effectiveness of the land redistribution stated that those who had received agricultural land had realized significant livelihood improvements as a result. There were, however, some exceptions. One farmer (who had not himself received land) reported that households in his village who had received land had not realized significant benefits because they lacked implements and thus were not able to put the land to good use. The same farmer claimed that some of those beneficiaries had mortgaged their land away to larger farmers. A farmer in another village who had received vested land reported that while the former owner had produced three crops per year, he was only able to produce one crop per year".[2]

Two farmers interviewed had received homestead plots. The homestead plots allocated were extremely small, typically 0.04 acres (about 1700 square feet) or less. Even such tiny plots, we observed that these interviewees and other who had received tiny household plots were growing vegetable or had planted fruit trees for household consumption (Rural Development Institutes, Washington, USA).

The Department of Land & Land Reforms, Government of West Bengal complemented the finding of study by RDI, USA which is in line with the approach of Government of West Bengal on the issue.

Under 'Green Revolution', the contribution of human labour was reduced to about 11 per cent so also of animal labour to 11 per cent (approx). Is required credit available for the poor in rural India like in green revolution ? On the other hand, according to a Chinese proverb, the more number of times a farmer visits his field, more will be production. The small land holder or sharecropper has nothing else to do. He will certainly visit his field more number of times irrespective of the fact that his landholding is very small.

Similar experimentation in Bangladesh has met with grand success where three stage cultivation is being undertaken on small plots of land. On the ground, some crop requiring less solar energy is sown and followed by fruit hearing plant and then followed by trees with lot of height. Even in small pots of 16 decimal, one family could earn its livelihood.

Thus, the theory of minimum economic holding size has been exploded through experimentation and practical experiences. In the estimates of economic size holding, the major component of agricultural production is human labour ranging from 25 per cent to 30 per cent and animal labour or mechanical implements from 30 per cent to 50 per cent.

There is no solution because surplus land is not available to satisfy the land hunger of ever growing landless population in rural India. Land is the most precious asset of a villager and is his identity in the village. Land as a resource, cannot be extended like rubber. The present political environment not ripe to lower down further ceiling limit in rural India as middle class has asserted itself and is hankering for more goods and services further at par with its counterparts in the developed world. In the present scenario, no government can run smoothly being on war-path with the middle class.

Government of West Bengal has come out with a solution. Where there is no surplus government land available and there are people at the brink of starvation, i.e. much below the poverty line, the government will go for purchase of land from the willing land owners where the landless and the poorest mainly tribals, scheduled castes and dalits reside.

The scheme is summarized below:

Name of the Scheme

Chas-O-Basobaser Bhumidan Prakalpa (Cultivation & Homestead Land Donation Scheme).

Objective of the Scheme

(i) Economic Development through Agriculture and Rehabilitation of Landless and Homeless Persons of Rural Areas by distributing agricultural land to them after purchasing the same from intending raiyats.

(ii) Providing inputs of all other line-departments for other developmental schemes, like construction of houses under the Indira Awas Yojana, formation of Self Help Groups to take up other economic activities with the help of DRDC and Banks, etc.

(iii) Providing logistic support and basic services in the compact block within the land to be settled to the group of beneficiaries by constructing road, supply of drinking water, electricity, community toilets, etc. under different Rural Development Schemes.

Manner of Implementation

(i) The scheme was introduced in the year 2005-06. Under this scheme, after giving wide publicity, agricultural lands are purchased at the market price from the intending raiyats for distribution of the same to the landless and homeless persons.

(ii) Locations of land are selected in the vicinity where the prospective beneficiaries are residing.

(iii) Purchasing of land is made through registered instrument in favour of Government as per existing norms.

(iv) A beneficiary is allotted more or less 16 decimal of land on permanent basis by executing deed of settlement. No premium is charged for such settlement.

(v) There is a Block Level Committee in each Block of this state under the chairmanship of the Sabhapati of the Panchayat Samiti. Other members are Block Development Officer, Agriculture Development Officer, Karmadhakshya of Bon-O-Bhumi Sthayee Samiti of Panchayat Samiti, Addl. District Sub-Registrar and Block Land & Land Officer (Convenor member). The role of the Block Level Committee for implementation of the scheme properly is to identify the eligible beneficiaries, to assess the requirement of land, to settle the purchase of land, and to settle the distribution of land to their approved beneficiaries.

(vi) Funds are placed to the District Magistrates for disbursement towards cost of land.

***Achievements of Schemes*[3]**

Year	Fund Allotted	Fund Utilised	Land Purchased	Land Distributed	No. of Beneficiaries
2005-06 & 2006-07	1000 lakh	72.20 lakh	80.70 acres	80.70 acres	193

During 2007-08, the funds are being utilized and the scheme is in operation in full swing.

Problems

(i) Normally suitable lands are not available. The lands which are available generally have some encumbrances like sharecroppers etc. Land with sharecroppers are not allowed to be purchased under the scheme.
(ii) Beneficiaries fail to cultivate land properly which were allotted to them which is very far from their residences.
(iii) Agricultural land available amidst fields of agriculture cannot be used for residential purpose.
(iv) After offering lands, some land owners withdraw their offers. That creates lot of complications.
(v) The offer rate and market rate of lands may differ considerably.

Lessons

Block level committee should be strengthened and they should expedite their activities and involve local farmers'. societies or organizations if any, for proper selection of land. Mostly, the beneficiaries should be selected and then lands should be identified because the people in villages do not want to move very much far off from their present abode or habitation. This is applicable in all rural development schemes. This is being followed as one of the important guidelines in the Scheme.

Conclusions

This is one of the unique schemes undertaken by the Government of

West Bengal in the country towards land reforms. I am sure that the other states will follow this scheme and Government of India will come in a big way for financial assistance by providing cent-per-cent grant under the Scheme because under the land reforms and revenue sector generally non-plan schemes are undertaken by State governments and such schemes can only be taken under the planned budget.

Secondly, the state governments are starved of the funds. Therefore, it is with the help of Government of India such a scheme can be taken off. West Bengal has always been speareheading movement of land reforms in the country. This is one of the steps of Government of West Bengal. Even the ex-Orissa Chief Minister, Mr. Biju Pattanaik,[4] while inaugurating the seminar on "Poverty Elimination in Rural Development" has said "Orissa should follow West Bengal in implementing land reforms to achieve substantial increase in agriculture production and productivity. The West Bengal Government's recording the rights of sharecroppers on the tenanted lands had helped them in availing of bank credit for investment on land under cultivation. This, in turn, had helped them increase agricultural production by a phenomenal 70 per cent in recent years."

1 am sure, that this scheme can be one of the welcome steps towards land reforms.

REFERENCES

1. Agrawal, Dr. P.K.: *Land Reforms in India, Constitutional and Legal Approach*, p. 206.
2. Hamstad, Tim & Lokesh, S.B.: *Allocating Homestead Plots as Land Reforms: Analysis from West Bengal*, Published by Rural Development Institute, 2002, New York, USA.
3. *Government of West Bengal Land and Land Reforms Department*: A booklet published on Chas Besohaser Bhumider Prakalpa, year 2007-08, Writers Buildings, Kolkata-700001.
4. *Ibid.* 1: *Ibid.* p. 206.

27

Streamlining Revenue Administration for Implementation of Land Reforms

The implementation of land reforms is done by the oldest government department popularly known as the Revenue Department. The department is very popular with the countrymen specially with the rural folk as this is the department which is the maker and custodian of land records in the country and has stood with the people in times of needs like drought, flood or other natural calamities. Its key functionary is the collector of the District who is also in-charge of law and order in the district. In his latter role, he is popular in urban areas except in metro town, which have Police Commissioners in-charge of law and order.

Traditionally and historically, none has ventured to disturb the hegemony of this institution. On the other hand, there are banquet of praises from all quarters including foreign researchers and international agencies how the district administration in India operates successfully with the most limited resources at its command by any national or international standard. Therefore, tinkering with this administrative set-up, will be a great risk, which may prove to be the biggest blunder in history of India.

The revenue department in a state is headed by the Principal Secretary or Chairman, Board of Revenue, whosoever is senior. In U.P. Chairman, Board of Revenue, is in-charge of revenue administration whereas Principal Secretary does the policy making job. In states like Madhya Pradesh, Rajasthan and few other states, Board of Revenue hears and disposes of revenue appeals and revisions only before cases go to the High Court. Below the state level apex structure, there is divisional level structure where Commissioner of a division consisting of four or five districts is the head. Under Commissioner, is the District Collector. Then, there are sub-divisional level officers known as SDO and then Tehsil or block level officer known by different designations—like Tehsildar or Block Land and Land Reforms Officer. Below the block level, there are revenue inspector/Kanungo consisting of two or three villages. In each village or revenue mauza or more, there is patwari, lekhpal, talathi—who keeps the village land record and keeps on updating it as per system prevalent from State to State. He is a basically an Amin or a technical person who is expert in land measurement and keeping of land records. A revenue inspector above him is also helped by an Amin who is an exclusive survey man.

There are two systems of revenue administration. One is the revenue machinery from top to down, which is in-charge of records as well as management. There is a second system in West Bengal where there is a separate machinery to update and maintain the records periodically and the other agency is for management purpose which records changes in land records by way of disposal of mutation and conversion petitions. In West Bengal, these two agencies have also been merged but at the district level, one post of ADM is kept as District Land & Land Reforms Officer who is exclusively for land reform purposes under Collector. As Collector is one of the busiest functionaries in the country, DL&LRO does all the land reform works on his behalf without formal delegation from the Collector. As a result, land reform work does not suffer. But due to merger of survey and settlement and management wing, maintenance and updation of land records work has suffered a lot because Collector utilizes them for multifarious pressing jobs at hand which are emergent in nature. Therefore, there is a case to separate two wings again. If two wings, i.e. Settlement and Management wing cannot be separated, at least employees engaged in Settlement work should be kept immune from the firefighting jobs of the Collector with a very strict and clear order from the Government to implement the same in the field. They shall not be engaged in protocol, land acquisition, elections and other twenty odd works of District Magistrate. Apart from arms licensing, maintenance of food and supplies, treasury, the District Magistrate is the Chief Development Officer who looks after development works mainly rural development like the Prime Minister Rojgar Yojana, NREGA [National Rural Employment Guarantee Act], Indira Awas Yojana etc.

Problems Faced and Solutions Suggested

(1) As Collector is overall in-charge of the revenue administration, he engages the revenue machinery in all his odd jobs. For instance, in Utter Pradesh, revenue administration is mainly busy in protocol duties and VIP matters, revenue administration of Bihar and Rajasthan are busy in attending land matters of the politically powerful landed persons. In Madhya Pradesh, the revenue administration at one time was doing its real work of measurement of land and giving over possession to the patta holders, but now the machinery has become awefully busy in demarcation of disputed plots and attending to earmarking lands for industries, urban settlement etc. In Punjab and Haryana, the revenue machinery is busy in mutations and conversions apart from land acquisition. In Orissa, the land revenue administration is busy in settling land disputes projected by NGOs and displaced persons due to land acquisition. In south, the land revenue administration of Karnataka and Tamil Nadu are doing their original jobs and are trying to modernize the system. In Andhra Pradesh, the Naxalites keep land revenue administration busy in attending law and order related land problem yet land records machinery is doing its job independently and successfully. In Gujarat, Maharashtra and West Bengal, land revenue administration is attending to the needs of industrialization of the states. Thus the main focus of land revenue administration is different in different states. There is a separate land acquisition wing under the Collector. That wing should only do land acquisition. It should be strengthened as per needs. The survey and settlement machinery should be left for updating of land records, maintenance of land records and recording of sharecroppers etc. Distribution of government vested land should be handled by the management wing of land revenue machinery because it involves everybody.

(2) The total strength of land revenue administration has not improved with the passage of time and increase of population. As there is fragmentation of plots continuously more personnel will be required by the land revenue wing because each owner is to be recorded separately in khatian and record-of-rights [Khasra] is to be given to him separately. As a result, no state government ventures into the thorough revision of record-of-rights, which takes 10 to 20 years if continuous work is done. Suppose required personnel are recruited for survey and settlement work, then where will they go after completion of operation? Therefore, what is being done in the name of updating of records, is just a tip of iceberg or polishing of land records. For example, Bihar has less than half of number of staff and officers of West Bengal. Due to poor financial position of majority of state governments including Bihar, Orissa, Assam, Punjab, U.P., the central funds for updating or computerization of land records are either not utilized or are diverted. Government of India has adopted one Central Scheme known as "Centrally Sponsored Scheme" of strengthening of Revenue Administration and updating of land records [SRA & ULR] in 1987-88 on 50 : 50 sharing basis between the Centre and the States.

The main objectives of the Scheme were:

(i) Strengthening survey and settlement organizations for early completion and preparation of land records in areas where this work is yet to be completed.
(ii) Setting up survey and settlement organizations especially in the north-east, where no land records exist.
(iii) Imparting pre-service and in-service training to revenue, survey and settlement staff and strengthening training infrastructure for this purpose.
(iv) Providing facilities for modernization of survey and settlement operations, printing survey maps, reports and documents and storage, copying and updating of land and crop records using, among other things, latest science and technology inputs.

(v) Strengthening revenue machinery at the village and immediate supervisory levels on a selective basis to make the work load of functionaries manageable.

Under the scheme, States and UTs have been given assistance for purchase of modern survey equipment, [like Global Positioning Systems (GPS), EDM, total stations, theodolites, work stations], carrying out aerial surveys, office equipment [like photocopiers, laminating machines and binding machines] and basic facilities to improve work efficiency at lower levels of revenue administration, construction of record rooms for proper storage of land records, construction of office-cum-residence for patwaries and construction, repair and renovation of training institutes and equipment for training.

Release of funds during first four years of Xth Plan:[1]

Year	*Funds Released [Rs. in Crore]*
2002-03	20.73
2003-04	24.21
2004-05	19.43
2005-06	39.49
Total	**103.86**

Thus, the allocation of fund for delivery system of land reforms is minimum as compared to other sectors. How can then the results be expected higher?

For further improvement, a scheme entitled NLRMP (National Land Resources Management Programme) has been adopted by the Central Government. For every ill in the administration, there is only one pill available with the high echelon of administration that is computerization. This is also going to be implemented to up-date land records irrespective of the fact that the land revenue machinery is farthest from the computer as they are deep rooted in the village. Secondly, computer cannot *suo motu* update a record. If garbage is fed in the computer, garbage will come out of it. But computerization can certainly help in current and future work of updation of land records.

The NLRMP will, *inter alia*, focus on citizen services like computerized Records-of-Rights (RoRs) with maps; web-based "anytime-anywhere" access to land data; services through facilitation centers in tehsils and other places; speedy and efficient property registration; automatic initiation of mutation notices; land passbooks—smart cards with all land information including charges and encumbrances; facilitated access to land-based credit/ Cooperative Banks, etc. It envisages creation of core GIS with cadastral layer for the entire country, 100 per cent digitization of cadastral maps, integration of textual and spatial data, updating of land records using modern technology (aerial photogrammetry, DGPS, ETS), National and State Land Data Banks with specific plot IDs and details, use of uniform land data codes with Indian language script computing, integration with National Spatial Data Base (NSDB) and National Natural Resources Management System (NNRMS), full training and capacity building of the functionaries and National and State Missions for effective implementation.[2]

However, in piecemeal survey work will have to be undertaken by all States, which is long over due. There is no escape from it as far as old records are concerned. Advance administrative set-up will have to be drawn up with investment jointly by the Centre and the States. The survey trained personnel are not available in the market. Therefore, the governments will have to recruit from the open market. Even setting up of survey institutes are to be promoted. Then through computerization current and future revisions in record-of-rights will be duly incorporated without disturbing the whole record of a village or mouza.

3. The Land Revenue Minister now-a-days is not generally a Senior Minister in the State Cabinet. He cannot ensure his voice being heard at the highest policy-making body. If his Secretary or Principal Secretary puts some unorthodox suggestions to implement land reforms, the vested interests at once work against him and get him removed. The Chief Minister is generally surrounded by the industry lobby and

is pleased to listen how the industries are developing in his state on papers. The media is very much averse to cover land reform field. In fact, one in hundred in media knows a b c of the land reform. In such a situation, land reform becomes the last priority of the state government and the first casualty in the present run of government. The state government does not like to disturb the *status quo* in the rural areas, which may prove to be explosive. As a result, the portfolio of and Revenue Minister may be blown away. None is interested to disturb the *status quo*. Everybody criticizes yet everyone likes to behave like a bureaucrat in India. Nobody likes to take the responsibility for backlash by the land owning class including middle class who are quite vocal adequately supported by the media. Thus, firefighting goes on. If there are incidents of Naxalite violence, police tackles them and everybody forgets until a fresh incident worth nothing occurs. Thus, the bureaucratic country is happy indulging in fire fighting. Even the Land Revenue Commissioner is happy to shirk his responsibility by saying that law and order is the police domain. They can do some tangible or proactive work of land reform only when peace is restored in the area. And this peace bird eludes everybody. As a result, land revenue department sits idle.

However, everything is not lost in India. There are some nationalist and patriotic officers and officials who work and continue working for the rural poor without any appreciation from their bosses because of their self-commitment and mental make-up. These reform personnel or change-agents are present in administration in a sizeable number who also keep on suffering for their genuine causes and convictions for the poor. Pen is in their support and will continue bleeding for them. It is hoped that their lone battle will bring good sense among the rest of bureaucracy and the political elite who at least will allow them to work impartially and objectively without unnecessary and unwanted interference from the top. The blessing eyes of the dumb majority of the dalits and the adivasis are enough sources of inspiration, which will keep them and their families happy in long run because they are serving the 'daridranarayana' of Gandhiji.

New technologies can also be employed like aerial survey for preparation of rough photo record of the plots of lands and then K-B, attestation, etc. can follow.

The Naxalite agitation at least keeps the administration alive.

If the state governments are serious, they should post men of statesmanship or high status in the political hierarchy as Land Revenue Minister who is known for his work by the people in the field. The Revenue Minister shall be such a senior person who cannot be cowed down easily by his Cabinet colleagues or the Chief Minister. This Minister will be able to protect his reform oriented secretary or officers and staff of the department. Otherwise the opponent side is so apt in making complaints couched in a logical language that the Revenue Minister or Chief Minister will be taken by their rhetoric and will punish his reform oriented personnel who will then be demoralized and frustrated and leave the initiatives. It does not mean that all is well with the land revenue machinery. It is already branded corrupt. But abolition of posts of patwaris could not solve the problem. Someone at the lowest level has to keep the land records which is the basic duty of every government so that two raiyats or owners or occupiers or claimants of one piece of land do not fight and disturb public peace and tranquillity. Time is ripe to add more personnel without any interference to the Revenue Department and make it an efficient vehicle of land reforms in the interest of the poor and the downtrodden. The same machinery when strengthened will take care of updation and maintenance of land records in urban areas including metropolitan towns. There are common service centres at Gram Panchayat level which will keep the latest records-of-rights on computer. Any person/owner can verify his R-o-R there.

If political interference is reduced, motivated and efficient officers will opt for posting in the Revenue Department because this is basically their parent department. It has been at present made so unattractive and dull that none likes to shoulder the responsibility. If the surplus land of the department is to be allotted among the industries, real estate people or among the service organizations, the Chief Secretary of the State will jump in and will become the Chairman of the allotment committee. Any how, if Chief Secretary does not have time, he will entrust this work to his most trusted lieutenant as per instruction of Chief Minister so that Chief Minister can control fruits of land department. If above could not be done through one window clearance, industry department will control the surplus land of the revenue department. The revenue department's job will continue to make records and handover to somebody else. In case of land acquisition, the land Revenue Department cannot question the real requirement of industry or service or commercial sector, which is forwarded to him by the concerned department in a balloon form. All hell will let loose on him and the Revenue Department will ultimately lay down arms. Is that the environment, in which the land reforms can be implemented?

Implementation of land reforms requires strong political will which will permeate upto the last ladder of the revenue administration The land Revenue Minister should be a person of high status who can say 'No' to anybody. He is the custodian, protector and leader of all the patta-holders and sharecroppers (tenants) in the State and he should discharge this role in a true spirit and with devotion to the teeming millions of India who hardly have their spokesman left. They also spoil their golden opportunity during elections when they throw their precious vote on the basis of caste, creed or some greed.

Conclusion

It is a fact that there are insurmountable difficulties in gearing up revenue administration in the country firstly because the subject is exclusively with the State Government and secondly because it requires huge investment which may not be forthcoming easily due to present financial position of most of the states. Therefore, the Central Government should immediately intervene for grant of financial assistance otherwise the Central Government will have to spend many more times funds on containing Naxalite violence in rural areas or other problems of unrest including divisive tendencies and flare-ups.

Without gearing up delivery agency, i.e. the Revenue Department, the discussion about implementation of land reforms will be like beating the drums behind the bush.

It is high time that the Revenue Department once again realizes its role of seat-anchor in the country and plays it well which it had done after the independence in nineteen fifties and nineteen sixties and in West Bengal in nineteen eighties and nineties under the Left Front Government. If reform is seriously intended, the traditional machinery is required to be thoroughly geared up or given a parallel new support of personnel and technology which will meet the new challenges properly.

It is hoped that there will be requisite political will at the highest level, which will generate required administrative will. As a result, Naxalite like agitations will evaporate soon.

REFERENCES

1. Government of India, Ministry of Rural Development: *Annual Report, 2006-07*, p. 145.
2. *Ibid*, p. 146.

Bibliography

Agrawal, P.K. (1993): *Land Reforms in India, Constitutional and Legal Approach*, M.D. Publications Pvt. Ltd.

Aziz, Abdul and Krishna Sudhir (1993): *Land Reforms in India, Karnataka, Promises kept and missed*, Vol. 4, Sage Publications, New Delhi.

Bandyopadhyay, *Commission on Land Reforms in Bihar*: Internet, 2008.

Bergmann, Theoder (1984): *Agrarian Reforms in India*, by Agricole Publishing House Academy, New Delhi.

Deshpande, R.S. (2008): *Contract Farming and Tenancy Reforms*, Centre for Rural Studies, Lal Bahadur Shastri National Academy of Administration & Concept Publishing Company, New Delhi.

Ekta Parishad (2008): Internet.

Gill, Sucha Singh (ed) (2001): *Punjab & Haryana,* Vol. 6, Sage Publications, New Delhi.

Goswami, Atul (ed) (1986): *Land Reforms and Pleasant, Movement, a Study of North-east India*, Osmons Publications, Guwahati.

Jha, Praveen K. (ed) (2002): *Land Reforms in India, Issues of equity in Rural M.P.* Vol. 7, Sage Publication, New Delhi.

Palkhivala, N.A. (1976): *We the people*, Strand Book Stall, Bombay.

Rajiv Gandhi Foundation: *Issues in Land Reforms*, RGICS, Working Paper Series No.18, 2000, Rajiv Gandhi Institution For, Contemporary Studies.

Sarkar, Bikram (2008): *Land Reforms in India*, Ashish Publishing House, New Delhi.

Shah, Ghanshyam, Sah D.C. (ed) (2001): *Land Reforms in India,*

Vol. 8, Performance and Challenges in Gujarat and Maharashtra, Sage Publications, New Delhi.

Sharma, Purushottam (2008): *Internet, Land Seizure Movement in Almora district, A historical background.*

Sinha, B.K. Pushpendra (ed) (2000): *Land Reforms in India*, Volume 5, An unfinished Agenda, Sage Publications. New Delhi.

Sunder, Nandini (2006): Bastar, Maoism and Salwa Judum, *EPW* July 2006, pp. 3187-92 Vol. XLI No. 29.

Venkaleswarlu, Pivatla English Readering by RVB Sarma (2000): *Red Terrorism in India*, Krishna Kishore Publications, Hyderabad.

Yugandhar, B.N., Iyer, K. Gopal (1993): *Land Reforms in India*, Vol. I, Bihar-Institutional Constraints, Sage Publication, New Delhi.

Yugandhar, B.N. Dutta, P.S. (1995): *Land Reforms in India*, Vol. 2, Rajasthan and Change, Sage Publications, New Delhi.

Report, Papers

Government Publications, Journals, Periodicals, Magazines, News papers

Annual Report: 2006-07, Government of India, Ministry of Rural Development, (www.rural.nic.in), 2007.

Annual Report: 2007-08, Government of India, Ministry of Home Affairs, 2008.

Department of Land Resources, Ministry of Rural Development, Government of India: *Quarterly Progress Report* (cumulative) on implementation of ceiling laws for the quarter ending December, 2007.

Economic & Political Weakly: Editor, C. Ram Manohar Reddy, EPW Research Foundation, Mumbai.

Government of India Gazette: The Scheduled Tribes and other Forest Dwellers (Recognisition of Forest Rights) Act, 2006, Extra Ordinary Gazette [No. 221, Part-II, Section I, January 2, 2007], New Delhi,

Government of India, Ministry of Rural Development (1991): Land Reforms in States, *Gramin Vikas Newsletter*, February, pp. 20-32.

Government of Tamil Nadu: The Tamil Nadu Land Reforms (Fixation of Ceiling of Land) Act, 1961, (Tamil Nadu Act 58 of 1961), Law Department, Government of Tamil Nadu, 1997.

India 2008: A Reference Annual, Ministry of Information and Broadcasting, Government of India, Publication Division.

Iyer, K. Gopal: Paper on Land Reforms and State Repression presented in Hyderabad Convention entitled Status of Land Reforms in Andhra Pradesh and the need to Implement Radical Land Reforms."

Jansatta: Hindi Newspaper, Kolkata.

Land Reforms in India: An Emperical Study, 1989-90, Vol. I: (Ed.) Prof. Gopal Iyer, Land Reforms Unit, Lal Bahadur Shastri National Academy of Administration, Mussoorie, 1990.

The Telegraph: Calcutta, Daily English Newpaper.

Index

Aboriginal Tribal Land, 224
Aboriginal Tribes, 224
Activist Organization, 7-8, 136, 140
Adhiadars, 217
Adhikar Abhiyan, 131
Adivasis, 156, 161, 166, 243
Administration machinery, 175
Aerial photogrammetry, 55, 242
Aerial surveys, 52, 79, 241, 244
Affluent owner, 35
Agragami Krishak Sabha, 40
Agrarian economy, 184
Agrarian Reforms Act, 45, 182, 184
Agrarian Reforms Law, 183
Agrarian reforms, 4, 113, 183, 187-8
Agricultural drought, 130
Agricultural family, 187-8
Agricultural Labour Organizations, 8
Agricultural labourers, 13, 30, 38, 44, 57-9, 112, 114, 119, 137, 141, 145, 183-4, 219, 229
Agricultural land ceiling schemes, 99
Agricultural Tenancy Act, 193
Agricultural Tenancy Rules, 193
Agriculture and Rehabilitation of Landless and Homeless Persons, 233
Agro-climatic conditions, 179
Ahoms, 199
Akas tribal, 206
Alienated tribal land, 4, 204-5
Alienation, 3, 20, 68, 82, 86, 99, 100, 107, 115, 124, 129, 155, 204, 208-9, 211, 218
Alienation of Tribal Land, Position of, 155
Almora, 62-5
Ancestral lands, 122
Andhra Pradesh Land Reforms Ceiling on Agricultural Holdings Act, 101
Andhra Pradesh Land Titling Act, 108
Angamis, 215
Anti-ceiling provisions, 176
Anti-land reform, 116
Apex Court, 21-2
Apple growers, 189
Arms licensing, 238
Artificial conditions, 131
Ashraya scheme, 146
Assam State Acquisition of Lands, 197
Assam State Acquisition of Zamindaris Act, 195
Aurobindo Ashram, 228
Autonomous District Council, 208

Bandyopadhyay Commission on Land Reforms, 83
Banjar lands, 111, 126
Barga certificates, 29
Barga cultivation, 25, 28
Barga Operation, 57, 90, 148, 150
Bargadars, 5, 21, 25-30, 32, 34-6, 38, 43, 90, 92, 109-11, 170, 204-5
Bataidars, 5, 38, 56, 58, 81-2, 85, 128
Benami lands, 6, 13, 27, 32, 69, 136, 157
Bhil Rajas, 156
Bhoodan Act, 6

Bhoodan land, 4, 72, 77, 105, 124-6, 153, 163, 175
Big Landed Estates Abolition Act, 182, 184
Bihar Land Ceiling Act, 81
Bombay Tenancy and Agricultural Act, 69
Bureaucracy, 96, 130, 163, 165, 243

Cadastral maps, 47, 55, 242
Cadastral survey, 6, 51, 84, 207, 217-18
Capitalism, 3
Card indexing, 85
Cashew nut, 192
Ceiling Acts, 13, 44, 68, 125, 176, 189, 196
Ceiling on Land Holdings Act, 60, 187
Centrally Sponsored Scheme, 44, 52, 240
Charitable Institutions of Public Nature Act, 197
Charitable trust, 31, 60-1, 111
Chhattisgarh Mukti Morcha, 128
Chhota Nagpur Tenancy Act, 81
Chinese invasion, 206
Chula tax, 190
CLR scheme, 46-8
Code of Civil Procedure, 124
Colonization, 20, 228
Common Property Resourses, 130
Constitution Amendment Act, 19, 38, 143
Constitution of India, 3, 99, 168, 212
Contract farming, 56, 59, 148-9, 174, 178-80
Contracting agencies, 179-80
Cooperative Banks, 55, 242
Cooperative fanning, 9
Criminal justice system, 95
Crops
  cash, 168, 171, 192, 220, 223, 228
  contract, 179-80
  -credit finances, 14
  fellow, 179
  food, 171-2, 182, 192, 226
  fruit, 187, 226
  irrigated, 60
  rice, 130
  vegetable, 178
  wheat, 178
Cropsharing patterns, 138
Cultivable land, 8, 163, 215
Cultural ethics, 129
Customary laws, 214-15

Dadra & Nagar Haveli Land Reforms, 225
100 days employment scheme, 126, 199
Debt Relief Regulations and Money Lending Regulations, 100
Delhi Land Reforms Act, 226
Department of Land and Land Reforms, 33, 39, 40
Devasthan and Wakf Inam, 67
Dharni Project, 193
Diamond brother States, 219
Digitization of maps, 46, 48, 80
Directive Principles of State Policy, 3
Displaced persons, 72, 239
Domicile certificates, 54
Drinking habit, 37
Dwelling houses, 44, 193

Earthquake, 223
East Bengal State Acquisition and Tenancy Act, 2
Economic Factors, 19
Egalitarian society, 3, 27, 60, 62, 186
Eklavya Sangathan, 156
Ekta Parishad, 124, 160
Employment Generating Schemes, 13
Encroachments, 3, 7, 59, 108, 111, 145, 155, 158, 177
Enron and Sardar Sarovar Projects, 72
Equitable distribution, 17, 60, 148, 171, 196, 218
Ex-servicemen, 143-4, 223
Ex-zamindars, 76

Fair rent, payment of, 138, 140, 228
Fake certificates, 176

Family ceiling, 31, 72, 110
FAO, 23
Farmers
  large, 91, 154, 212
  medium, 91
  small, 91, 114, 141, 166, 186-7, 212
  co-operative, 13, 17, 37, 64, 73, 149, 227
Feudalism, 134
Forest Act, 123, 156
Forest Conservation Act, 123
Forest dwellers, 122, 126, 155
Forest management, 121-2
Fruit cultivation, 146, 187

Garbage, 241
Garden cultivation, 38
Government machinery, 107, 120, 133
Government regulation, 224
Government subsidies, 14, 145, 212
GPS, 52-3, 241
Gram panchayats, 17, 27, 58, 94, 125-7, 155, 244
Gram Sabha, 127, 193
Green revolution, 220, 231-2

Halka, 82, 86
Himalayan district, 63
Homesteads, 6, 38, 43, 114, 145-6, 193, 218, 223, 229
Human labour, 22, 232-3
Hydel projects, 190-1

Informal tenancy, 39, 102, 146, 163-5, 190
Institutional credit, 103
Integrated Tribal Development Programme, 126
International agencies, 237
Irrigated land, 44, 60, 68, 72, 141, 183-4, 219

Jagannath, 160, 163, 165
Jagirdars, 148, 184
Jan Adalats, 90
Jhum land, 206
Kalahandi, 160, 164
Kanungo, 30, 57-8, 148, 238
Kazis, 217-18
Kerala Land Reforms Act, 168-70, 172, 228
Kerala Land Reforms, 171
Khas possession, 76

Lakshadweep, 222, 226
Land-based credit, 55, 242
Land Ceiling Acts, 128, 152-3, 196
Land Ceiling Laws, Implementation of, 20, 161
Land ceiling programme, ineffectiveness of, 101, 104
Land distribution scheme, 95
Land Records, 46, 53, 94
Land Reform and Productivity, 93
Land reform beneficiaries, 5, 105, 116, 150, 154, 171, 226
Land reform machinery, 31, 33
Land Reforms Act, 4, 45, 111
Land Reforms in
  Andhra Pradesh, 98
  Manipur, 207
  Mizoram, 212
  Nagaland, 214
  Sikkim, 217
  Uttarakhand, 62
Land revenue machinery, 58, 148, 227, 239, 241, 244
Land Rights of Tribals, Protection of, 160
Land Tribunal, 9, 43-4, 82, 103, 114, 116, 135, 146, 150
Landed properties, redistribution of, 3, 141
Landless
  beneficiaries, 94, 153
  peasants, 65
  persons, 7, 27, 34, 59, 69, 94, 96, 110-11, 125, 135, 145-6, 164, 173, 175, 215-16
  tenants, 102, 177

Landowners
affluent, 219
rural, 164
tribal, 163, 212
unscrupulous, 158
Left Front, 25, 96

Madhya Pradesh land reform, 122
Maharajas, 134, 141-2, 191
Maharashtra State Farming Development Corporation, 69, 73
Mahe region, 228
Manipur Land Reforms and Land Revenue Act, 207
Maoist Communist Centre, 89
Maoists, 106, 131-3
Maps digitisation, 79-80, 110
Marginal farmers, 8-9, 43, 57, 68, 91, 106, 114, 117, 155, 160, 191, 205, 212
Militancy, 101, 184, 186
Mizo District Council, 212-13
Mobile banks, 87
Modern survey equipment, 52-3, 241
Money lending, 9
Mortgage, 32, 37, 131, 136, 145, 163, 200, 217, 224
Mutation, 49, 54, 79-80, 85, 109, 150, 190, 193, 238-9

National Informatic Centre, 80
National Land Resources Management Programme, 53-4, 241
Naxalism, 75, 84, 88-91, 95-7, 112, 121, 123, 127, 131, 146, 149-51, 231
IXth Schedule, 4-5
Nodal agencies, 9, 179-80
Non-tribal cultivation, Rehabilitation of, 205

Occupancy rights, 44, 139-40, 22
Occupancy tenants, 102, 119, 164, 200-1, 223
Operation Barga, 25, 27-30, 34-5, 38, 80, 82, 119, 205
Operation Bataidar, 58
Orchards, 32, 184, 189, 197, 203
Orissa Estate Abolition Act, 163
Ownership rights, 2, 5, 16, 70, 114, 119, 200-1, 214, 228

Panchayat functionaries, 32, 94, 110
Panchayat samity level, 127
Patta distribution camps, 32-3, 94
Pattadars, 13-4, 30-3, 36-8, 59, 76, 110-11, 116-17, 130, 155
Pattas, 32-3, 38, 69, 95, 145, 202, 207
Peasants, 9, 25-6, 30-1, 33, 40, 101, 147, 219
Personal cultivation, 21, 44-5, 70, 82, 89, 101-3, 111, 118, 143, 180, 183-5, 204, 210, 228
Pioneer states, 56
Plantations, 111, 160, 170, 220, 223
Pod cultivation, 166
Political affiliation, 16
Political backlash, 69
Political sufferers, 144
Pondicherry Cultivating Tenants Protection, 228
PRIs, 78, 119, 127, 130-1, 155, 158
Protected belts, 196
Punjab Land Reforms Act, 174-5

Rajasthan Tenancy Act, 134
Real estate boom, 35
Refugees, 183-4
Resettlement, 73, 157-8
Restoration of Tribal Lands, 162
Revenue machinery, 51-2, 64, 123, 126, 178, 230, 238-9, 241
Revenue villages, 223
Rice cultivation, 168
Rural artisans, 114
Rural Development Institutes, 94, 146-7, 232
Rural development schemes, 8, 82, 91-2, 150, 201, 234-5

Salwa Judum, 131-3

Sardar Sarovar Project, 157
Self-cultivation, 8, 71
Semi-government institutions, 131
Separatist agitations, 37
Settlers, 223
Sharecroppers, 5-9, 25-6, 56-7, 69-71, 77, 81-3, 92, 117-20, 130, 136-9, 141, 143-4, 148-50, 163-5, 199-202
  exploited, 25
  non-recording of, 128
  record, 164
  recording, 36, 92
Shifting cultivation, 206-7, 214
Skewed distribution, 1
Social justice, 3-4, 19
Spatial data, 54-5, 242
State Land Ceiling Law, 114
State Land Data Banks, 55, 242
State of Rajas, 134
STORFA, 126-7, 157
Stridhan, 116-17
Structural reforms, 1, 2
Surplus land, 4-5, 15, 21-2, 32, 44, 60, 81-2, 99, 106-7, 135-6, 174-5, 183, 218, 229-30, 244-5
  distribution of, 4-15, 30, 56, 59, 90, 183, 229
  government, 30, 33, 36, 56, 59, 94, 106, 111, 135, 145, 158, 209, 211
  possession of, 106, 229
Survey of India, 79

Taluk computer centres, 47
Tamil Nadu Land Reforms, 115
Tea cultivation, 196, 202
Tea estates, 205
Tea gardens, 190-1
Telengana, 101, 103, 106, 152
Tenancy Act, 101, 103, 196, 199, 213
Tenancy cases, 44, 70, 213
Tenancy prohibition policy, 147, 150
Tenancy reforms legislation, 139, 154
Tenants
  cultivating, 118-19, 170, 192, 200, 228
  informal, 8, 69-70, 83, 148, 164
  khatedar, 137
  non-occupancy, 9, 140, 196, 199-200
  recorded, 117, 137, 177
  tribal, 164
  unrecorded, 57, 92, 177
Terrace, 215-16
Terrorist violence, 89, 96, 199, 231
Thikader, 217-18
Tourism, 141, 192, 219
Tribal Agriculture Societies, 124
Tribal land, restoration of, 15, 124, 162, 203-4
Tribal Welfare Department, 86, 204
Tribals
  aboriginal, 224
  illiterate, 123
  primitive, 222
Tripura Land Revenue and Land Reforms Act, 202, 204

Under-raiyats, 165, 200, 204
Uttar Pradesh Zamindari Abolition and Land Reforms Act, 57

Vested land, distribution of, 32, 36, 39, 112, 225, 239
Vidarbha, 40
Village Councils, 207, 212, 214-15, 217
Voluntary Organizations, 7-8

Waste land, 59, 105, 113, 115, 145, 158, 172-3, 189, 193, 199, 210, 227
  distribution of, 6, 71, 76, 203
West Bengal Land Reforms Act, 29-31, 86, 110
West Bengal Land Reforms Rules, 27-8

Zamindari Abolition and Land Reforms Act, 62, 226
Zamindars, 1, 62-4, 76-7, 113, 141, 148-9, 170, 217